FROM ITALIAN VILLAGES
TO GREENWICH VILLAGE

FROM ITALIAN VILLAGES
TO GREENWICH VILLAGE
Our Lady of Pompei, 1892–1992

Mary Elizabeth Brown

1992
Center for Migration Studies
New York

The Center for Migration Studies is an educational, non-profit institute founded in New York in 1964 to encourage and facilitate the study of sociological, demographic, historical, legislative and pastoral aspects of human migration movements and ethnic group relations. The opinions expressed in this work are those of the author.

From Italian Villages to Greenwich Village
Our Lady of Pompei, 1892–1992

First Edition
Copyright © 1992 by
The Center for Migration Studies of New York, Inc.
All rights reserved. No part of this book may be reproduced
without written permission from the publisher.

Center for Migration Studies
209 Flagg Place
Staten Island, New York 10304-1199

Library of Congress Cataloging-in-Publication Data

Brown, Mary Elizabeth.
    From Italian villages to Greenwich Village: Our Lady of Pompei, 1892–
1992 / by Mary Elizabeth Brown. —1st ed.
        p. cm.
    Includes bibliographical references.
    ISBN 0–934733–69–4 (cloth).—ISBN 0–934733–68–6 (paper)
    1. Our Lady of Pompei (Parish : New York, N.Y.)—History. 2. New York
(N.Y.)—Emigration and immigration—History. 3. Italy—Emigration and immigration—History. 4. Italians—New York (N.Y.) 5. Immigrants—New York
(N.Y.) 6. Greenwich Village (New York. N.Y.)—Emigration and immigration—History. 7. Greenwich Village (New York, N.Y.)—Church history. I.
Title.
BX4603.N60873   1992
282'.7471—dc20   92–24247
                                                                          CIP

Printed in the United States of America

Contents

Preface

When Our Lady of Pompei celebrated its parish centennial, its plans were much like other New York City parishes. All the groups of parishioners—Italian Americans, Filipino Americans, Vietnamese Americans, senior citizens, parochial school alumni and current students—had their places in the year-long calendar of events. During 1991–1992, there was a May crowning, a health fair, a Filipino Santo Nino Festa, the annual Festa Italiana, a Vietnamese centennial cultural presentation, a tour of Ellis Island for the school children, centennial fundraisers, a special observance of the annual Feast of the Holy Rosary, an alumni dance, a Christmas fair and novena, a service honoring those who had married at Pompei, a luncheon, two Communion breakfasts, two concerts, and two special Masses. A more unusual form of celebration was this book, which is intended for two audiences: parishioners and scholars.

I began researching Pompei at the Center for Migration Studies Library and Archive, where Diana Zimmerman, Maria Del Giudice and Richard Del Giudice, made me welcome. CMS director Father Lydio Tomasi, C.S., got me in touch with Pompei's pastor, Father Tarcisio Bagatin, C.S., who made this project into the centennial history. Father Ezio Marchetto and Joan Mancuso of the Center readied it for publication.

Pompei funded portions of the research and the writing. Pompei's staff also gave of themselves—housing me, feeding me, and sharing office space and supplies. Thanks are due to Father Tarcisio Bagatin, C.S., Mrs. Helen Brizzolara, Mrs. Maria Mandarino, Brother Michael La Mantia, C.S., Mrs. Rose Schiavone, Mrs. Lena Scuderi, Father Bernabe Sison, and Father Giulivo Tessarolo, C.S. I would also like to acknowledge those who sat for interviews.

Several individuals helped. Father Charles Zanoni, C.S., prepared the way for this study. He set up Pompei's archive room, edited its newsletter, *The Village Bells,* with an emphasis on parish history, and brought many things to my attention. Father Andrew Brizzolara, C.S., lent a copy of his master's thesis on Bishop Scalabrini's American visit. Sister Margarita Smith helped find Pompei materials in the Archives of the Archdiocese of New York. Professor Gerard Innocenti helped with Italian history and Italian translations. Sister

Mary Louise Sullivan, M.S.C., shared her research on Mother Cabrini. Messrs. Paul Kalinsky and William Motsavage proofread the text.

Some background information may be helpful in understanding the footnotes and index.

1) The Archives of the Archdiocese of New York has material regarding the building of Pompei's present church. Items identified as AANY came from there.

2) Pompei's rectory has Saint Raphael baptism and marriage registers, Pompei baptism and marriage registers, and a wide variety of documents. The collection is fairly solid from 1952 to the present, and excellent for the period 1981–1989. The citation for materials found at Pompei is OLP Box Name, Folder Name.

3) The Center for Migration Studies has several relevant collections of material. It has a collection of Pompei's material which is fairly solid from 1892 to 1937, and excellent for the period 1899–1933. The citation for Pompei's collection at this location is CMS Box Number, Folder Number.

4) Former parishioner Ralph Stella's hobby is compiling scrapbooks, and he has generously donated to Pompei a series of scrapbooks with clippings and souvenirs of events at the parish and in Greenwich Village. Material taken from this source is cited as OLP Scrapbook.

5) Two sets of dates may help in using the index. Pompei has had the following addresses: 113 Waverly Place from 1892 to 1895; 210 Sullivan Street from 1895 to 1898; 210 Bleeker Street from 1898 to 1927; and the corner of Carmine and Bleeker Streets from 1927 to the present. The parish has had the following pastors: Pietro Bandini from 1892 to 1895; Francesco Zaboglio from 1896 to 1899; Antonio Demo from 1899 to 1933; John Marchegiani, as administrator from 1933 to 1934 and as pastor to 1937; Ugo Cavicchi from 1937 to 1947; John Bernardi from 1947 to 1952; Mario Albanesi from 1952 to 1964; Anthony Dal Balcon from 1964 to 1967; Guido Caverzan from 1967 to 1970; James Abbarno from 1970 to 1974; Giulivo Tessarolo from January to July 1975; Edward Marino, as administrator from August, 1975, to February, 1976, and as pastor to 1981; Charles Zanoni from 1981 to 1989; and Tarcisio Bagatin since 1989.

In the course of my research I got a chance to read this letter:

Please say a Mass for my grandfather . . . at your earliest convenience. He's of that special breed: a strong-willed, kind, family-oriented Italian immigrant who embraced this country whole-heartedly. . . . It's clear that your parish is filled with this extraordinary generation.[1]

The word "extraordinary" struck me. There are no miracles connected with Pompei; Mother Cabrini spent only a brief time there, it's not on any official list of historic landmarks, and the research failed to uncover anything earth-shaking. And yet, after reading the records, one gets a sense of Pompei's participation in dramatic events: the immigration and resettlement of thousands of people, raising a new generation in a new place, adding another community to the mix of people in Greenwich Village, establishing a tradition of charity. The more my research progressed, the more apt the word "extraordinary" seemed.

In writing the history of Our Lady of Pompei, I have tried to be accurate, balanced, and thorough, but here in the preface it is possible to say something from the heart as well as from the head. It was a privilege to work on this project. I hope it is a pleasure for all those who read the results.

NOTES

[1] To Charles Zanoni, May 31, 1989, OLP Papers 1988, January 1989 Folder.

1

Before the Beginning

Several elements came together to make Our Lady of Pompei parish possible. Had there been no migration from Italy, and had the Italian migrants been received into American society differently, there would have been no need for Pompei. Had there been no Bishop Giovanni Battista Scalabrini and no Archbishop Michael Augustine Corrigan, the need might have been met in another way. Had there been no Greenwich Village and no Italian community developing there, Pompei might have fulfilled its purpose long ago and become a historical monument rather than a vital place.

In the 1990s, there were people whose families had been members of Pompei parish for generations, and who were very attached to their homes. If one knows that, one begins to wonder what it must have been like for their ancestors, who had been rooted in their Italian homes longer than their descendants have been rooted in the Village. Yet these ancestors shook loose from those roots, left their homes, and ventured to a place where there was as yet no Italian community to receive them.

Why leave home? By the standards of its political leaders, nineteenth century Italy was doing well. In 1870, the national government completed the unification of the peninsula. The national government set out to make Italy one of Europe's great powers. The price of becoming a great power was paid by the middle-class and the poorer citizens.[1] Centuries of land use and competition from other agricultural countries made Italy's agriculture less productive. The industrial sector didn't grow enough to absorb the surplus agricultural workers. Those who found jobs in Italy's industries faced long hours, poor pay, and unhealthful conditions. The national government levied heavy taxes, and the army drafted young men into service during their most productive years.

The statistics describing Italian immigration to the United States are a little different from those describing the Italians who became members of Our Lady of Pompei parish. However, since Pompei began as part of a traveler's aid agency serving all Italian immigrants, the general statistics are important.

In the 1840s northern Italians began traveling in search of work. A few thousand each year found their way to the United States. A few hundred settled in New York. The 1865 state census counted 955 persons born in Italy residing in New York City. American-born children were counted as Americans, so the total Italian American community was larger.[2]

The northern Italian immigrants divided into two classes.[3] The upper class was composed of two groups. There were merchants and professionals, such as Mozart's sometime librettist Lorenzo da Ponti, who migrated to New York to sell their goods and their services to a similar class of native New Yorkers. There were political activists, such as Giuseppe Garibaldi, who found it expedient to be out of Italy for a while. Neither group had connections with the poor who invested their earnings in passage to the United States, and ended up as casual laborers, or who fashioned livings for themselves as street musicians and entertainers.

Unification brought to the south of Italy the problems that had driven northerners to migrate, and provided Southerners with easier access to trans-Atlantic steam ships. In 1880, the number of Italians arriving in the United States in one year exceeded ten thousand for the first time. In 1900, the number of Italians arriving in the United States in one year exceeded one hundred thousand. In some years before World War I, the annual total of Italian immigrants to the United States exceeded two hundred thousand.[4] In this flood of immigrants, the small group of professionals, entrepreneurs, and activists was completely outnumbered by large numbers of working people.

The United States was a popular destination for southern Italian immigrants: 80% of all Italians entering the United States between 1880 and 1930 hailed from Sicily or from the peninsula south of Rome.[5] In any given decade between 1880 and 1930, about 70% of all Italian immigrants were between fourteen and forty-four years old. Until 1910, over 70% of all Italian immigrants were male. As many as 90% of all Italian immigrants in any given year told the immigration officials they were unskilled laborers.

From about 1880 to about World War I, Italian immigrants were highly transient. One-and-one-half million of the Italians came to the United States returned to Italy in that time.[6] Three events ended this period of transiency. First, World War I disrupted travel. After 1921, United States immigration law made entry into the country much more difficult. After 1922, Italian immigration law made it more difficult for men of military age to leave the country. Men who had come to the United States temporarily decided to bring over their families permanently. (This meant that when women and children travelled, they often travelled without husbands and fathers.)

Even a single Italian man travelling without his immediate family wasn't entirely alone. Italian migration's pioneers explored the way for others, and whole communities came from a particular spot in Italy to a particular spot in the United States. Even immigrants without friends and relatives had recourse to *padroni*, bilingual contractors who hired and supervised labor gangs for others.[7] Observers, though, thought the Italians were terribly vulnerable and badly needed protection against three dangers.

The first danger was from accidents. Immigrants had to travel from their home towns to port cities, get tickets, get on ships, land, perhaps journey to their final destinations, find housing, and find jobs—all without losing their luggage, health, money, traveling companions, or passports. Most immigrants proved themselves resourceful travelers, but there were bound to be problems.

The second danger was from governmental interference. Until 1922, Italian officials were not pleased with the depopulation immigration caused, but they did nothing about it, because they thought migration took away the poorer people most likely to become political radicals and revolutionaries. Until 1921, the United States had a more open immigration policy than it later would have, but from the point of view of immigrants, admission was difficult enough.[8] Beginning in 1882, Congress began passing laws to weed out people it considered undesirable immigrants. Officials questioned each person entering the United States, and turned back people who didn't meet the requirements. Immigrants needed help with American immigration procedures.

The third danger was from con artists. Even honest *padroni* didn't assist immigrants out of kindness. They derived their profit from the difference between what clients paid to find a labor gang and what it cost to hire the labor, between what it cost to feed and house workers, and what workers were willing to pay for their accommodations. There were enough dishonest *padroni* to give all of them a poor reputation. They sold immigrants fake transportation tickets, cheated them when changing currency, overcharged for all sorts of services, underpaid them and otherwise exploited their labor. Pompei was founded as part of comprehensive system of assistance protecting immigrants from the dangers just described.

Italian immigrants would have normally banded together to be near people who spoke the same language and who shared the same customs. Like all immigrants, Italians had an additional reason for banding together: they encountered bigotry in the United States. In the Italians' case, it was a double burden of prejudice, against their nationality and against their religion.

At the end of the nineteenth century and the beginning of the twentieth , the theories of scientific racism took hold in the United States.[9] According to these theories, every human trait was inherited, whether it was physical feature or a mental ability or a personality characteristic. Even tendencies toward representative government were supposed to be inherited, and Americans reasoned they had inherited their love of liberty from their colonial ancestors. Americans also reasoned that Italians, whose history was very different from their own, must be an undesirable "race."

Americans also had religious prejudices. The United States had a long history of anti-Catholicism, and Italy was home to the pope himself. The complicating factor here was that both Protestants and Catholics were prejudiced against Italian Catholics, each for their own reasons. The American Catholics' anti-Italian sentiments had three causes.[10] First, in the process of unifying the peninsula, the Italian government had taken lands which belonged to the papacy. American Catholics blamed all Italians for the government's action. Second, there were profound cultural differences between American Catholics, who at the time of the Italian migration were usually of Irish ethnic background, and the southern Italians who comprised the majority of Italian immigrants. The Irish were particularly embarrassed by southern Italian festas, feast-day celebrations for patron saints that lasted several days and included outdoor processions and festivities. Third, Italian men were caught in the middle of Italian church-state conflicts. Some rejected religion and proclaimed themselves atheists. Even these men, though, had wives and children who kept up the faith.[11] Other men simply left religious duties to their wives.

Their employers did not make it easy for Italians to practice their faith. Italian men labored at sites far away from churches, and had their wages held until their work was complete. Even if they lived near a church, they worked long hours and did not take time for Mass. Nor did they take money from their small earnings to give to the collection. Nor did parishes accept them when they did come to Mass. Pastors complained that Italians smelled from their hard work and their poor living conditions, and that they huddled in the back of the church to avoid the collection plate.

Protestants reacted to Catholic prejudices against Italians. Here were Catholics whom even co-religionists didn't consider to be very faithful, so they must be ripe for conversion. Judson Church, south of Washington Square Park was established to have a Protestant presence among the Village Italians.[12]

Catholic clergy in Italians neighborhoods were in a quandary. The clergy shared the general anti-Italian prejudices. The Archdiocese of New York expected each parish to support itself, and the clergy expected parishioners to contribute their share; they couldn't afford to have parishioners who didn't contribute to the Church.[13] So, the clergy didn't want Italians converting to Protestantism, but they didn't want them in the American parishes either. The Italians wanted their own parishes, but they were also pushed into their own parishes. Pompei was founded partly to help Italians preserve their faith, and partly to protect them from proselytism and prejudice.

In Italy, immigration was not only a personal problem for immigrants and their families, it had pastoral and political ramifications. The man who did the most to identify the problems of immigration, and to work out possible solutions, was Giovanni Battista Scalabrini.[14] Scalabrini was born July 8, 1839, in

Fino Mornasco in northwestern Italy and ordained a priest in 1862. The turning point in his life came January 30, 1876, when he was consecrated bishop of the Diocese of Piacenza in Lombardy. He served in this post until his death on June 1, 1905.

As he got to know his diocese, Bishop Scalabrini began to realize the double risk immigrants faced. The new home might prove no more prosperous than the old; the immigrants would not fare as well as those who exploited them. Also, whether they failed or succeeded, what became of their spiritual lives while they were on this quest for material subsistence?

Having decided where the risks to emigrants lay, Bishop Scalabrini tried to do something about them. In 1887, he published a pamphlet on *L'Emigrazione Italiana in America,* and in 1888, a second pamphlet on *Il Disegno di Legge sulla Emigrazione Italiana* [*A Plan for Italian Emigration Law.*] Bishop Scalabrini's suggestion for cooperation between church and state to aid immigrants was radical for its time and place. The Italian government provided some funds for immigration agencies, but Bishop Scalabrini was left to develop the agencies himself.

Bishop Scalabrini organized two institutions to serve Italian immigrants. The longer lasting of the two was a community of priest and brothers dedicated to the immigrant apostolate, whose first members professed vows November 28, 1887. Bishop Scalabrini called them the Pious Society of Saint Charles, after their patron saint Saint Charles Borromeo (1538–1584), cardinal archbishop of Milan during the Reformation, and model for bishops everywhere. The missionaries were better known as Scalabrinians. (There is also a community of women religious, but no representatives of that sisterhood served at Pompei.)

Bishop Scalabrini also wanted to create a traveler's aid society for Italian immigrants. There was a precedent for such a society. In 1871, German layman Peter Paul Cahensly had organized the Saint Raphael Society for the Protection of German Emigrants, named for the archangel who appears in the biblical book of Tobit and who is regarded as the patron saint of travelers.[15] Bishop Scalabrini proposed a similar Saint Raphael Society for the protection of Italian Emigrants in 1887. The New York branch, the one that led to the founding of Our Lady of Pompei, was established in 1890.

Canon law assigned responsibility for immigrants to the bishops through whose dioceses immigrants passed and in which they settled. Bishop Scalabrini's suggestions had to be taken up by his episcopal colleague to whose dioceses Italians came. Such a colleague was Michael Augustine Corrigan.[16] Archbishop Corrigan was born in Newark, New Jersey, in 1839, was ordained in 1863 in Rome, and was consecrated Bishop of Newark in 1873. In 1880, he was appointed coadjutor, auxiliary bishop with the right of succession, to New York's archbishop, John Cardinal McCloskey. As the cardinal's health failed, his coadjutor became more active in archdiocesan administration. Cardinal McCloskey died in 1885, and Corrigan became archbishop in his own right, a position he held until his death in 1902.

Some of Archbishop Corrigan's colleagues in other dioceses assumed the immigrants would not Americanize unless they were placed in "American" parishes with English-speaking pastors.[17] In New York, the assumption was the immigrants would inevitably Americanize, and the clergy's responsibility was to keep them in the Catholic faith during their Americanization. Archbishop Corrigan used the history of immigrant pastoral care in New York to guide him in planning for the Italians. Usually, a Catholic parish is a territorial unit, and Catholics attend the parish in which they reside. For immigrants, American Catholics had a variation, "national" parishes with linguistic borders and permission to minister to individuals who spoke a certain language, regardless of where that person lived. National parishes were staffed by clergy from the same country as the lay immigrants. Sometimes these were immigrant clergy. More often, religious orders with foundations in the home country sent missionaries.

The Italians were New York's largest non-English-speaking Catholic ethnic group in Archbishop Corrigan's time, and so required many more clergy. Archdiocesan clergy were even more suspicious of Italian clergy than they were of Italian laity. Not until the early twentieth century were Italian clergy promoted from assistants to pastors. As a result, the New York's Italians had more religious orders than usual involved in their ministry.

The large number of religious orders was due to Archbishop Corrigan. He solicited religious orders to send Italian-speaking clergy and sisters, and gave from his own funds to support them during the difficult early years. When he heard about the Scalabrinians' founding, he sent congratulations, a donation, and a request for two missionaries.[18] Pompei was founded as part of these two bishops' ministries: Bishop Scalabrini's mission to those leaving Italy, and Archbishop Corrigan's mission to those arriving in New York.

Beginning in the 1870s and continuing through to the 1920s, New York developed not one Little Italy, but many, each peopled by immigrants from a different part of the peninsula.[19] Greenwich Village was not well known as an Italian neighborhood.[20] The area called Greenwich Village was farmland to the Indians, the Dutch, and the English. Just before the American Revolution, real estate there became a popular investment. Between 1820 and 1850, Greenwich Village grew into a suburb for middle-class and wealthy people. Almost immediately after the Civil War, the large cast-iron facade buildings in what is now SoHo began going up, and the Village changed to a neighborhood of warehouses and factories.

The most noticeable residents, as far as outsiders were concerned, were the non-ethnic "bohemians," who combined artistic excellence with a passion for reform. Some actually lived in the Village. More came to visit. Even more tourists came to see where the artists and reformers lived. Many Village landmarks became attractions because of their association with these star residents. But consider this description of a Village landmark which appeared next to a photograph of a restaurant in a museum exhibit on the "bohemian" Village:

> The Cafe Bertolotti on West Third Street was among the most popular of the back street bistros to attract the bohemian art crowd. Well into the teens, Signora Bertolotti, affectionately known as "Mama," served a famous lunch of thick minestrone soup, bread and butter, and red wine for fifteen cents, tip included. Those who couldn't pay were often fed on the house.[21]

Mrs. Bertolotti led another life besides restauranteur for bohemian artists. She was an Italian immigrant. She probably opened her restaurant for another sort of clientele, for transient Italian laborers who needed cheap meals and a nice place to sit with their friends. It turned out that artists also needed bargain dinners and places where they could talk as well as eat. The bohemian patrons brought Cafe Bertolotti fame, but did not influence Mrs. Bertolotti's basic values. She probably attended Pompei, and one of her daughters returned to Italy to enter a Roman convent.[22]

Other Italian business people had stories similar to Signora Bertolotti's. What they considered a shop serving a Little Italy, outsiders considered a part of the Greenwich Village life style. If the Italians did not maintain cultural institutions that were completely separate from what bohemians and tourists considered part of Greenwich Village, they would have dissolved completely into the Village's bohemian culture. Pompei was founded partly to help Italians preserve their distinct culture in the Village melting pot.

Earning a living in the early twentieth Village required enormous effort.[23] Employers blamed the workers themselves for the low wages of the day: when so many competed for jobs, the jobs went to those willing to work for the least amount of money, thus driving down the general wage rate. There was no job security: workers were hired for the busy season and let go for the slack season. There was no time off with pay, no vacations, sick days, or paid holidays. There was no insurance against unemployment or on-the-job accidents. There was little attention to preventing such accidents. One tragic event in Pompei's history was the Triangle Shirtwaist Factory Fire, in which 146 people were killed for want of a clean and safe place to work. The New York Factory Commission estimated that in the years before World War I, a New York City family needed an income of $876 per year. The average unskilled working man earned $1.25 to $1.50 per day. This would have added up to only $456.25 to $574.50 in a 365-day year—but lay-offs were so frequent that no one worked 365 days a year. The average annual earnings for an unskilled man were $390.

The above statistics may make the Italians sound like poor people. It might be better to think of them as struggling, and to observe that they had a variety of strategies for improving their family's standard of living.

One was to have more family members work. The most common candidates for work were adolescents, who forswore the additional schooling that would have given them well-paying jobs in favor of the immediate, but low, returns from unskilled work. There were no modern household appliances and so the married woman's burden of housework was exhausting, yet some women combined housework with paid labor. Even children under fourteen were pressed into service augmenting family income. All this work didn't bring the family any closer to a living wage. Women earned about half what men did, children about half what women did. If the adult males' income didn't equal a living wage, the family could not just send the mother out to work: it took the mother and at least two children to equal one man. And if the head of the household couldn't work, even all the rest of the family working together couldn't compensate for that lost income.

A second strategy was to open a family business, but the economic system served the small capitalist not much better than it served the laborer. People went into debt to open their businesses, interest payment ate up their profits. The only way to compete for customers was to lower prices, which also lowered profits. Like laborers dealing with *padroni*, businesses dealt with criminal exploitation. Loan sharks lent money, but at high interest rates. Gangsters extorted "protection" from vandalism and "insurance" that goods would arrive for stores or that construction work would proceed as scheduled.

A third strategy, using education to get better jobs, was one the Italians learned in America. In Italy, the poor could not afford the time for education, and one needed to become very well educated for the education to pay off financially. In New York, though, even the poor could afford education at public schools and private agencies. Even the smallest amount of education—learning English—was profitable. After World War II, Italian youngsters began staying in school, to prepare for better jobs.

A final strategy was to use community institutions to sustain family life. If the family lost one parent, the surviving parent might have to put the children in a home temporarily. If the parents had poorly-paying jobs, fresh-air camps gave the children the summer outings they needed. If there was no institution to meet their needs, the Italians created them: their own mutual benefit societies for insurance, their own day care centers for working mothers' pre-school children. Pompei was founded to meet the diverse social needs of a struggling community.

One might argue that so far, this chapter has discussed things *around* Pompei, but not Pompei itself. Pompei is not just a community service center, nor a historic monument honoring the Italians among America's immigrants. It was built and remains open, to enable Catholic Christians to practice their faith. The argument is well made. Faith on earth, though, is always in dialogue with its particular setting, sometimes in tension with it, sometimes growing from it. What follows is the story of setting in which Pompei's Christians lived out their faithful lives on earth, and how their faith developed in that setting.

NOTES

[1] Robert F. Foerster, *The Italian Emigration of our Times* (Cambridge, Massachusetts: Harvard University Press [Harvard Economic Studies, volume XX], 1924), 47–126.

[2] Ira Rosenwaike, *Population History of New York City* (Syracuse : Syracuse University Press, 1972), 67.

[3] Howard R. Marraro, "Italians in New York in the Eighteen-Fifties," *New York History* XXX (1949), 181–203, 276–303.

[4] United States Department of Commerce Bureau of the Census, *Historical Statistics of the United States, Colonial Times to 1970*, 2 volumes (Washington: Government Printing Office, 1975), 1:105–106.

[5] Silvano M. Tomasi. C.S., *Piety and Power: The Role of the Italian Parishes in the New York Metropolitan Area, 1880–1930* (New York: CMS, 1975). Chapter 2 has statistical tables.

[6] Betty Boyd Caroli, *Italian Repatriation from the United States, 1900–1914* (New York: CMS, 1973).

[7] Humbert S. Nelli. "The Economic Activities of Italian Americans" in Winston Van Horne and Thomas V. Tonnesen, eds., *Ethnicity and the Work Force* (Madison: University of Wisconsin [Ethnicity and Public Policy Series], 1985, 193–207.

[8] Leonard Dinnerstein and David M. Reimers, *Ethnic Americans: A History of Immigration*, third edition (New York: Harper and Row, 1988), 218–219.

[9] John Highan, *Strangers in the Land: Patterns of American Nativism, 1860–1925* (New York: Atheneum 1969), 131–157.

[10] Rudolph J. Vecoli, "Peasants and Prelates: Italian Immigrants and the Catholic Church," *Journal of Social History* II (1969), 217–267.

[11] J. Francis McIntyre to John Marchegiani, 29 May 1934, CMS Box 9, Folder 104.

[12] Joan Jacobs Brumberg, *Mission for Life: The Story of the Family of Adoniram Judson, the Dramatic Events of the First American Foreign Mission, and the Course of Evangelical Religion in the Nineteenth Century* (New York: Free Press, 1980). *See also* John McNab, "Bethlehem Chapel: Presbyterians and Italian Americans in New York City," *Journal of Presbyterian History* LV (1977), 145–160.

[13] Stephen Michael Di Giovanni "Michael Augustine Corrigan and the Italian Immigrants: The Relationship between the Church and the Italians in the Archdiocese of New York 1885–1902" (Ph.D., Gregorian Pontifical University [Rome]. 1983), 126.

[14] Marco Caliaro and Mario Francesconi, *John Baptist Scalabrini: Apostle to Emigrants,* translated Alba I. Zizzamia (New York: CMS, 1977).

[15] Colman J. Barry, O.S.B., *The Catholic Church and German Americans* (Milwaukee: Bruce Publishing Company, 1953), 30.

[16] Di Giovanni, 143–162.

[17] Richard M. Linkh, *American Catholicism and European Immigrants, 1900–1924* (New York: CMS, 1975).

[18] Michael A. Corrigan to Giovanni Battista Scalabrini, 10 February 1888, reproduced in Constantino Sassi, P.S.S.C., *Parrocchia della Madona di Pompei in New York: Notizie Storiche dei primi Cinquant'anni dalla sua Fondazione, 1892–1942* (Rome: Tipografia Santa Lucia, 1946), 17.

[19] John Horace Mariano, *The Italian Contribution to America Democracy* (Boston: Christopher Publishing House, 1921), 19–22.

[20] Joyce Gold, *From Trout Stream to Bohemia: A Walking Guide to Greenwich Village History* (New York: Old Warren Road Press, 1988).

[21] "Within Bohemia's Borders: Greenwich Village, 1830–1930," exhibition pamphlet distributed by Museum of the City of New York, 1990–1991.

[22] Emma Bertolotti to Antonio Demo, Rome, 9 November 1924, CMS Box 5 Folder 32; 29 March and 10 May 1925, Box 5, Folder 33; 14 December 1925, Box 5, Folder 34; and 8 August 1927, Box 5, Folder 37.

[23] The statistics that follow come from Foerster, p. 379; Louise C. Odencrantz, *Italian Women in Industry* (New York: Russell Sage, 1919); and Louise Boland More, *Wage Earners' Budgets: A Study of the Standard and Cost of Living in New York* (New York: Henry Holt and Company [Greenwich House Series of Social Studies #1], 1907).

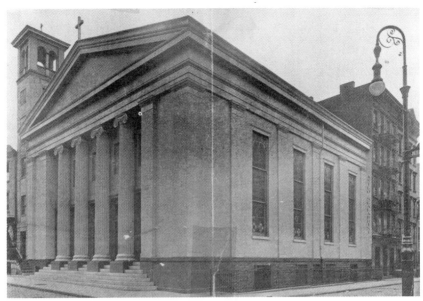

210 Bleecker Street, Pompei's home from 1898 until its demolition in 1927. Erected in 1836 for a Unitarian Universalist Congregation, the church was occupied from 1883 until its sale to Pompei by the African–American Congregation of Saint Benedict the Moor.

210 Bleeker's interior in 1909. Papal Countess Annie Leary donated the funds for the painting of the Madonna of the Rosary, a copy of the one in Pompei, Italy.

THE SOCIETY FOR THE PROTECTION OF ITALIAN IMMIGRANTS

Entrance to the City from the Ellis Island Boat at Battery.

Here "Runners" formerly fleeced the Newcomers.

Courtesy of Leslie's Weekly

OFFICE,

17 PEARL STREET, NEW YORK.

TELEPHONE, 3641 BROAD.

Cover of a pamphlet of the Society for the Protection of Italian Immigrants, which was one of the voluntary agencies engaged in defending the inexperienced immigrants from the speculation of unscrupulous *padroni*.

2

The First Pompei in America, 1892–1898

Easter Sunday was no day for a priest to travel. Yet it was Easter Sunday, March 29, 1891, that Father Pietro Bandini arrived in New York Harbor, aboard a steam ship loaded with freight and with immigrants from Europe. If Father Bandini travelled first or second class, his journey ended at the East River piers, where the steam ship docked and the immigration officials checked off those passengers. If he travelled third class, he and his fellow "steerage" passengers (so-called because their accommodations were below the water line, with the freight and the ship's steering mechanism) were taken by barge and tugboat to a building in Battery Park called the Barge Office, where other immigration officials waited to process these poorer and less-desirable newcomers. If Father Bandini didn't see the Barge Office when he landed, he would see it soon enough. He had come to work there.

Father Bandini arrived in New York by a roundabout route.[1] He was born in Forli, in the Italian province of Romagna, March 31, 1852. He entered the Society of Jesus, or Jesuits, September 24, 1869. After assignments in Monaco and Romagna, the Jesuits sent him to the United States, as a missionary to American Indians in the Rocky Mountains, where he was ordained in 1878. In 1889, the Jesuits called him back to Italy as rector of Thomas Aquinas School, in Cuneo, Turin. He and the Jesuits parted company in July 22, 1890. Judging from his later life, Father Bandini had an adventurous streak and preferred to be out in the mission field—the further out, the better.

On Christmas Eve, 1890, Father Bandini took vows to join the Scalabrinians. The order, had an assignment tailor-made for him. In 1888, the Scalabrinians sent their first missionaries to New York City, to open parishes for the city's Italians, and to start a branch of the Saint Raphael Society for Italians passing through its harbor. New York's Archbishop Corrigan was sufficiently supportive of the idea that on July 10, 1890, he published a pastoral letter introducing the Scalabrinians and the Saint Raphael Society to his non-Italian clergy and laity.[2] However the Scalabrinians had a surplus of projects and a shortage of resources, and the Saint Raphael Society had not progressed. Father Bandini came to turn the Saint Raphael Society from a proposal to a fact.

Soon after his arrival, Father Bandini took up his duties at the Barge Office. He was not the only priest there. Other ethnic Catholics had their own travelers' aid societies. One was the Archdiocese of New York's Mission of the Holy Rosary for the Protection of Irish Immigrant Girls. The mission occupied the site of the present Mother Seton National Shrine. Its chaplain, Father Callahan, helped Father Bandini learn his new job.[3]

Federal officials opened a new immigration station on Ellis Island on New Year's Day 1892. One reason for choosing an island for the immigration station was to separate the immigrants from those who exploited them. Only people with passes were allowed on Ellis Island. Father Bandini secured a pass, and continued with his work. The Ellis Island building in which Father Bandini began his work burned June 15, 1897, and was replaced with the present one December 17, 1900. Near the stairs immigrants descended when they finished their processing were offices for immigrant aid agencies. Father Bandini may have had an office there.

Father Bandini published the first Italian language Saint Raphael Society annual report in July 1892, and the first English language report in 1893. By reading them, and reports from later years, one can watch Father Bandini at work.[4] At the point at which Father Bandini and the other Saint Raphael agents met the immigrants, the process of clearing the immigrants had already begun. Ship captains kept manifests of their cargo, including immigrants in steerage, and they issued each steerage passenger a tag with a number showing on which line of the manifest the immigrant's name appeared.

Father Bandini or another agent met each barge load of Italian immigrants as they trooped down the gang plank and shepherded their children and baggage toward Ellis Island's main building. If luggage got lost or stolen, Father Bandini tried to find it. As the immigrants headed upstairs to the Great Hall, or waiting room, they encountered the first of many medical inspectors checking to see if they were healthy enough to find work in the United States. If they were ill, the medical inspectors sent them to one of the island's hospitals, and Father Bandini visited them there. In the Great Hall, families and individuals waited for interviews which determined their fitness to enter the United States. When the number on their tag was called out, the individual, or the entire family, came forward for a interview with an official. Ellis Island had interpreters, but Father Bandini helped with some translations. People who were not admitted were entitled to hearings, and Father Bandini provided access to legal aid. If immigrants planned to travel beyond New York, Father Bandini helped map out their routes and determine a means of transportation. He insured they paid fair prices for their tickets, and telegraphed relatives to meet them. If immigrants planned to stay in New York, Father Bandini told them about American wages and working conditions so they could negotiate with *padroni*. When they changed their Italian for American currency, Father Bandini made sure the exchange rates were fair.

Pompei's baptismal and marital records show Father Bandini performed pastoral as well as charitable work. He said Mass on Sundays on Ellis Island. He baptized babies born while their parents were travelling, or who for some other reason had not received the sacrament. He witnessed marriages between women arriving on Ellis Island and the sweethearts who sent for them. Presumably he heard confessions and performed the last rites, or Extreme Unction, for those unfortunate enough to die in the hospital within sight of the end of their long ocean journeys.

Some immigrants had special needs. Because immigration officials suspected, with some reason, that there was an international prostitution trade, females were usually detained unless a male—husband, father, brother—promised to support them. If the man supposed to meet the woman failed to appear, Father Bandini sent him a telegram or message. (Some time after Father Bandini left Saint Raphael, the society was called upon to assist a woman just arrived from Italy and looking for her fiancé, who was supposed to meet her in New York. It turned out he had indeed been on his way but aboard the *Titanic*.[5])

Children travelling alone posed two problems. Immigration officials detained them until their parents called for them. Being kept for an indefinite period on Ellis Island was bad enough. What was worse was that not everyone who came to claim children had good intentions toward them. Unscrupulous people imported children to use as beggars, newspaper hawkers, or street performers, exploiting their labor, mistreating them, and denying them the education they needed. Father Bandini kept an eye out for the children's welfare.

Father Bandini thought the Italian immigrants needed more extensive services than he could provide from an Ellis Island office. He went house-hunting, and found a four-story residence in Greenwich Village for sale. It was three miles to Battery Park which was quite a distance considering Father Bandini's clients would not have known their way around New York, and would have wanted to walk to save money. However, it was spacious, the price was right, and there were Italians in the neighborhood. Archbishop Corrigan donated three thousand dollars from his personal funds, and early in 1892, Father Bandini opened the New York headquarters of the Saint Raphael Society at 113 Waverly Place. (The building was still standing in the 1990s.)

Now that he had the space, Father Bandini engaged the Pallottine Sisters of Charity, an Italian community which had come to New York in 1884, to manage the house. He set aside rooms for lodging Italian immigrant women and children in transit, and a labor bureau for Italians looking for jobs. On the ground floor, in a room about sixteen by sixty-five feet, Father Bandini opened a chapel, which he dedicated to Our Lady of Pompei. He said the first Mass there May 8, 1892. This date is usually given as the founding of Our Lady of Pompei parish.

How did Father Bandini choose the name? That story starts with Bartolo Longo (1841-1926), a lay man from Latianio, near Naples.[6] A devout man interested in encouraging the recitation of the rosary, he conceived of the idea of a shrine to Our Lady of the Rosary. On November 14, 1875, as a gift from a cloistered convent of Dominican nuns at Port Medina, he acquired the perfect centerpiece for his planned shrine. In terms of its antiquity or its artistic value, it was an ordinary painting, but it showed Mary, the Child Jesus on her lap, giving the rosary to Saint Dominic (1170–1221, on the left in traditional pictures), and Saint Catherine of Siena (1347–1380, on the right). He brought the painting of Our Lady of the Rosary to Pompei, where he set up the shrine. The shrine became well-known throughout southern Italy, from whence came many of the Italians Father Bandini saw on Ellis Island. Father Bandini may have chosen the name to give the southern Italians a touch of home in their new surroundings.

The people who lived in Greenwich Village and attended Mass at the new chapel had a different demographic profile than the people Father Bandini saw at Ellis Island. Pompei's earliest parishioners were from Genoa, a port city in northern Italy that had already contributed one important Italian to American history: it was the birth place of Christopher Columbus. Baptismal records for 1893, the first full year of operation, indicate many parishioners came from Chiavari, a port southeast of Genoa.

The chapel had four Sunday Masses, the earliest at 5:30 a.m., to accommodate those who had to work on that day. In its earliest days, Pompei followed the southern Italian custom of including prayers for the deceased at the end of every Mass, but by the early twentieth century, the southern Italians had already begun assimilating to the northern Italian and the American way of doing things, and dropped the custom.[7] By the time the last Mass was said it was time for dinner, the largest and most relaxed meal of the day in most Italian families. After dinner Father Bandini performed baptisms. Then he departed for house calls while the chapel was given over to catechism classes and pious society, or sodality, meetings. At the end of the day came a vespers service, with a sermon and benediction.[8]

By the end of the 1893, Pompei's first full year, the sacramental registers recorded 87 baptisms and about 13 marriages.[9] The balance sheet showed how valuable the chapel was for supporting the Saint Raphael Society financially. Saint Raphael took in $1,933 between September 1892 and February 1893: $299.91 from miscellaneous sources, $147.90 from donations to Saint Raphael, $379.25 from a benefit concert, and $1,105.94 from the chapel.[10]

Father Bandini pressed Archbishop Corrigan to let him open a parish separate from Saint Raphael. A parish would have a definite set of parishioners, from whom it could expect support. A separate building would allow for expansion of services. Archbishop Corrigan was skeptical. In the same period that Saint Raphael took in $1,933, it spent $2,133, and fell so far behind on its mortgage payments that creditors initiated legal action. However, Archbishop Corrigan also recognized the value of Father Bandini's work at the port, and the long-term need for Italian parishes in the city. He made another gift from his personal funds to satisfy the creditors, and Father Bandini again went house-hunting.

This time he found a lot and two buildings on 214 Sullivan Street. One building was a red brick church built in 1810 for an African-American Baptist congregation. In 1842, it became Bethel Methodist Colored Church. By 1895, the Methodist congregation was also gone, and the property owners extended Father Bandini a lease that included an option to buy. Father Bandini signed the lease March 6, 1895. (The structures Pompei occupied have since been replaced by a loft building.)

Archbishop Corrigan dedicated the church for Pompei's use April 28, 1895. Auxiliary Bishop John Murphy Farley, who became archbishop upon Corrigan's death in 1903 and a cardinal in 1911, celebrated the first Mass. Another guest, a Father Mulcahy of Waterbury, Connecticut, led the evening vespers. Apostolic Delegate Francesco Cardinal Satolli, Pope Leo XIII's diplomatic representative in the United States, said a few words in Italian after vespers. He reminded the Italians to live up to their faith, since they were from the same country in which was located the center of the Catholic Church.[11] Pompei was still a chapel, not yet legally distinct from Saint Raphael, but in terms of its organization and services, it was becoming more and more like a parish.

Like other pastors of his day, Father Bandini organized his parishioners into sodalities or societies according to their age, sex, and marital status.[12] Parish sodalities played a special role in American churches, as Father Constantino Sassi, one of Pompei's later priests and author of its golden anniversary history, explained:

When a sodality is large and well regulated, its people are bound together in the practice of Christian life, in frequent attendance at church, in frequent reception of the sacraments, in giving a good example to others, and in unity with the pastor, to whom they are especially close. Besides, sodalities also give fair sums to the church and add to the dignity of the church, because on many occasions, such as processions or solemn functions, they participate as groups with banners and standards. Religious sodalities are the soul of the church.[13]

Father Bandini's most important sodality was the Saint Joseph Society. After the 1917 Bolshevik Revolution, Saint Joseph, a carpenter, was frequently upheld as a model for working people.[14] In the late nineteenth century, he was the model for husbands and fathers, and the Saint Joseph Society was open to the married men of the parish.

There were more societies for married women. Two societies were incorporated into Pompei's regular devotional schedule: Our Lady of Pompei and the Honor Guard of the Sacred Heart, the ancestors of Pompei's present Three Societies. After Pompei moved to its Sullivan Street church, an Altar Society helped to keep the church clean.

The traditional patron saint of youth was Saint Aloysius Gonzaga (1568–1591). He is best known for rejecting the life of the young nobleman and soldier in order to become a Jesuit. However, he was also a fellow countryman to Italians, because he was born in Lombardy. The Italians called him Saint Luigi. Father Bandini organized a Saint Luigi Society, but such a society had an inherent element of instability. At a certain age, its members automatically got too old for it. Thus young men's societies went through numerous transitions during Pompei's history.

Young unmarried women joined the Children, or Daughters, of Mary. Parish women wanted such a group when the parish was still located at Waverly Place, but there was no meeting space, so they waited until the move to Sullivan Street.[15] The Daughters of Mary was more stable than the young men's groups. An announcement regarding it appeared in Pompei's bulletin as late as 1967.[16]

Pompei operated on a schedule designed to foster the individual's religious life. The most important acts of religious life were participation in the sacraments. Each sodality had its assigned Sunday for communion, which meant each sodality also had its unofficial Saturday for confessions. On Sunday evenings, Pompei celebrated Vespers, usually including a sermon and benediction.

Vespers were part of the Divine Office, or daily cycle of prayers, which, like Mass, were part of Catholicism's liturgy. In addition to the liturgy, there were devotions, or pious practices, designed to be done privately, or by people gathered in groups. Pompei had weekly and annual devotions. On the first Friday of each month there was an exposition of the Blessed Sacrament, a practice popularized by Saint Margaret Mary Alacoque (1647–1690). Every Friday evening there were Stations of the Cross. In December there were novenas, or nine consecutive days of special devotions, to prepare for the feast of the Immaculate Conception and for Christmas. (*Perpetual* novenas, weekly devotions, came in the 1930s.) Some devotions indicated Pompei's parishioners' Genoese origins. Saint John the Baptist was the patron of Genoa, and his feast day was marked with a Mass for deceased members of the parish and a special benediction service. The women from San Stefano, near Genoa, attended services in honor of Our Lady of Guadalupe each August.

Pompei was established to allow the Italians to use their familiar language and customs in their worship. However, as soon as they got their Italian parish, Italians found out they couldn't operate it unless they adopted some American ways. Father Sassi recalled one of the most unusual and important Americanisms:

> The American custom is that at every Sunday and holy day Mass, the celebrant ascends the pulpit, after the Gospel, for the reading of the weekly announcements, in which are recorded the upcoming feast days, days of fast and abstinence, sodality meetings, and the dates of the sodalities' monthly communions.[17]

Children Americanized quickly, even where Christmas customs were concerned. Or, perhaps especially where Christmas customs were concerned. As early as 1895, Pompei had a Christmas tree for its catechism classes, a decoration that did not appear in homes in Italy. These patterns of adapting to American ways, especially where the running of the church was concerned and especially where children were concerned, were repeated throughout Pompei's history.

There were some customs, especially those that touched upon family life as well as religious life, that were too precious to give up. Christmas brought back so many memories of family and of home that it made sense to preserve as many Italian Christmas customs as possible. Pompei's parishioners had one Christmas practice that was unusual in American churches. Every Christmas season, Pompei put up in the church a creche. At some point between Christmas and Epiphany, parishioners visited the church to kiss the face of the Infant Jesus lying in the manger. When in 1915 the Archdiocese of New York began permitting midnight Mass on Christmas Eve, Pompei incorporated into that Mass a ritual like the contemporary Good Friday veneration of the cross, except instead of the cross, parishioners filed to the altar to kiss the statue of the Infant Jesus.[18]

Under Father Bandini, Pompei derived most of its income from the pastoral care of parishioners. At every Mass, ushers stood by the doors to accept offerings from people entering the church. As far as the Italians were concerned, this door fee was an unpleasant American custom which made the church resemble a theater with an admission price.[19] It was indeed an American custom. American Protestants rented pews in their churches. Each church-goer paid an annual fee, which varied according to the seating's desirability. Some Catholic churches rented pews, but, Pompei never did. Instead, it followed customs many parishes established for their poor parishioners. Each Mass-goer either paid a small sum at the church entrance, or stood in the back throughout the Mass. Pompei kept its door fee until 1969.[20]

Ushers passed the basket during Mass, and, when the parish had an extraordinary expense, took up a second collection as well. Those who gave a dollar at Sunday Mass were entitled to enter their names in a book kept near the door, and Mass was said on Monday for their intentions. Before holy days such as New Year's, Pompei distributed donation envelopes, which were collected at the holy day Mass. Sodality members paid dues regularly, and, on feast days, took up special collections.

Pompei also raised money in a more American way, by sponsoring socials. The parish celebrated Labor Day 1895 with a parish picnic, the proceeds of which went to benefit the church. Pompei had discovered another element of American Catholic life that became an important part of its own life. The surest way to strengthen a parish financially was to strengthen it spiritually, socially, and in terms of its service to others.

Despite the effort to raise money, debts were piling up. Also, Father Bandini's fancy had been caught by another missionary challenge.[21] A wealthy investor named Austin Corbin was looking for either a new investment or a charity—it was never clear which. At that time, most of the United States' African-American population lived in the former Confederate states and many earned their living by sharecropping, renting land to live on and to farm, and paying the rent with a portion of their crop, which their landlord then sold on the commodities market. Coincidentally, *mezzadria* was also practiced in Italy. Mr. Corbin thought he could transplant Italians to the American south to practice sharecropping on cotton plantations there. He bought a tract of land in Sunnyside, Arkansas. He recruited the labor for it with the help of Prince Emmanuel Ruspoli, who owned a lot of land in the Marches, in central Italy, but who had even more people than he had land. Prince Ruspoli convinced some of the families to go to Sunnyside and form a community there.

Father Bandini saw in the newspapers the plans for the Sunnyside project, and wrote Cardinal Satolli of his interest. Separately, Mr. Corbin, who knew of Father Bandini's work at Saint Raphael, wrote Cardinal Satolli requesting Father Bandini's services. Cardinal Satolli had his own reasons for supporting Sunnyside. Like many of his colleagues, he thought that farming was more secure than factory labor, and that in the country Catholics would be safe from Protestant proselytization and secular temptation. Cardinal Satolli got in touch with the Scalabrinians' vicar general in New York, Father Francesco Zaboglio, about sending Father Bandini to Arkansas. Father Zaboglio protested he needed Father Bandini in New York, but there was nothing he could do. Father Bandini's five-year temporary vows with the Scalabrinians came to an end in 1895. In January, 1896, Father Bandini was on his way to Arkansas.

On June 4, 1896, shortly after Father Bandini's arrival, Mr. Corbin died and his heirs abandoned his sharecropping experiment, Father Bandini could have left, too, and gone off in search of his next missionary adventure. Instead, he found his life's work in Arkansas. When Sunnyside was liquidated, he remained with the remnant of the sharecroppers. Through the Saint Raphael Society he purchased land in the Ozark Mountains, and sold plots to the sharecroppers, who then became owners instead of tenants. The new community took the name Tontitown, after Enrico Tonti (1650–1704), an Italian who was part of Robert Cavalier de la Salle's exploring party and thus the first Italian in what is now Arkansas. Father Bandini was Tontitown's pastor, its teacher, and its post office manager until his death in 1917.

Back in New York, Father Zaboglio took over Father Bandini's duties at Saint Raphael and at Pompei. Father Zaboglio was born February 15, 1852, at Campodolcino, Sondrio, Italy.[22] He was ordained a diocesan priest in 1876 and joined the Scalabrinians April 10, 1888. He had helped Bishop Scalabrini draft the plans for the community and its immigrant apostolate, and, shortly after he joined, he departed for the United States as the Scalabrinians' vicar general. Until coming to Pompei, he was kept busy as an administrator for the Scalabrinians. After his pastorate at Pompei ended in 1899, he returned to Italy, where he died September 3, 1911.

Despite his administrative experience, Father Zaboglio despaired of Pompei. Pompei and Saint Raphael were still one legal entity, and that legal entity was heavily in debt. Father Zaboglio thought he could stabilize the situation by creating two legal entities, Saint Raphael and Pompei, keeping Saint Raphael, and getting some other religious order, or the archdiocese, to take care of Pompei. Neither the archdiocese nor the other religious orders involved in the Italian ministry felt able to shoulder the debt burden.

At this point, Annie Leary stepped in. Miss Leary (1830–1919) was a wealthy heiress who specialized in contributing, financially and in terms of personal involvement, to Catholic project. She was given the title papal countess and buried beneath Saint Patrick's Old Cathedral in recognition of her largesse toward Catholicism in the Archdiocese of New York and in Italy.[23] Her Italian work began when she financed Mother Cabrini's Missionaries of the Sacred Heart so that they could teach sewing and catechism to Italian immigrant girls in Greenwich Village.[24] From the children, Miss Leary's interest expanded. Father Zaboglio listed her contributions:

If it had not been for her, our church of the Madonna of the Rosary of Pompei would have closed. She gave her own money, had a concert for the church, last Sunday she had another entertainment, she had the facade repaired, mended the stairs in the church and in the house, ordered a painting of the Madonna of Pompei from Italy, she is repairing and furnishing all the rooms and maintaining the work school for Italian children. But what is most important, she had the intention to found industrial schools even for the young men and to acquire new sites.[25]

The painting Father Zaboglio described is probably the one in Pompei's sanctuary.[26]

Thanks to Miss Leary's support, Father Zaboglio took confidence in Pompei's future. The next step was to separate Pompei from Saint Raphael. The new parish had to have a name. As it had been calling itself Our Lady of Pompei for four year, Father Zaboglio wrote Bartolo Longo at the Pompei shrine to formally request permission to use the name. The reply came in a letter written in Italian and signed with a stamp of Bartolo Longo's signature: "I do not see any difficulty and so approve that the church of which you are rector may become the center of the cult and of the veneration of Our Lady of the Rosary of Pompei for all the United States and for all of North America."[27] Hence Pompei became a "shrine," although the phrase wasn't much used until the 1980s.

By this time, the owners of the property at 214 Sullivan, fearing Pompei would never become a reliable, rent-paying tenant, let it be known they would neither renew the lease nor permit Pompei to exercise its option to buy the site. Father Zaboglio had to find a new home before the lease ran out in May 1898.

Coincidentally, another Village congregation was in the process of relocating, and willing to sell its Village property. At 210 Bleecker Street there stood a Greek Revival temple of a church.[28] The structure had been erected in 1836 as the home of the Third Unitarian Universalist Church. In 1883, the Unitarians sold it to Saint Benedict the Moor, an African-American Catholic congregation. By the 1890s, the African-American population was moving uptown, the area west of Columbus Circle and Lincoln Center. Saint Benedict the Moor bought another old church at 342-344 West 53rd Street. Arrangements were made for Saint Benedict the Moor to transfer its Bleecker Street church to Pompei in 1898.

Pompei probably could have used an earlier transfer date. On July 14, 1897, someone smelled gas rising from the basement of the church at 214 Sullivan. Father Zaboglio, sexton Samuel Vincentini, and Saint Raphael agent Francis Isola descended to the cellar to find the leak. It was late afternoon, it was getting dark, and they struck a match. The resulting explosion killed Messrs. Isola and Vicentini.[29] Damage to the church is more difficult to estimate. The explosion ignited a destructive fire, but the congregation continued meeting at 214 Sullivan until May 1898. Similarly, the extent of Father Zaboglio's injuries are difficult to determine. He was near death for two months, and he never fully recovered his health. On the other hand, either an optimistic assessment of his recovery, or a sense of duty, or a decision by his superiors, led him to remain at Pompei until 1898, and to be its official pastor until June 1899.

Perhaps the explosion destroyed some records. Perhaps Father Zaboglio's poor health led him to rely more heavily on the lay men for assistance. Perhaps the lay men themselves became alarmed by the mounting debts and the pastor's declining health. In any case, the earliest surviving minutes from a parish society meeting are dated January 20, 1898. The name of the meeting was not recorded, but it seems to be an ancestor of Pompei's present Finance Committee.

This was evidently the first meeting of the new year, for it began by electing officers: E. Siccardi, president; Luigi Lango, corresponding secretary; Riccardo Lorenzoni, vice-secretary; Father Zaboglio, treasurer; and Michele Pepe, secretary of finance. Next, the meeting appointed a committee, consisting of Emilio Ballerini, Dominico Gazzola, Vincenzo Cinque, Angelo Cuneo, Giuseppe Miele, Giuseppe Gregughia, and Eduardo Franceschini, to accompany Pompei's clergy on visits to the laity's homes to take up a collection for the church. Mr. Gregughia moved, and the meeting agreed, to leave up to Father Zaboglio the decision as to when to call a general parish meeting to discuss finances. Mr. Pepe moved, and the meeting agreed, to send a circular letter to other Italian communities, inviting them to contribute.[30]

The group met again January 29.[31] The minutes added a few new names: Luigi Fugazy, Eduardo Bergonzi, and Giuseppe Gregughia were mentioned as constituting a committee of *curatore*, trustees. Given the recent explosion at the Sullivan Street church, it is no wonder the group met again on February 3, and appointed a subcommittee, consisting of Michele Pepe, Giuseppe Miele, Eusebio Pazzo, Pietro Alpi, and Father Zaboglio, to research insurance for the new building at 210 Bleecker.[32] The meeting also discussed the matter of retaining a good lawyer.

On March 7, 1898, Pompei was incorporated as a parish, a separate entity from Saint Raphael, and, although it had debts stemming from the operation of the church, it was no longer tied to the debt stemming from the operation of the travelers aid society.[33] Under New York State law, every Roman Catholic parish is incorporated separately, each with a four-man board of trustees. The archbishop and pastor are always two members of the board, and the other two always lay men from the parish. Pompei's first two trustees were Luigi Fugazy and Eduardo Bergonzi. Mr. Fugazy was sufficiently well-known in the Greenwich Village Italian community that a scholar later used him as an example of ethnic group leadership.[34] Mr. Bergonzi's family was involved in Pompei for two generations.

The men who attended these early 1898 meetings established another pattern of life at Pompei. They were a small core of loyal parishioners. Over the years, such small cores formed around various parish societies and activities. Sometimes these groups lasted only so long as they were useful, as Pompei once had, but no longer has, a group to put on an annual Passion Play. Sometimes, the group changed with the times and survived as the group of men described above evolved into the Parish Finance Committee. The existence of these groups is an important part of Pompei's history.

A formal procession from 214 Sullivan to 210 Bleecker marked Pompei's taking possession of its new church on May 8, 1898.[35] When Pompei's parishioners photographed the church at 210 Bleecker, they tended to let the church fill the photograph frame, which gives the impression it was more prominent than it actually was. There is a landscape called *The City from Greenwich Village,* painted in 1922 by artist John Sloan (1871–1951), that shows how Pompei fit into its landscape.[36] "The city," that is, the downtown lights, are far away in the upper left corner. The foreground is taken up with a view of the Village from a point above Sixth Avenue, following the elevated line as it curved at Fourth Street. Pompei's roof and tower are barely visible, peeking over four-story tenements along Bleecker Street.

The best photographs of 210 Bleecker during Pompei's stay there were published in a 1922 pamphlet, and probably taken about then.[37] In architectural style, Pompei's church resembled the present day Saint Joseph's Church on Sixth Avenue. (Saint Joseph's was built just three years before Pompei's church, in 1833.) Like Saint Joseph's, Pompei's building had a slightly sloping roof, with the ends of the crossbeam at the altar and the front door. Unlike Saint Joseph's, Pompei was built of some kind of monochromatic stone, probably lime stone or smooth granite. Its porch roof columns roof ran across the entire front of the building. Three shallow steps rather than a steep staircase led to the front door.

The interior also resembled Saint Joseph's. There was one big room with galleries on both sides, again running from the altar to the front door. Across the space over the front door hung a choir loft with an organ. There was no main aisle; rather there were three sets of pews, east center, and west. Above the altar was the legend "Gloria in Excelsis Deo," with Christian symbols on either side.

The sanctuary marked the building as an Italian church dedicated to Our Lady of the Rosary. The copy of the shrine painting of the Madonna of Pompei went into a rectangular frame and hung over the altar. Beneath the altar was a Corpus Christi, a statue of the dead Christ resting in the tomb. On the altar was the tabernacle. Immediately adjacent to the altar stood statues of the Sacred Heart and Saint Joseph with the Infant Jesus. Further to the sides were two more altars, one with a painting of the crucifixion, and the other with a painting of the Assumption. Around these paintings were more statues; one of Saint Luigi is especially noticeable. All around the sanctuary area were candle stands bearing not modern votive candles in little glasses, but shorter versions of dinner table candles.

Now that Pompei had a long-term home, Miss Leary began work on the school Father Zaboglio had mentioned in his description of her activities. Miss

Leary's school brought Pompei into contact with American Catholicism's most famous Italian immigrant, Mother Frances Xavier Cabrini.

Mother Cabrini (1850–1917) was born at Sant' Angelo Lodigiano, in Lombardy. She founded the Missionary Sisters of the Sacred Heart in 1880, hoping at that point to go to China. In a famous audience pictured in one of Pompei's stained glass windows, Pope Leo XIII directed her westward to assist Italian immigrants. Mother Cabrini and her first missionaries arrived in New York City in 1889, and began teaching at the Scalabrinians' Saint Joachim. Mother Cabrini herself soon left the city. She was a legendary traveler. Only recently has a biographer, Sister Mary Louise Sullivan, M.S.C., figured out exactly when Mother Cabrini was where. According to Sister Mary Louise, it was on a trip to New York in 1898-1899 that Mother Cabrini arranged for her Missionary Sisters to staff Miss Leary's *Scuola di Lavoro,* or sewing school for Italian girls, and teach Christian Doctrine at Pompei.[38]

The earliest surviving parish bulletin dates from February 1899. At that time, parishioners got information about parish happenings from the Sunday pulpit announcements. The bulletin, in English, attracted non-Italians, and kept donors such as Miss Leary informed as to Pompei's progress. According to this bulletin, Sunday was Pompei's busiest day. There were Masses at 6:00, 8:00, 9:00, 9:30, and 11:00, with an explanation of the Gospel at each Mass. At 2:00 came catechism and baptisms, presumably in separate parts of the church. Confessions were heard daily at 4:00. Regular devotions to patron saints weren't yet common, but every Sunday Pompei had a service with vespers, a sermon, and benediction. There were several sodalities: Saint Joseph, Saint Louis, Pompei, the Children of Mary, Poor Souls (in purgatory), Sacred Heart and Church Debt. Two lay people appeared on the parish schedule: Miss Leary and Miss Minnie Mooney, the organist.[39]

With the huge debt, the frequent moves of the first two years, the first pastor heading out to adventure in Arkansas, and the second pastor blowing up the church, it might not seem as though Pompei were off to a good start. If there were enough room to go into more detail about the situation in which Fathers Bandini and Zaboglio worked, and to compare them with other New York clergy of the same time period, one would see that nearly every parish had a similar story of a rough beginning.

Under Fathers Bandini and Zaboglio, Pompei established important patterns. Although Pompei was an Italian church, it adopted American customs regarding financial matters and children's programs, thus ensuring its continued survival and starting on the long road to assimilation. From its earliest days, Pompei did not completely divide the spiritual, social, and material aspects of running a parish, but interwove them to strengthen community life. Pompei soon acquired a core of loyal parishioners, gathered around particular parish societies or activities. What Pompei needed next was stability: an address that lasted longer than three years, and a pastor that lasted longer than five. Both these needs were soon met.

NOTES

[1] Edward Claude Stibili, "The St. Raphael Society for the Protection of Italian Immigrants, 1887–1923" (Ph.D., University of Notre Dame, 1977), 149ff.

[2] Sassi, 20.

[3] Pietro Bandini, *First Annual Report of Saint Raphael's Italian Benevolent Society* (n.p., 1893), 27.

[4] P.M.A. Bandini, *Relazione Della Società Italiana di San Raffaele in New York* (Piacenza: Marchesotti e L. Porta, 1892). This was reprinted in *Studi Emigrazione* V (1968), 303–323.

[5] *Società San Raffaele per gl'Immigranti Italiani, XXI Rapporto Annuale* (n.p., 1913),15.

[6] *Village Bells* (Winter 1981), 2–3.

[7] Sassi, 54.

[8] DiGiovanni, 361.

[9] "About" 13 because Father Bandini apparently recorded them elsewhere and then transferred them into the permanent record in 1895, mixing them in with the 1894 and 1895 weddings.

[10] "Statement of Saint Raphael's Home from 11 September 1892 to 28 February 1893," AANY, Saint Raphael's Society New York City, Folder E–11.

[11] New York *Times*, 29 April 1895.

[12] DiGiovanni, 481–497. These pages contain the parish announcements for 1894–1895.

[13] Sassi, 53.

[14] *La Messa D'Argento: Discorso Recitato Dal Rev.mo Francesco Canonico Castellano . . . .* (New York: Il Carroccio Publishing Company, 1923), unpaginated.

[15] Private communication, Bridgeport, Connecticut, 9 November 1917, Box 3, Folder 20.

[16] Weekly bulletin, 24 September 1967, OLP Bulletins I.

[17] Sassi, 53–54.

[18] Caroline Ware, *Greenwich Village, 1920–1930: A Comment on American Civilization in the Post-War Years* (New York: Houghton Mifflin, 1935; reprint, New York: Harper, 1965), 313.

[19] Vecoli, 237.

[20] Weekly bulletin, 17 November 1968, OLP Sunday Bulletins I.

[21] "A Model Italian Colony in Arkansas," *Review of Reviews* XXXIV (September 1906), 361–362; Robert Schick, "Father Bandini: Missionary in the Ozarks," *Ave Maria* LXVI (20 December 1947), 782–786; and *Village Bells* (Spring 1985), 1–3.

[22] *Village Bells* (Spring 1987), 2–3.

[23] *New York Times,* 27 April 1919, I:22:4.

[24] New York *Herald*, 30 July 1905.

[25] Di Giovanni, 373.

[26] Mario Albanesi to Henri Bon, 25 March 1955, OLP Papers before 1975, 1950–1959 Folder.

[27] Bartolo Longo to Francesco Zaboglio, Pompei, Italy, 30 May 1896, CMS Box 1, Folder 1.

[28] Jorge Coll, T.O.R., *Una Iglesia Pionera* (New York: Privately published, 1989), 49, 71, and "Saint Benedict's Church," *Our Colored Missions* IX:10 (October 1923), 147–149.

[29] *New York Times*, 15 July 1897, 10:4; Sassi, 32.

[30] Meeting minutes, 20 January 1898, CMS Box 18, Folder 205.

[31] Meeting minutes, 29 January 1898, *ibid.*

[32] Meeting minutes, 3 February 1898, *ibid.*

[33] Incorporation Certificate #00174-98C* on file at 31 Chambers Street, Room 703.

[34] Victor R. Greene, *American Immigrant Leaders, 1800–1910: Marginality and Identity* (Baltimore: Johns Hopkins University Press, 1987), 126–128.

[35] Note on flyleaf of expenditure book in CMS Box 51.

[36] The painting hangs in the National Gallery of Art, Washington, D.C.

[37] *La Messa D'Argento.*

[38] Conversation with Sister Mary Louise Sullivan, M.S.C., 8 September 1991.

[39] Bulletin, February 1899, CMS Box 32, Folder 330.

3

The People and Their Pastor, 1898–1911

The 1897 explosion and Father Zaboglio's subsequent poor health presented the Scalabrinians with a dilemma. They didn't want to replace Father Zaboglio if he could still work. On the other hand, they didn't want to leave Our Lady of Pompei in the hands of someone who only *thought* he could still work. They needed someone to assist Father Zaboglio and, if necessary, take over. They found their man in Father Antonio Demo.

Father Demo was born April 23, 1870, at Lazzaretto di Bassano in the province of Vicenza.[1] His parents were Pietro Demo and the former Maria Merlo. He graduated from the Mander a Fonte Institute near his home, and entered the diocesan seminary. The Italian government required all men over twenty-one to serve the military, and Father Demo departed the seminary for a tour of duty from 1891 to 1892. Returning from the army, he transferred from the diocesan seminary to the Istituto Cristoforo Columbo, the seminary for Scalabrinians. In 1895 he again interrupted his studies for military service. Both tours of duty were with the *granatieri* or grenadiers. According to Father Demo's obituary, this was an elite unit "composed exclusively of tall, well-formed men," ideal for Father Demo, who stood six feet.

After ordination from Bishop Scalabrini's own hands on July 20, 1896, Father Demo departed for the mission field of Sacred Heart Church in Boston's North End. From there he came to New York as an assistant. Father Zaboglio's deteriorating health finally compelled him to resign in May 1899, and Father Demo's superiors appointed him Pompei's pastor July 19, 1899.[2] Father Demo always kept his Italian passport, never became an American citizen, and made several long trips back to Italy. But Pompei was his real home for the rest of his life.

One minor mystery is the state of Father Demo's English when he first came to Pompei. In a letter written in 1924, Father Demo mentioned that many Scalabrinian missionaries coming from Italy to Pompei did not speak English at the time of their arrival. Father Demo may have had some English in school, or he may have started learning it in Boston. When he came to New York, he befriended the family of Joseph Scarinzi, who was a professional translator and who may have helped Father Demo with his English.[3] Father Demo used Italian almost exclusively during his early years at Pompei, switching to English as his parish children grew up and as Pompei became more involved in Village activities.

When he became pastor, his superiors carefully advised Father Demo on the importance of good record keeping.[4] Father Demo seems to have filed away everything that crossed his desk. When he died, he left Pompei thirty-five years worth of advertisements, announcements, balance sheets, bills, brochures, correspondence, flyers, form letters, invitations, newspaper clippings, minutes from meetings, notes, personal letters, photographs, play bills, post cards, programs, sodality dues records, solicitations, and other pieces of paper. Many parishes have had pastors who built them their churches and schools, or who started some annual event that became a parish tradition, but few parishes have the rich legacy of history Father Demo left his people.

From Father Demo's records, one can sketch a profile of Pompei as he found it in 1900.[5] As we saw when Father Bandini began keeping baptismal records, most of Pompei's earliest parishioners were from Genoa. Other northern Italian provinces were also represented. The Michelini clan came from southern Tyrol near Trento.[6] Andrea Sabini came from Parma, and, before coming to New York in the early 1880s, he often visited an aunt who was a nun at a convent near Father Demo's home town.[7]

Most parish leaders arrived ahead of the mass migration out of Italy. Luigi Fugazy, who signed Pompei's incorporation papers, came to New York in 1869.[8] Charles Baciagalupo arrived so early he left before most other people came. He migrated with his family at age seven, and returned to Italy in 1905. He left a business on Mulberry Street, and took with him savings amassed in New York.[9]

Parish leaders tended to be in business for themselves. Some were sufficiently successful to merit inclusion in New York's Italian Chamber of Commerce publications. Angelo and Pietro Alpi manufactured artificial flowers. Mr. Baciagalupo was a mortician, Mr. Fugazy a banker, Joseph Personeni a pharmacist. There were scores of smaller businessmen.[10] Being in business for one's self was not absolutely necessary, though. John A. Perazzo, who was head usher and parish trustee even longer than Father Demo was pastor, was a life time employee of the post office.[11]

Parish leaders were family men. Charles Baciagalupo's sister Caroline married Giovanni Battista Perazzo (no relation to John A., above), who worked with Mr. Baciagalupo in the undertaking business and who in 1908 opened a funeral parlor of his own, which he passed on to his sons and grandsons.[12] Angelo and Marina Michelini had ten children, which may have contributed to their decision to make their business a boarding house.

Parish leaders involved themselves in Italian Village social life. Angelo Michelini's sons August and Leon followed him in the Tyrol–Trentino Benevolent Society, which was formed to provide insurance, but which also fostered the sense of community among immigrants from the same area.[13] Mr. Leon Michelini was also prominent in Tiro a Segno, an Italian target-shooting club founded in 1866, which ran social activities and a charitable foundation. The Progressive Era Association, which was incorporated January 10, 1929, included several names familiar to Pompei's records: Victor A. Fontana, Italo A. Fugazy, and G.B. Perazzo.[14]

There were similarities between Pompei and small businesses and social clubs. Like a business or club, Pompei called upon the skills and talents these men had: trustees required an understanding of business and legal documents, and fund raising chairmen needed to know about public relations. Like successful businesses or club affairs, successful parish activities added to the men's sense of themselves, and to the community's respect for them. This is not to say parish *prominenti* thought of Pompei only as another business or club. It is to say that their attachment to their faith was expressed in their attachment to Pompei, and their attachment to Pompei was expressed in doing for the parish the things they did best—which were usually things they learned in the business and club world.

There were three groups through which men involved themselves at Pompei. The earliest was the Saint Joseph Society, which was a combination Fathers' Club and Finance Committee. It advised Father Demo on parish business and legal matters, and helped with fund raisers.[15] There was also a "Church Aid Society," which was like a modern "friends of the museum" group. It included people like Mr. Fugazy. Its members were not necessarily parishioners. They were people who interested themselves in Pompei, donated money, contributed time and talent, and lent their good names to improve public relations, and so received membership in this society as a form of recognition.[16]

The most visible group of parish men were the *colletori*. The dictionary translates *colletore* as "collector," especially "tax collector." Parishioner Leon Michelini translated the word as "usher." Mr. Michelini was issued his *colletore* badge, a pin in the shape of a Maltese cross with the word *colletore* inscribed in its center, by Father Demo in 1908.[17] Mr. Michelini was only fourteen at the time, so the *colletori* could be quite young. A pulpit announcement for August 26, 1900, thanked a *colletrice* for gathering $35.51 at the San Stefano women's observance of the feast of Our Lady of Guadalupe, but women were not ushers at the Sunday masses, only at services primarily for other women.[18]

Membership in the *colletori*, the Church Aid Society, and the Saint Joseph's Society overlapped. Andrea Sabini, for example, was in all three.[19] All three helped support Pompei, each in different ways. Pompei had to be creative in its fund raising in the early twentieth century. It had many needs, and many poor parishioners without much money to give. Also, there were limits as to what

Pompei could do to raise money. New York State Law prohibited certain games of chance.[20] The chancery's ethical code forbade parishes to raise funds through sponsoring balls and dances, lest the dancing descend to an unacceptably low moral level.[21]

Nor could Pompei hold street fairs similar to its present Festa Italiana. First, the Festa has some points in common with the old southern Italian outdoor celebrations of patron saints' feast days. In the early days of migration, those feast days were organized by mutual benefit societies composed of lay men from the town where the saint was patron, not by parishes. Second, Americans, even Catholics, were sufficiently prejudiced against Italians that it is doubtful many tourists would have come. Father Demo and the northern Italians at Pompei may have shared the popular distaste for southern Italian street festivals. Father Demo also worried that sponsoring such a feast would prejudice outsiders against Pompei, and would embarrass young people going through an adolescent rejection of their parents' ethnic and religious heritage.[22] Pompei did not hold outdoor events while Father Demo was pastor. Instead, it raised funds in other ways.

The *colletori* took donations at the church door and during Mass. Saint Joseph ran affairs such as parish picnics.[23] On May 30, 1900, the Church Aid Society mounted a more ambitious fund raiser, a "First Annual Entertainment and Reception."[24] This was a variety show worthy of Ed Sullivan, with solos, duets, trios, an "eccentric comedian," a "singing and talking comedian," a "Hebrew comedian," a banjoist, a buck-and-wing dancer, a slack-and tight-rope walker, an athlete, and a "boy wonder." Most of the program's organizers were familiar names from Pompei's records. At least one performer was a local person who volunteered her talent: Mrs. Luigi Fugazy sang with the duet and the trio. On the other hand, the fact that the program was printed in English indicates the "entertainment" was intended to reach an audience larger than Pompei's parishioners. Pompei spent $32.26 for the show, took in $109.74 in ticket sales, and netted $77.48, a good sum then.[25]

Mrs. Fugazy was unusual in appearing in the program, because parish wives paid their sodality dues and contributed their labor to the parish when they tended to the altar and sanctuary, but they did not take a prominent role in fund raising. Their unmarried daughters did, by putting on plays to benefit the church. Pompei has a program from a *Primo Trattenimento Drammatico*, which is undated but which must be quite early: Pompei hadn't yet fixed up its Bleecker Street basement for parish events, and so this affair was held at nearby Saint Joseph's.[26] The first dramatic program consisted of a melodrama and a farce, both in Italian. The next year, Pompei found a format which it used for many years: a melodrama or serious play in Italian and a farce in English.[27] All plays had musical selections sung or played between the acts.

Parishioners' fund raisers became more important after 1905. When Father Demo became pastor, Miss Leary's name was dropped from the front of the bulletin.[28] Miss Leary still had her *Scuola di Lavoro*, and the Missionary Sisters still taught there and at Pompei. Mother Cabrini herself is supposed to have taught at Pompei during Father Demo's administration, most likely in 1899, and to have come to Father Demo for confessions.

Reading through Miss Leary's letters to Father Demo, one can see a potential for trouble. Miss Leary seldom called on Father Demo. Either she asked him to visit her (she lived on Fifth Avenue near the Metropolitan Museum of Art), or she sent her maid.[29] She overturned the usual order of things in which the clergy took the lead and the laity, especially women, cooperated. Then, on April 4, 1905, Father Demo saw a New York *Daily News* article about ""Big Stars at Miss Leary's Concert"[30] The stars were indeed big; the story was about how Miss Leary had booked Enrico Caruso to sing at a benefit for her projects, and mentioned Pompei. Apparently, the article disturbed Father Demo: did it make it seem as though he couldn't manage his own parish? He wrote Miss Leary about the article, but, unfortunately, did not keep a copy. She sent back a four-page note (she had small stationery and large handwriting) saying she was "shocked and *grieved*" at his letter.[31] This may have adversely impacted Pompei's entire financial future. When Miss Leary died in 1919, Pompei was not mentioned in her two-million-dollar will.[32]

Miss Leary turned her attention to her Pius X Art Institute, with which Pompei maintained cordial relations; a photograph of a class at the institute is included in a 1911 Pompei publication. However, Pompei had to rely more on its parishioners and their initiative in raising funds. The most regular source of funds besides the Sunday collections were dramatic performances staged by young parishioners. The first play bills with dates on them are from February 12–13, 1906, when a *Circolo della Madonna di Pompei* put on a four-act drama.[33] On June 4–5, 1906, the Daughters of Mary put on a play about Saint Bernadette of Lourdes, and a farce.[34] Besides their role in raising funds, the dramas fed the parishioners' appetite for devotional fare by choosing plays with religious themes. As we shall see in the next chapter, the plays were an important part of Pompei's youth ministry.

Pompei did not raise funds only for itself. The Catholic Church began its annual Peter's Pence collection during Pius IX's reign, to help compensate the pope for revenue lost when his land was confiscated by the new Italian government, and Pompei participated in that collection.[35] Proceeds from the February, 1906, play were divided between Pompei and a fund to assist victims of a devastating earthquake in Calabria.

Fund raising was only one aspect of parish life at Pompei. In the early twentieth century, Pompei had numerous important liturgical services. Perhaps the most important event of Father Demo's early years occured in 1901, when Bishop Giovanni Battista Scalabrini came for a pastoral visit to his missionaries and their parishioners. Father Andrew Brizzolara, who studied the newspaper accounts of Bishop Scalabrini's visit, observed that the bishop's tour increased the respect accorded to the entire Italian population of the United States; with the press commenting enthusiastically on the Italians' economic and social progress.[36] Bishop Scalabrini visited Pompei August 8. He returned October 10 to preside over the First Communions and Confirmations of 750 candidates from Pompei and from Saint Joachim's, another Scalabrinian parish in New York.

During his stay in New York, Bishop Scalabrini ordained several candidates for the priesthood in the Scalabrinian community. One of them was Pio Parolin. Father Pio, as everyone called him, was born in Casoni, a rural town in Vincenza, April 25, 1879. He completed his studies at the Istituto Cristoforo Columbo, and sailed to the United States for his ordination, which took place November 4, 1901. He said his first Mass at Pompei. In 1904, Father Pio was assigned to Pompei as an assistant, and served there for the next ten years. His musical and dramatic talents were very much appreciated, as he formed a children's singing and dramatic group, and played the piano to accompany Pompei's variety-show fund raisers.[37]

Apparently it was under Father Demo that Pompei began one of its oldest annual liturgical traditions. The earliest mention of it is an advertisement which is probably from the 1920s; it mentions Anna Carbone as a singer, and she began singing at the parish about then. At that point, the event was titled *Tre Ore d'Agonia di Nostro Signore Gesu Cristo,* referring to the three hours of the Crucifixion. Catholicism's official Good Friday service took place from noon to three o'clock. Most American businesses didn't observe Good Friday, and not many people could take time off from work to attend. Pompei took an old Italian custom and used it for a service held from 7:00 to 10:00 p.m., when more people could come.[38]

The service's centerpiece was the Corpus Christi which usually rested beneath the main altar. On this occasion, the statue was laid on a bier, carried into the church by men acting as pall bearers, and placed before the altar rail, as if for a funeral Mass. The service consisted of a reading of the Gospel account of Crucifixion, with an emphasis on the Seven Last Words spoken from the cross. The priest gave a short discourse on the Gospel, and the musicians played and sang Mercadante's *Le Sette Parole.* The exact form has varied over the years, but Pompei has sponsored this Good Friday service at least since the 1920s, and probably before.

Father Demo brought the first "mission," or week of special preaching and spiritual renewal, to Pompei. During the 1910s, the Archdiocese of New York had an Italian Apostolate, which sent one or two Italian priests to parishes for one- or two-week missions. Pompei's first mission was November 15–29, 1914, one week for men and a second for women. Each mission was set up the same: daily Mass at 5:00 a.m., Mass with a sermon at 9:00 a.m., an evening service with a rosary, catechetical instruction, an invitation to meditation, and benediction, and opportunities for confession throughout the day.[39]

Besides special events, Pompei took steps to enhance its regular Sunday Masses and devotions. The earliest document about liturgical music at Pompei dates from 1904, and indicates that Miss Minnie Mooney, who had been Pompei's organist for some time, was leaving the parish for Corpus Christi Monastery in the Bronx.[40] The second earliest document is significant for many parishes besides Pompei. It is a form letter from Archbishop Farley, dated September 22, 1904, explaining Pope Pius X's recently released *motu proprio,* or directions concerning liturgical music.[41] People who study liturgical music consider this document an important step in restoring Gregorian chant. Implementing the directions, though, posed problems. American parishes relied on women to assist with the singing, but the *motu proprio* emphasized that church singing was, like serving at the altar, men's work, and that only men (or, for the high parts, boys) should sing at liturgies.

In 1908, Giovanni Batista Fontana arrived at Pompei. Maestro Fontana was born in Cremona, Italy, about 1873, entered the musical profession, and worked his way up to the post of director of the Ponchielli Institute of Music at Cremona. He was acquainted with Bishop Scalabrini, and perhaps with Father Demo as well, for he emigrated to New York when he was offered the position of organist and choir master at Pompei. Maestro Fontana supplemented his Pompei income by offering private lessons in piano, organ, voice, and music theory, but Pompei kept him busy enough. He played the organ at all Masses, weddings, funerals, and devotions, directed the adult and children's choirs, accompanied the fund raising shows, and wrote compositions. The one thing he did not do was replace the female singers with males. A 1911 photograph shows him surrounded by his choir, all young women. One of his pupils was Anna Carbone LaPadula, another Pompei musician. Maestro Fontana died in 1945.[42]

On a typical Sunday at Pompei early in the twentieth century, there were six morning Masses. One was principally for children, and another featured the choir. The Sunday school took over the main body of the church at two, while the clergy found a place to perform baptisms. After an hour of catechism, the teachers turned over their classes to the clergy for more instruction and Benediction. The laity ended their day with a corporate rosary and Vespers. The priests ended theirs with a benediction with the Blessed Sacrament.[43] On week nights there were also sung Vespers.

As parish functions increased, Pompei put its resources into creating a plant sufficient for all its activities. About March 1907 Pompei renovated its rectory, and at some point that same year altered its basement to accommodate socials and fund raisers.[44] Pompei still didn't have enough room. Twenty-five-hundred seats in the church times six Masses on Sunday meant 15,000 people could have seats at Mass—but Father Demo estimated he had 30,000 parishioners.[45]

Father Demo's records allow us to sketch out the history of Pompei *parish:* identify leaders, watch Pompei inaugurate its annual traditions, see the buildings go up. Father Demo's records also allow us to look at Pompei's *parishioners.* We can see a little of what it was like to be an Italian immigrant in New York city in the early twentieth century, and a little of what it was like to be a pastor.

Four general observations before we begin. First, life in the early twentieth century was not compartmentalized. Parish families did not have "spiritual" problems or "practical" problems—every problem had spiritual and practical aspects. All problems were brought to one person, the priest, who handled all aspects of the problem. Writing about the Irish, one observer noted that "If a poor man wants a favor asked of some great man, he gets the priest to ask that favor of him; if he is in distress or difficulties, he goes to his priest, and looks upon him as a friend and protector."[46] The Italians had a word for such an intercessor, a *padrone.* Father Demo was a sort of community *padrone.*

Second, most of Father Demo's letters in this category were from women. It was not that men didn't write, and not that men didn't ask for favors. It was that in Italy women were the traditional link between the Church and the family. Through their prayers and through their requests for practical assistance, women supported and strengthened their families.

Third, to say immigrants went to their pastor for help was not to say they could not cope with their problems and needed someone to do everything for them. Most people who wrote to Father Demo did not need *advice.* They needed something more concrete: a baptismal certificate, perhaps, or a reference letter. They explained their needs to Father Demo, and he tried to accommodate them.

Finally, to say that immigrants wanted help is not to call them beggars. Some idea as to how the Italians themselves thought about asking Father Demo for assistance comes through in a letter from a social worker who visited a parishioner to see if she qualified for welfare. The social worker wrote Father Demo that the parishioner "resented our inquiry, saying that she . . . would only accept aid from her Church."[47] To call on outsiders for aid was disreputable. The proper thing was to call on the pastor, who provided Christian charity in a dignified way.

What did Father Demo's correspondents want? Most of all, they wanted help with their spiritual lives. Some correspondents described how difficult it was to keep up one's faith. People living in isolated areas had trouble getting to Mass. One man, at a sanitarium in upstate New York, wrote that the Catholics gathered on Sundays for the rosary, but could not go to Mass: a chaplain came during the week for Mass, and the Catholics went to Confession and Communion then.[48] Poor parents struggled to purchase the white outfits which made First Communion and Confirmation so special.[49]

Since Pompei was the center of a Marian cult, people wrote from all over the country asking Father Demo to say Mass at the shrine church in the Virgin's honor for their intention.[50] In the 1970s and 1980s, Pompei developed a far-flung congregation of devotees. Such an element was present almost from the beginning of the parish. Pompei occasionally received requests from mutual benefit societies to hold services on the feast day of the patron saint of the Italian town from which the society members came.[51] The feast of Our Lady of Guadalupe continued through Father Demo's administration. One woman, whose mother was one of that first generation of devotees, sent an annual donation for Our Lady of Guadalupe for thirty years, although she lived all that time in Stamford, Connecticut.[52]

Correspondents also wanted help with their private devotional lives. They wrote when they wanted to know how to say the Pompei *supplica*, or when they were starting Pompei societies in their own parishes and wanted books and medals.[53] They requested other sorts of prayer aids, such as Italian-language Bibles, rosaries, and instructions on how to say certain prayers.[54] The traffic in devotional aids ran both ways, for parishioners sent Father Demo and Father Pio items such as scapulas.[55] Parish sodality women asked Father Demo to ask their sodality to pray for them.[56]

What did people pray for?[57] Sometimes they prayed for situations past earthly help, for example, when someone died.[58] Sometimes, they prayed for situations the solutions to which depended on chance as well as effort; as in the case of the housekeeper praying for a new job because the people she worked for would not let her practice her faith.[59] Sometimes they prayed for successful recovery from illness or injury; this was a situation where reason told them that doctors and medicine helped, but faith taught them that healing ultimately came from God.[60] Sometimes they prayed for situations that in the early twentieth century seemed to require a miracle. One woman joined the Pompei society to pray for her husband's continued sobriety, and this worked so well that when the woman died, her niece continued the membership so she could pray for her uncle.[61]

Besides praying for their personal intentions, Catholics contacted their parish priest when they needed help with the sacraments. There were no baptism *classes* like those parishes now sponsor for parents and godparents, but supplying baptismal *certificates* was an important part of Father Demo's work.

Catholics needed baptismal certificates to be married in the Church or to enter a religious order or the priesthood. Baptismal certificates substituted for birth certificates, providing proof of age for working papers and pensions.

Catholic marriage in Father Demo's day was easier than it would later become, as there was no Pre-Cana for engaged couples. However, the paperwork could be almost more than some people could manage, as can be seen in a case involving a widow's second marriage. The widow had to prove her husband had died before she entered a second marriage. Rather than get a death certificate, a letter from the priest who said her husband's funeral Mass, or something from the cemetery that buried him, she submitted the one piece of paper she had on hand that proved her husband was dead: the bill for his embalming.[62]

Father Demo's funeral correspondence is touching. The sacrament for those facing death was Extreme Unction, which was performed free of charge. Father Demo once returned a check for fifty dollars that Fiorello LaGuardia sent him for his services at the time of LaGuardia's first wife's death. LaGuardia wanted to thank the priest for his assistance, but Father Demo explained it was inappropriate to accept money for attending death beds.[63] There were, though, fees for funeral Masses. Some people found the fees difficult, and negotiated to pay on the installment plan.[64] Despite the expense, people wanted to honor their dead. Father Demo once received a note from a social worker concerning a family the father of which had recently died. The social worker recommended letting the city bury the body for free, but the family refused, for it meant a pauper's grave. Could Father Demo arrange an inexpensive burial for a family with no money?[65]

Besides helping people with the sacraments and the paperwork attached to some of them, Father Demo helped them conduct business with the secular world. Parishioners often asked him to be their interpreter. Sometimes, the translation service was between members of the same family. One parish couple, who had no telephone and did not read or write Italian or English, stayed in touch with a niece in Boston because Father Demo received letters from the niece, read them to the couple, wrote down their reply, and mailed it back to the niece.[66]

Father Demo also translated communication between his parishioners and the various city bureaucracies with which they dealt. Some translations were amusing: Father Demo had to explain to the Health Department that Lucia was a girl's name, and request officials please change his parishioner's birth certificate to read "girl".[67] Other translations were tragic. On July 8, 1918, a family asked Father Demo to find a cousin who was admitted to Bellevue December 5, 1916, and, last the family heard, transferred to another city hospital on

January 6, 1917. Father Demo finally found out, on November 23, 1918, that the patient had died—fifteen months earlier, on August 1, 1917.[68]

Pompei did not yet have a Saint Vincent de Paul Society, so parishioners who needed financial assistance asked Father Demo himself, and he responded to such requests.[69] He also did something conventional charities didn't do: he made small loans, usually for expenses like a trip to a sister's wedding which could then be repaid.[70]

Like any *padrone*, Father Demo found people jobs. He had some jobs at his direct disposal, for he employed people about Pompei as musicians at Mass, or as housekeepers.[71] His work brought him into contact with numerous offices which required the bilingual skills some of his parishioners had.[72] Two kinds of jobs required character references from one's pastor. People looking for servants advertised among pastors so as to ensure the trustworthiness of the people they took into their homes.[73] Requests for character references for candidates for clerical positions indicated Italians were moving up the occupational ladder.[74]

Office jobs for women were just beginning to open up, and were still restricted to single women. One woman, who was supporting a tubercular husband, found this utterly frustrating. When she told Father Demo she had listed him as a reference on her job application, she warned him: "Being as [the place where she applied for work] doesn't take married women, I didn't mention I was married . . . . You know how I stand financially, so I had to do it."[75]

Besides job references, Father Demo supplied other types of character references. A woman once wrote him for a character reference on a potential husband.[76] A parishioner requested a credit reference so she could borrow money to complete her schooling. This particular reference worked out splendidly. The woman went on to a responsible position which allowed her to request Father Demo recommend some more people for work as bilingual clerical help.[77] A particularly important character reference, referring people to welfare agencies, will be discussed in the next two chapters.

As might be expected in an immigrant community, parishioners needed help with immigration matters. Family members got separated during migration, and wrote to Pompei to be put back in touch with each other.[78] People got stuck in the immigration process and needed expert advice to figure out the laws and procedures.[79] Money orders sent home went astray, and needed to be traced.[80]

Immigrant communities were young communities, but there were some senior citizens in need of care. Care of the elderly was especially important. Most social welfare agencies assumed adult children could and would take care of the elderly parents, but families did not always have the money to support the elderly, and their were no pensions to allow them to support themselves.[81] Nor did growing young families have space for grandparents in crowded tenements. Father Demo once spent two months writing to four different rest homes, waiting for replies, and then writing some more letters, trying to find a home for an elderly woman.[82]

Interceding for those in trouble with the law was a delicate part of Father Demo's ministry. He received requests from people, or from their relatives, to get them out of jails and prisons.[83] Father Demo was willing to help, especially when it was a matter of getting a man back to work to support his family.[84] Prison officials, though, usually replied to his letters about how mothers and children needed their men at home with explanations about how parole worked.

There were other services for those in prison which Father Demo could, and did, perform. He wrote reference letters for the recently arrested and for those up for parole.[85] He tracked down relatives.[86] He found jobs for people about to be released.[87] Sometimes, the best thing he could do was be a good listener. One of the saddest letters in his collection came from a man who began "Since I saw you last affairs have not progressed to my benefit." Indeed not; the man was writing from a federal prison in distant Deer Lodge, Montana, which permitted prisoners to send only one letter per month. Apparently this man had few friends or kin, for he used one of his monthly letters to express his "hope you will write me a letter as soon as you read this one."[88]

Father Demo's work with those in trouble with the law should not be taken as supporting the stereotype that all Italians were criminals. All ethnic neighborhoods had young men barred by poverty and poor education from many legitimate ways of advancing to better-paying jobs. After 1920, Prohibition turned drinking wine, one of the most common aspects of Italian culture, into a federal crime. Other pastors had more menacing contacts with criminals who threatened to dynamite churches or harm pastors.[89] Pompei's contact with persons in jail was usually in the context of charity.

Among Father Demo's vast output of recommendations are two with wording like this: "This is to recommend the poor widowed [mother] of this parish. She [has] already one son in the United States Army, and needs this one home for her support."[90] Letters requesting that men be released from the military may show that Father Demo and his parishioners thought the United States was like Italy, where one could make such requests. They may show that the parishioners thought a letter from Father Demo could do just about anything. They may also show how earnestly Father Demo tried to be of help to his parishioners. Once, a parishioner wrote him a couple of letters, in rambling Italian, from Columbus Hospital. Father Demo admitted "I really did not understand what she intended to say." But he wrote to Columbus Hospital anyway, a nice letter introducing the woman and asking the sisters to take special care of her.[91]

Not only did parishioners consult their *padrone* pastor when they wanted a favor done, people trying to help parishioners also asked Father Demo's aid. When a doctor found out a patient had no one at home to care for her, he asked Father Demo to get her admitted to a Catholic sanitarium.[92] When Gimbel's Department store had openings for 150 people at the start of one Christmas season, it sent a circular to Father Demo to recommend as many parishioners as he could.[93] When a hospital wanted to move a little girl patient to its country rest home, hospital officials requested Father Demo explain the situation to the reluctant parents so they would permit their daughter to go.[94]

There were a few requests for help which modern priests get which Father Demo did not. Few people asked him for what is now called pastoral counseling, helping people resolve emotional problems. There were psychiatrists, but there was not yet training in counseling for the clergy. Nor did many people request help with marital problems. Perhaps people who were afraid their marriages were in trouble were reluctant to talk to a priest, for fear of what they might hear. Usually by the time Father Demo was called in to help with a marriage, one spouse was already gone and could not be traced, and the remaining spouse needed help with the children.[95]

Father Demo's parishioners generally valued him, were grateful for all his work. They sent few complaining letters, the most serious being one from a mother and daughter who found out, eight months after a death in the family, that they owed $22 for the funeral. (Father Demo explained that he hadn't wanted to bother the grieving family, and so hadn't written them about the debt sooner.)[96] There were many more appreciative notes. There were occasions, such as Father Demo's twenty-fifth anniversary as a priest and when he returned from trips to Italy, which the parishioners turned into festive events for him. As for Father Demo's feelings towards his parishioners, there is no one letter to quote, but there is one event which shows better than any letter how Father Demo understood his relationship to his parishioners and his responsibilities toward them.

At about 5:30 p.m. on Saturday, March 26, 1911, fire broke out in the Triangle Shirtwaist Company factory, located on the eighth, ninth, and tenth floors of the Asch Building, at the corner of Washington Place and Greene Street. The building itself was fire proof, but the factory, which made women's blouses, was a fire trap, and there were few escape routes. This fire, the single worst indoor industrial accident in United States history, claimed 146 lives, mostly those of young Italian and Jewish immigrant women.

The clergy heard confessions at that hour, so they may not have known about the fire until early evening. The fire first appears in Pompei's records Tuesday, March 28, when Father Demo said Mass for Eulalia Prato, a twenty-one-year-old woman who was identified in the newspapers by her American nickname,

Millie.[97] One of the three curates at Pompei at the time, Father Giuseppe Quadranti, said Mass for seventeen-year-old Isabella Tortorella. On March 30, Father Demo said one Mass for three of the deceased: Anna Treue; a married woman of twenty-four named Irene Ginnastasio; and thirty-one-year-old Rose Bassino. On April 3, Father Pio Parolin said Mass *per bruciati fuoco Washington Place*. By April, Father Demo counted eighteen parishioners dead in the fire, and there may have been more. The last person to be identified, several months after the fire, was from an Italian family this accident had cut in half: the mother and daughters died, leaving the husband and sons behind.[98]

On April 26, 1911, Pompei held a month's mind for all those who died in the fire. Father Demo sent out English-language black-bordered announcements to people beyond the immediate parish community.[99] He sang the Solemn High Requiem Mass, and Father Ernesto Coppo, a Salesian missionary who was pastor of Transfiguration on Mott Street, gave the sermon. The church was crowded with Italian women mourning their friends and kin. The sermon was traumatic. According to the newspaper account: "Father Coppo, who delivered the sermon, spoke eloquently of those who perished in the fire, and his auditors several times broke into sobs, which were once so violent that the sermon was interrupted."[100] One woman wrote to let Father Demo know how grateful she was for his pastoral care of the bereaved: "I was eye-witness to this awful tragedy and can never forget its horrors."[101]

There was an unusual conclusion to the Mass. The Women's Trade Union League, which brought together upper-class ladies and working-class women to improve working conditions for the latter, distributed circulars calling for a campaign to enforce existing fire safety laws. Mary Kingsbury Simkhovitch, who lived at Greenwich House near Pompei and who participated in the Women's Trade Union League, recalled that Father Demo gave his "cordial permission" for the circulars.[102]

Father Demo's reaction to the Triangle Fire contains all the elements of his pastoral work. He was priest who provided spiritual care for his people. His spiritual care was made real in the charitable services he performed for his parishioners. He shaped Pompei's programs to serve parish families and their needs. And, when necessary, he reached beyond the parish to find other community services to aid his parishioners.

NOTES

[1] *Biglietto di Licenza*, CMS Box 11, Folder 132; *La Messa D'Argento*; New York *Catholic News,* ca. 2 January 1936; Remo Rizzato, P.S.S.C., *Figure di Missionari Scalabriniani* (New York: D'Alatri's Press, 1948), 107–112; and *Village Bells* (Winter 1985), 1–3.

[2] Giacomo Gamberra to Demo, Boston, 19 July 1899, CMS Box 7; Folder 62, and Demo, note dated 23 April 1925, in CMS Box 5, Folder 33.

[3] Letters between the Scarinzi family and Father Demo can be found in his papers as follows: 7 January 1909, CMS Box 1, Folder 10; 12 January 1912, Box 1, Folder 12; 5 August 1911, Box 1, Folder 12; 6 May 1914, Box 2, Folder 15; and 29 June 1916, Box 2, Folder 17.

[4] Di Giovanni, 377.

[5] *See also* Patrizia Salvetti, "Una parrocchia italiana di New York e i suoi fedeli: Nostra Signora di Pompei (1892–1933)," *Studi Emigrazione* XXI (March 1984), 43–64.

[6] *Village Bells* (Fall 1982), 4.

[7] CMS Box 11, Folder 134.

[8] S.v. "Luigi Fugazy," in *Gli Italiani negli Stati Uniti* (New York: Italian Chamber of Commerce, 1906).

[9] S.v. "Charles Baciagalupo" in *ibid*; and Victor R. Greene, *American Immigration Leaders, 1800–1910: Marginality and Identity* (Baltimore: Johns Hopkins University Press, 1987), 122–137.

[10] *See* the advertising in *Souvenir Journal, Grand Bazaar, Church of Our Lady of Pompei* (New York: L'Italiano in America, 1911).

[11] *Village Bells* (Fall 1984), 3–4.

[12] *Village Bells* (Winter 1983), 3.

[13] Sparks, Nevada, to Zanoni, 21 January 1985, OLP Papers 1980–1987, January 1985 Folder.

[14] Progressive Era Association, *Sixtieth Anniversary Dinner,* brochure dated 28 January 1989.

[15] Minutes of Saint Joseph Society, CMS Box 26, Folder 297.

[16] *New York Times*, 10 August 1930, 23:6. This is Mr. Fugazy's obituary. It notes he was not buried at Pompei. It also notes that he was involved in scores of activities benefitting New York Italians.

[17] Leon Michelini to Edward Marino, 15 May 1978, OLP Papers 1975–1980, near Correspondence 1977 Folder.

[18] Sunday announcement, 26 August 1900, CMS Box 28, Folder 309.

[19] Saint Joseph Society meeting minutes, 26 March 1899, CMS Box 26, Folder 298; CMS Box 12, Folder 144; and *Grand Bazaar.*

[20] Anthony Comstock to Demo, 15 February 1912, CMS Box 2, Folder 13.

[21] Farley, circular, 14 June 1916, CMS Box 8, Folder 91.

[22] Ware, 312.

[23] Sunday announcement, 8 July 1900, CMS Box 28, Folder 309.

[24] Program dated [30 May] 1900, CMS Box 12, Folder 144.

[25] Sunday announcement, 15 July 1900, CMS Box 28, Folder 309.

[26] Program for *Primo Trattenimento Drammatico,* CMS Box 12, Folder 144. There are several undated programs in the same box.

[27] Program for *Secondo Trattenimento Drammatico*, CMS Box 12, Folder 144.

[28] Monthly bulletin, October 1899, CMS Box 32, Folder 330.

[29] Annie Leary to Demo, 26 May and 4 August 1904, CMS Box 1, Folder 5.

[30] New York *Daily News*, 4 April 1905.

[31] Leary to Demo, 15 April 1905, CMS Box 1, Folder 6.

[32] *New York Times*, 4 May 1919, 22:5.

[33] Program dated 12–13 February 1906, CMS Box 12, Folder 144.

[34] Program dated 4–5 June 1906, CMS Box 12, Folder 144.

[35] Farley, circular, 30 March 1908, CMS Box 8, Folder 84.

[36] Andrew Brizzolara, C.S., "One Hundred Days: The Visit of Bishop Scalabrini to the United States and its Effects on the Image of Italian Immigrants as Reflected in the American Press of 1901" (Master's thesis, Fordham University, 1983).

[37] CMS, Pio Parolin Papers (Collection 073), Box 1, Autobiography Folder.

[38] Program for *Tre Ore d'Agonia di N.S.G.C.*, undated, CMS Box 12, Folder 144, and interview 0006. *See also* Daniel David Cowell, M.D., "Funerals, Family, and Forefathers: A View of Italian-American Funeral Practices," *Omega* XVI:1 (1985–1986), 69–85.

[39] Program, 15–29 November 1914, CMS Box 12, Folder 144.

[40] Minnie Mooney to Demo, 10 August 1904, CMS Box 1, Folder 5; and Mooney to Demo, 16 March 1905, CMS Box 1, Folder 6.

[41] Farley, circular, 22 September 1904, CMS Box 8, Folder 84.

[42] *Village Bells* (Fall 1984), 1–3.

[43] Sassi, 54.

[44] Demo, circular, 13 March 1907, CMS Box 1, Folder 8; and program, 18 December 1907, Box 12, Folder 144.

[45] Farley, Circular, 20 September 1907, CMS Box 8, Folder 84.

[46] Quoted in Jay P. Dolan, *The Immigrant Church: New York's Irish and German Catholics, 1815–1860* (Baltimore: Johns Hopkins University Press, 1975), 64.

[47] E.A. McCutcheon to Demo, 4 January 1907, CMS Box 10, Folder 108.

[48] Annex Loomis to Demo, 21 May 1908, CMS Box 1, Folder 10. *See also* Jersey City, New Jersey, to Demo, 25 June 1902, Box 1, Folder 3.

[49] 8 Jones to Demo, 23 May 1923, CMS Box 4, Folder 29; and 281 W. 11th to Demo, Box 5, Folder 37.

[50] *E.g.*, Orange, New Jersey, to Demo, 13 September 1907, CMS Box 1, Folder 8. Many of these are in Italian.

[51] Rosario Vitale to Demo, 1 May 1925, Box 5, Folder 33.

[52] Stamford, Connecticut, to Demo, 19 August 1916, CMS Box 2, Folder 18; 10 August 1920, Box 3, Folder 25; 18 August 1921, Box 3, Folder 26; 18 August 1922, Box 4, Folder 28; and 17 August 1923, Box 4, Folder 30.

[53] *E.g.*, Chicago to Demo, undated and 21 October 1918, CMS Box 3, Folder 22.

[54] Sparkill, New York, to Demo, 1 February 1923, CMS Box 5, Folder 31; Denver, Colorado, to Demo, 26 June 1923, Box 4, Folder 29; and Doria, Italy, to Demo, 6 January 1928, Box 5, Folder 38.

[55] 164 W. Houston to Demo, 31 January 1912, CMS Box 2, Folder 13, and to Demo, no place, no date, Box 2, Folder 16.

[56] *E.g.*, Long Island City to Demo, 10 March 1915, CMS Box 2, Folder 16.

[57] Cf. Robert Anthony Orsi, "What Did Women Really Think When They Prayed to St. Jude?" *U.S. Catholic Historian* VIII:1–2 (Winter/Spring 1989), 67-79.

[58] *E.g.*, to Demo, 20 June 1922, CMS Box 4, Folder 27.

[59] Englewood Cliffs, New Jersey, to Demo, 8 September 1922, CMS Box 4, Folder 27.

[60] *E.g.*, Somerset City, New Jersey, to Demo 5 March 1908, CMS Box 9, Folder 9.

[61] Bedford Park to Demo, CMS Box 2, Folder 15; Wilmington, Delaware, to Demo, 6 March 1918 and 14 February 1919, Box 3, Folder 21; and 25 March 1927, Box 5, Folder 37.

[62] Thomas F. Murray to Demo, Brooklyn, 11 July 1916, CMS Box 2, Folder 18.

[63] Demo to Fiorello LaGuardia, 24 December 1921, CMS Box 3, Folder 26.

[64] 200 Bleecker to Demo, 1 November 1917, CMS Box 3, Folder 20; and 540 W. Broadway to Demo, June 1931, Box 6, Folder 41.

[65] Muriel H. Deane to Demo, undated business card, CMS Box 3, Folder 21.

[66] Boston to Demo, 11 November 1920, CMS Box 3, Folder 24; 13 June 1920, Box 3, Folder 25; 6 January 1921, Box 3, Folder 26; and 1 June 1932, Box 6, Folder 42.

[67] Demo to New York City Department of Health, 7 September 1933, Box 6, Folder 43. See also Louise C. Spaziano to Demo, 30 June 1925, Box 5, Folder 33.

[68] C.B. Bacon to Demo, 23 November 1918, CMS Box 3, Folder 22. *See also* William P. Richter to Demo, 11 March 1927, Box 5, Folder 37.

[69] *E.g.*, Mt. Sinai Hospital to Demo, 24 August 1917, CMS Box 3, Folder 20.

[70] *E.g.*, Troy to Demo, 8 July 1913, CMS Box 2, Folder 14.

[71] 403 W. 22nd to Demo, 8 May 1915, CMS Box 2, Folder 16, and Jersey City, New Jersey, to Demo 23 September 1915, Box 2, Folder 16.

[72] Carolyn A. Perera to Demo, 28 August 1923, CMS Box 4, Folder 30.

[73] Oakland, California, to Demo, 24 August 1914, CMS Box 2, Folder 15; Daniel Burke to Demo, 1 January 1918, Box 3, Folder 21; and Bayshore, Staten Island, to Demo, undated, Box 3, Folder 24.

[74] E.g., Henry Macomber to Demo 11 February 1918, CMS Box 3, Folder 21.

[75] Newark, New Jersey, to Demo, 25 January 1923, CMS Box 4, Folder 29.

[76] Chicago to Demo, 23 August 1917, CMS Box 3, Folder 26.

[77] J.T. Timmono to Demo, 2 April 1915, CMS Box 2, Folder 16; and Washington, D.C., to Demo, 23 October and 3 November 1917, Box 3, Folder 20.

[78] Pozzoleone, Italy, to Demo, 25 September 1920, CMS Box 3, Folder 26.

[79] 569 Hudson to Demo, 6 April 1927, CMS Box 5, Folder 37.

[80] 65 Broadway to Demo, 28 January 1919, CMS Box 3, Folder 23.

[81] Muriel Hudnut to Demo, 30 March 1925, CMS Box 5, Folder 33.

[82] Sister Athanase Joseph to Demo, 6 May 1915; Sister Josephine de Ste. Aurelie to Demo, 17 May 1915; Sister M. Veronica to Demo, Jersey City, New Jersey, 13 July 1915; and Sister Rose de Viterbe to Demo, Jersey City, New Jersey, 27 July 1915, Box 2, Folder 16.

[83] *E.g.*, 317 W. 53rd to Demo, 20 June 1920, CMS Box 3, Folder 25.

[84] *E.g.*, Demo to Superintendent of Prison, 10 March 1930, Box 6, Folder 40; and William A. Adams to Demo, New Hampton, New York, 3 December 1930, Box 6, Folder 40.

[85] *E.g.,* D.J. McMahon to Demo, 22 November 1910, CMS Box 1, Folder 11.

[86] Albert Garvin to Demo, Chesire, Connecticut, 18 January 1915, CMS Box 2, Folder 16.

[87] Eastern New York Reformatory to Demo, 1 August 1913, CMS Box 2, Folder 14.

[88] Deer Lodge, Montana, to Demo, 14 April 1909, Box 1, Folder 10.

[89] Father Demo saved numerous clippings from the 1903 case of Father Giuseppe Cirringione, who apparently took out a loan from the wrong agency, and was kidnapped as a warning to make prompt repayment. In 1909, New York Police Department Lieutenant Joseph Petrosino was assassinated while on a fact-finding mission in Sicily. When his body was returned to his parish, Saint Patrick's Old Cathedral, for burial, pastor John F. Kearney received dynamite threats. *See New York Times,* 12 April 1923, 19:5.

[90] Demo "To Whom It May Concern," 10 September 1918, CMS Box 10, Folder 129; and 8 May 1925, Box 5, Folder 35.

[91] Demo to 41 Bedford, 31 January 1933, CMS Box 6, Folder 42.

[92] James F. Navoni, M.D., to Demo, undated, CMS Box 2, Folder 17.

[93] Gimbel Brothers, circular, 7 October 1919, CMS Box 3, Folder 23.

[94] M.T. Simmons to Demo, 24 October 1922, CMS Box 4, Folder 28.

[95] *E.g.,* New York to Demo, 9 June 1924, CMS Box 5, Folder 31.

[96] Demo to 619 W. 204th, CMS Box 5, Folder 34.

[97] *New York Times* 28 and 29 March 1911, 2:4-7 and 4:4, respectively; and CMS Box 46, book labelled Messe 4, which is a register of sponsored Masses.

[98] Leon Stein, *The Triangle Fire* (Philadelphia: J.B. Lippincott, 1962).

[99] Box I, Folder 12.

[100] *New York Times*, 27 April 1911.

[101] 194 W. 4th to Demo, 25 April 1911, Box 1, Folder 12.

[102] Mary Kingsbury Simkhovitch, *Neighborhood: My Story of Greenwich House* (New York: Norton, 1935), 162.

Fr. Antonio Demo, Pompei's pastor from 1899 to 1933.

| NICODEMUS | CAIPHAS | PONTIUS PILATE |
| DOMENICK PETTI | FREDERICK ROCCA | DANTE NEGRO |

One of Pompei's most successful community event was the Passion Play, produced from 1923 to 1932. Parishioners in their costumes.

4

Raising an American Generation during Father Demo's Pastorate

In 1908, Our Lady of Pompei began thinking of a project so novel it didn't even have a word for it. When Father Demo explained it to the parishioners, he used the words *asilo* and *istituto*, asylum or institution, and *infantile*, for infants. When it opened, it was named the Asilo Scalabrini, in honor of the bishop. The English word Pompei used was recently imported from German: "kindergarten," or children's garden.[1] Today we would call Pompei's project a "day care center."

As we saw in the last chapter, Pompei held variety-show-style "entertainments," but so far those had not raised the amount needed for a day care center. Other New York Catholic institutions raised large sums by holding "fairs" or "bazaars" which lasted several days and combined several types of fund raisers.[2] Pompei took a step forward in Americanization, and decided to hold a bazaar, too.

The parish had a meeting to discuss the bazaar October 8, 1991. Father Demo took the minutes, and did such a thorough job that someone else, probably Giuseppe Pagliaghi, president of the Saint Joseph Society, must have chaired the meeting. The first step was to establish an organization to conduct the bazaar. Father Demo, Mr. Pagliaghi, and John A. Perazzo were the bazaar's general directors, with Mr. A. Michelini (Angelo or perhaps his son August) as corresponding secretary. Under these heads came a committee of four men and three women. The men were identified by their initials and last names: S. Prescia or Frescia, G. Baciagalupi, G. Savro, and G. Quarzite. The women were identified by the sodalities they represented: Bianca Caucifronicotti for the Rosary Society, Giulia Razzetti for the Daughters of Mary, and Julia Lipparelli for the Sacred Heart Society. This committee set the dates for the bazaar: November 26 through December 10, 1911. It assigned six selling tables: one each to the Daughters of Mary, the Rosary Society, the Sacred Heart Society, the Saint Joseph Society, the altar boys, and the catechism teachers. A male committee was appointed to conduct the public relations campaign, a female committee to provide refreshments, a third committee to decorate the church basement, and a fourth to handle the door prizes.[3]

The bazaar produced the first substantial Pompei publication, a souvenir journal. Although smaller than later such journals, this first one had the same format. Much of the space was taken up with advertising. Later journals carried advertising from families or individuals whose advertisements were gestures of support rather than business publicity. The 1911 journal was almost entirely business advertising. Many men associated with the parish advertised their businesses: Charles Baciagalupo, undertaking; the Bergonzi family; R. Michelini, wines and liquors; Raimond Michelini, wines and liquors; Serafino Michelini, trucking; Giuseppe Pagliaghi, newspaper agent; Michael and Vincent Pepe, real estate and insurance; G.B. Perazzo, funeral director; and G. Savro (or J. Savio), artificial flower manufacturer.

For the souvenir journal, Father Demo produced the first parish history. In two pages, he explained how the Scalabrinian missionaries came to New York and established several parishes and the Saint Raphael Society, and how Fathers Bandini and Zaboglio nurtured the parish. He finished with a description of Pompei's facilities and schedule. Statistics supplemented Father Demo's narrative, and showed that Pompei had become financially healthy. In the years since settling down at 210 Bleecker, receipts exceeded expenditures, in 1906 by as much as $3,474.65, or about 30% of that year's income.

There were also photographs showing how the parish, and the parishioners, looked in 1911. One photograph was especially touching. After reading the minutes of the earliest parish meetings, at which Andrea Sabini played a prominent role, it is sad to see a commemorative photograph with the explanation that Mr. Sabini died in 1910, at age 52. The commemorative photograph had a caption describing Mr. Sabini as a *zelante colletore*, "zealous usher." The frontispiece was the earliest surviving photograph of 210 Bleecker during Pompei's stay there, taken at Mr. Sabini's funeral, and showing the funeral cortege lining up in front of the church. The journal also had photos of young, dark-haired Father Demo, and even younger Father Pio Parolin. There was a studio portrait of organist Giovanni Battista Fontana with his summer straw boater and his walking cane, and group photos of Pompei's parish organizations.

With its bazaar earnings, its more regular fund raisers, and its savings account, Pompei was ready to look for a place for its day care center. In January 1913, the parish was fortunate indeed. It bought a tenement right around the corner from the church at 8 Downing Street. (The building was later torn down to widen Sixth Avenue). The building, bought at a public auction, cost $20,100.[4]

During the next year, Pompei prepared the building for its new use. Messrs. John A. Perazzo and Edward Bergonzi served as trustees for the day care center. Architect Anthony Vendrasco planned the changes necessary to convert the space into a day care center, and a contractor did the renovation work.[5] The day care center occupied only a portion of the building, and Pompei rented out the two remaining apartments. The parish also got sisters to act as day care attendants. The sisters were members of the Pallottine Sisters of Charity, the same order that staffed Saint Raphael's. The Pallottines sent two sisters to the day care center, at a stipend of $25 per month or $300 per year per sister.[6]

The day care center's opening was accompanied by two evenings of entertainment, October 24–25, 1915. The main event was a performance of a drama entitled *Il Pescatore di Balene*, with parishioners Michele Pavone, Antoinette Scagni and Luigi Laneri in the leading roles. The two evenings raised another $255.25 for the new project.[7]

Had the parishioners known how much trouble running a day care center was, they might have had second thoughts. Municipal ordinances required a physician inspect the Asilo Scalabrini; parishioner Filippo Isola, M.D. was appointed to the task.[8] Employees from the Health Department also inspected the Asilo. They then sent letters regarding repairs to be undertaken or changes to be made in the way the place was run.[9] One of the Health Department's complaints was the excessive number of children. Father Demo himself admitted the Asilo took in between 75 and 90 children per day, although the Board of Health said the day care center's capacity was only 79.[10] The overcrowding testified to the necessity of day care for Village families, and to the families' preference for day care near their homes and with day care attendants they trusted. It was especially useful for mothers who were the sole support of their young offspring.[11] Pompei maintained the Asilo Scalabrini until 1944. A second day care center started at the parish about 1976, and continues today.

The Asilo Scalabrini brought Pompei into contact with the larger world of social welfare workers. After Catholic Charities was founded, in 1922, it sponsored conferences bringing together representatives from parish day care centers to talk to experts on child care and to discuss common issues. As if to prove there's nothing new under the sun, a 1926 conference took up topics which continue to be controversial among social workers. Should day care centers be charities for families that were so poor even the mothers had to work, or should they assume mothers worked for personal fulfillment or supplemental income rather than necessity, and charge competitive rates? Should day care centers serve parents, and so save their spaces for parents whose jobs required they put their children in day care, or should they serve children, and so accept even those with mothers who were at home, in order to give them a better environment and opportunities to play with other children?[12]

Concern about children bridged a gap between the Italian Catholics at Pompei and native-born Protestant and secular philanthropies. Pompei received a circular letter from the National Federation of Day Nurseries inviting its representatives to a conference.[13] Apparently, Pompei was on a mailing list of day care centers that was shared within the field. It once received a circular soliciting cooperation "in our efforts to bring before the public the facts of the value of pure food gelatine in the dietary of the child" and inquiring about Pompei's use of jello as a food for the children.[14] (Father Demo didn't respond to the circular, but he did save Asilo Scalabrini's expenditure records, and from them we learn the youngsters had a good Italian diet of macaroni and tomato sauce).

Father Demo began receiving letters about family problems almost from the moment he arrived at Pompei, and the number of letters increased in the 1910s and 1920s. New York's Italian population was getting larger; 544,449 in the 1910 census, 802,946 in the 1920 census. An increasing percentage of that population growth was due to births within the Italian community. In 1910 about 40% of Italian-Americans in New York were born in the United States, and about 60% migrated there. By 1920, about half the Italian population was born in Italy, and the other half in the United States.[15] Pompei shared in this population boom. The souvenir journal noted Pompei had 20,000 parishioners. Its baptismal register indicates it christened over a thousand babies a year in the 1910s. With so many children, there was bound to be a generation gap at some point. In Greenwich Village, two factors exacerbated the generation gap.

The first was that poverty makes everything harder, and some families were depressingly poor. Consider these two letters, the first written by a girl in 1923 and the other by a boy in 1926:

> I want to go to work and I ain't got no father and mother has a baby and she can't go to work and if I ain't got the Baptist papers I can't go to work and we are poor.

> I am letting you know that we are all sick. My father has pains on his [illegible]. And my mother was to the City and the Charities said you was [born] in Chicago we [cannot] give you something to eat. Dear Father will you give us a pass to come to Chicago again. The little baby that was baptism in your church always [cries]. Dear Father she always wants milk. Milk is what she wants. Dear Father we pick up the bread from the streets and bring home all the bread to eat. We are all froze. We go pick the coal from the [garbage] and [burn] it. [The brackets are to correct spellings].

The first question a historian has to ask is: are these genuine? Social workers constantly worried that undeserving recipients ended up on welfare through pathetic, but fake, descriptions of their condition. However, in the case of the letter requesting a baptismal certificate ("Baptist papers"), Father Demo found the girl in Pompei's records. In the case of the letter requesting passage to Chicago where the family met the residency requirements for welfare, he contacted the family, and jotted down the name of the person with whom he spoke. These people, and their desperation, were quite real.

Both letters were written in the 1920s, generally considered a prosperous decade. Why was it not so for these families? Perhaps some accident left them poor. Perhaps they were not industrious in their work, or thrifty with what they did earn. On the other hand, in one family the father was absent, in the other he was disabled, and in both the mothers were limited in their ability to work because both had babies. Baby formulas were just beginning to be widely used, and were not yet popular among immigrant women.[16] Finally, although both letter writers could use more education, at least one wanted to go to work, thus cutting off chances for eventually getting a better-paying job. There were reasons for poverty besides misfortune or personality traits: fathers unavailable to work, mothers busy with little babies, and poor preparation for the labor force.

The second reason for Pompei's wide generation gap was that the older generation was raised in Italy and the younger in America. Children stayed out later than their parents wanted, and used the church donations their parents gave them to skip Sunday School and go to the movies instead.[17] Father Demo had some personal experience with caring for such youngsters when his niece lived in New York in the late 1910s and early 1920s. He boarded her at a convent but the girl moved out to a friend's house nearby, since she wanted to keep later hours than the convent allowed.[18]

Pompei's parishioners tried a number of strategies to care for their children. One possible solution was to work at home while watching the children, but this did not usually bring in enough money. In one family, the husband died of tuberculosis, leaving a pregnant wife and three children, two of them under ten, so the mother got a job assembling artificial flowers at home. The work brought in $16 per month, and the rent alone was $15 per month.[19] Having one person be both bread winner and care taker did not work well.

A second possible solution was to remove children from school as soon as they qualified for working papers. Father Demo received letters from families in which the husbands and fathers were too ill to work, the wives and mothers were nursing them, and so wage-earning responsibility devolved on a teen-ager.[20] He also received letters from parents who did not indicate they needed their children to work, but who were following Old World customs.[21] In Italy poor children didn't spend long years in school, partly because their families couldn't afford to send them, and partly because no one expected people to use education as a way out of poverty.

Father Demo realized that the old ways had to change in the new world. In a speech given about 1914, he outlined the disadvantages of leaving school early. One passage, translated into English, reads:

> After the first few years of mandatory schooling, when the boy has just grasped the fundamentals of learning, then, pressured by his parents, or by family necessity, or by the attractions of the world, he abandons study for work. Intelligent youths confined to the factory surrounded by machinery . . . lose their best years for developing their mental faculties. School, gentlemen, school and study are the true

factories of great civilized peoples. The study of science, of art, and of morals makes the man capable of self-control and the leadership of others.[22]

However, not all families felt they could afford to follow Father Demo's advice.

A third way to rear children was to share the burden with relatives.[23] A fourth way was to place the youngster in an orphanage, correctional institution, or boarding school. Father Demo received numerous requests to help place children in institutions. Sometimes parents could not handle the child's behavior and so were looking for assistance in discipline.[24] More often, parents could not provide for their children, or, if the mother was the sole breadwinner, she could not care for her child at the same time, and so boarded the child at a school.[25] Organizations such as the Catholic Guardian Society and the Girls' Service League did not board youngsters, but acted as employment services, placing girls in homes where they did housework and received the guidance of Catholic families.[26]

One problem with putting children *in* institutions was getting them *out* again. Catholics accused Protestant and secular agencies of breaking up families, but Catholic agencies, too, kept children in their institutions if they feared the youngsters would not do as well at home.[27] Parents and even other clergy asked Father Demo to write letters for them, hoping he might carry some weight with child care institution managers.[28] They rehearsed with him the arguments that might convince the institution managers and restore their children. One woman reasoned that since her husband and son had jobs, the family had a store, they had moved to a small town where the air was good, and the mother was at home to provide constant attention, surely the hospital would let her have her daughter back.[29]

There were people who sincerely thought that if a family was very poor, or if one parent had died, it was best to remove the children to institutions or to foster care. Apparently, neither Father Demo or his parishioners agreed. In one instance, a parish family with seven children lost the wife and mother, and one child, a three-year-old girl, was placed with a suburban Catholic family. The suburban parish priest asked Father Demo to persuade the widowed father to let the foster couple adopt the child. The suburbs were better than the city, and the couple were good Catholics who gave the girl every spiritual and material advantage. Father Demo replied that not only was the father unwilling to consent to adoption, but he wanted his daughter home immediately.[30]

If children were going to remain in their families, the parents needed their parish to help them. Pompei developed a comprehensive program of pastoral care for school-age children and for teenagers, beginning with catechism. Immigration and poverty disrupted many children's religious education, a serious matter for Catholics.[31] Pope Pius X stressed the importance of making one's First Communion early in life, about the age of seven years. Pompei celebrated First Communion and administered Confirmation about the same time. Since one went to Confession prior to receiving Communion, a lot of information about the Catholic faith had to be inculcated in a short time.

It seems that about 1905, Pompei's Sunday School was reorganized. The Missionary Sisters withdrew, and the Christian Brothers, under Brother Eliphus Victor I, took charge of Pompei's catechism classes. Brother Victor was born John Joseph McConnel in Philadelphia October 27, 1860. On August 23, 1876, he entered the Christian Brothers. He came to New York in August 1893 to teach at the Brothers' La Salle Academy on East Second Street. One woman who recalled teaching catechism under his instruction called him "our dear joyous Brother Victor."[32] Brother Victor died July 27, 1913.[33] The connection between Pompei and the Christian Brothers continued for many years, and opened the way for many young men at Pompei to attend the Christian Brothers' schools.

Brother Victor trained parish women to assist with the teaching. A photograph in the 1911 souvenir journal shows there were at least twenty-seven women teachers at that time. Since Pompei had only the church on Bleecker Street, the classes were seated in different areas of the church.[34] Not only did the women teach, they sponsored, and acted in, shows to raise funds for the school.[35] Being a Sunday School volunteer required sufficient commitment of time and energy that only single women taught, and left when they took on the additional responsibilities of married life. When they left, the parish showed its gratitude with certificates of appreciation.[36]

Catechism was almost a full day's activity. The children and teachers attended Sunday Mass at 9:30 a.m., and listened to an English-language sermon. At two o'clock the students and teachers reassembled for an hour of catechism. In the 1920s, the lessons were followed by an hour of movies, as a sort of reward. School children took part in special events. A group of thirty elementary school girls sang vespers with Anna Carbone at Christmas, 1923, and another 25 recited poetry in English, Italian, and Latin.[37]

Father Demo took an interest in individual children preparing for their First Communion, and encouraged them with presents of religious books and rosary beads.[38] The youngsters received the sacraments in as festive an atmosphere as possible. The participants wore white, the boys in suits with long trousers, the girls in dresses with veils. The girls carried flowers, and the use of the organ, choir, and incense as well the presence of the bishop administering Confirmation, added to the solemnity of the occasion.[39]

When the younger generation entered its teens, a new danger arose. Their quick assimilation raised the possibility teenagers might reject Catholicism as part of their Italian immigrant parents' lives unsuitable for young Americans.

Pompei had to be "Italian" enough to be a source of spiritual comfort to the older generation, and "American" enough that its younger generation grew with the parish, rather than away from it.[40] It had to have special programs for youths outside of catechism.

One activity which attracted parish boys from childhood through adolescence, was serving at the altar. The souvenir journal included a group photograph of sixteen altar boys, ranging from small lads to tall young men. Altar boys added to the dignity of the services by assisting the celebrating priest. Like a modern volunteer coordinator, Father Demo thanked the boys by doing something special for them, taking them on outings.[41]

Once youngsters finished formal religious education, sodalities encouraged them in their faith. Under Father Demo, the parish boys reorganized their traditional youth sodality. The earliest surviving minutes from a Saint Luigi Society meeting at Pompei are dated April 14, 1912. In contrast to the Saint Joseph Society, and to a young women's society of the same time period, the Saint Luigi Society always kept its minutes in English, a sign of the young men's swift assimilation. These were not, though, young men whose assimilation led them away from their faith: The meeting's acting chairman was August Michelini, and the temporary secretary was his younger brother Leon.[42] By 1914, Father Demo thought Saint Luigi had 200 members.[43]

The Holy Name Society was another popular young men's society. It descended from a confraternity founded in 1274 in Rome by John Gargella of Vercelli. It was associated with the Order of Preachers, or Dominicans, who started the first Holy Name Society in New York City in 1868 at their parish of Saint Vincent Ferrer. The Archdiocese of New York had an Italian branch of the Holy Name Society, in which Pompei's Holy Name participated, but Pompei's Holy Name was founded by young English-speaking men.[44] By 1921, the Saint Luigi boys had outgrown their society and were too old for its equivalent, the Junior Holy Name. That February, they elected officers for a parish Holy Name Society: president Leon Michelini, vice-president John Podesta, financial vice-president Victor Podesta, vice-financial secretary Americo Roscelli, and corresponding secretary Luigi Laneri.[45] The founding members sponsored a recruiting meeting and invited a Dominican priest to come talk about the society.[46] Pompei's Holy Name was accepted into the Holy Name structure in May 1921.[47]

Surviving minutes from a March 9, 1925, meeting give some idea as to the importance to the members of being a Holy Name man.[48] Like a sodality, the Holy Name had its assigned week for monthly Communion (which meant monthly Confession). At this particular meeting, the members discussed asking Father Demo to set aside a special section at one Mass so that the Holy Name men could sit together. The Holy Name urged its members to choose morally good companions, and thus encouraged them to socialize with each other outside of church through participation in athletics and by hosting receptions.

The traditional group for unmarried young women was the Daughters of Mary. Father Demo counted 300 parish Daughters of Mary in 1914.[49] Women took their membership seriously. Upon being told she had been elected the organization's president, one woman declined the honor, citing a demanding job and a sick mother.[50] The pride another woman took in the group was reflected in her telling Father Demo, in Italian, that "so far we have not had to annoy the public with a single collection" to cover the expenses of a banner the Daughters of Mary were making for the Rosary Society.[51]

A second women's group, *Circolo Gioventù Femminile,* or Young Ladies' Circle, held its first meeting December 10, 1912.[52] Unlike the young men, this group kept its minutes in Italian, perhaps because Father Demo acted as secretary. However, it was bilingual, because its purpose was to raise money for the church, and its chosen method was producing dramatic performances in Italian and in English.[53]

Pompei's dramatic program did far more than just raise money. It provided another way to reach youth. Young men and women such as Luigi Laneri, Concetta Mollica, Luigi Raybaut, and Antoinette Scagni enjoyed performing so much they acted in Pompei plays until 1932. Theatre was a popular leisure activity in the Italian community, with whole families spending dimes and quarters to buy tickets for an evening's worth of serious drama, melodrama, musical selections, and comic sketches.[54] Pompei's theatre also provided an alternative to Greenwich Village's secular theatre. The Provincetown Players came to MacDougal Street in 1916 performing new works by authors such as Eugene O'Neill. Today O'Neill is considered one of the world's great playwrights, but at the time his plays were new, daring, and suspect.[55] What Father Demo thought of modern drama is not known. It is clear from one letter that he thought people in show business had low moral standards; when a parish girl ran away to be an actress, he wrote a lengthy letter to persuade her to come home where it was safe.[56] But he had no objection to an activity that kept youngsters busy and exposed them to an important and popular element of Italian culture.

Pompei produced a couple of plays each year throughout the 1910s and 1920s, each new production running for a couple of nights.[57] Until 1922, when the players introduced an annual Passion Play, the productions followed the same general format. The headline event was in Italian. Judging from titles such as *L'Orfana Vindicata* [the Orphan Girl Vindicated] or *L'Eroismo di una Figlia di Maria* [Heroism of a Daughter of Mary], the plays centered around moral issues. Some plays may have been chosen not for their artistic merit but because Pompei had the correct number of actors needed for the performance. Other plays were among the best in Europe. The Young Ladies' Circle's first production, June 30–July 1, 1913, was *La Notte Del Sabato*, based on Goethe's Faust. In 1922, Pompei presented, in Italian, Shakespeare's *Othello*, and Emil Zola's *Teresa Raquin.*

Each solemn performance was accompanied by a short comedy in Italian or English. The plays themselves had musical accompaniment, provided by *maestro* Fontana or by Father Pio. During the intermissions, there were musical diversions for the restless audience. Once, in 1916, there was a film of Egypt and the Holy Land. Since this was the era of silent movies, a lecturer explained what the audience was seeing.

For youngsters not interested in drama, Father Demo tried everything else. Father Demo could not have played basketball as a youth himself, because the game was invented in 1891 in Springfield, Massachusetts, but he encouraged his boys, and girls, to play. Pompei's teams participated in the local leagues.[58] Similarly, the Boy Scouts started after Father Demo's own boyhood. At that time, the troops were sponsored by churches, and Father Demo may have become acquainted with them in 1917, when he was first asked to form a troop in his parish.[59] He later wrote to the Girl Scouts asking about a troop for Pompei.[60] Whether Father Demo followed up on these inquiries is unknown, but Pompei had troops under one of his successors, Father Ugo Cavicchi.

Besides programs and youth organizations, Father Demo provided informal counseling and friendship. Although Pompei did not send a young man into the Scalabrinians until Guy Nugnes entered the order in 1963, Father Demo was a mentor for young people making decisions about their religious vocations.[61] In 1920, sixteen-year-old Joseph Pernicone left the minor seminary in Sicily and accompanied his mother and siblings to join his father and two sisters in New York. The reunited family settled on Sullivan Street, and the teenager began learning English so he could enter Saint Joseph's Seminary. He was ordained December 18, 1926, and said his first Mass at Pompei. He and Father Demo kept up a correspondence the rest of Father Demo's life. Father Pernicone went on to be a curate and then a pastor in several Italian churches in the archdiocese. On May 5, 1954, he became the first man of Italian origin consecrated a bishop in the Archdiocese of New York. He died in 1985.[62]

Women considering the convent also confided in Father Demo. In one case, the woman had been part of Pompei's Daughters of Mary and had begun thinking about her vocation before her father relocated the family to Bari, Italy. The old country was disappointing after New York: the father opened a store, but the mother found the housework difficult without all the conveniences available in America, the son missed New York, and the daughter found her vocation hampered by her mother, who didn't want her to go too far away. The family returned to New York, and after several years, the daughter entered the convent—and when she did she invited Father Demo and the Daughters of Mary to attend the ceremony.[63]

Other youngsters at odds with their families' plans confided their frustrations to Father Demo. One family travelled from Italy to Uruguay to Saint Louis, Missouri. They settled in New York long enough for the children to develop a sense of home; then the father took them back to Saint Louis. One daughter described how the rest of the family dutifully went along, although they were all homesick for the crowds at all the Masses at Pompei. When the daughters grew up, they returned to New York and went into the restaurant business. Father Demo corresponded with them for years: he invited them to events at the parish and they sent him donations for his special projects.[64]

Youngsters separated from their families found Father Demo an anchor. Even very young children had a sense of home, and when they left Pompei they missed seeing Father Pio say Mass and inquired after their Sunday School teachers.[65] Other children reported to Father Demo on their new and interesting surroundings. It must have been disconcerting when one little correspondent was moved from the Catholic Protectory to the city's home for children and decided: "This is better place th[a]n Catholic Protectory. I am having a very nice time. I go to moving picture[s] twice a week and it is very nice." But the girl was also lonely, and asked Father Demo to tell her mother and siblings, "I am saying a very nice long prayer for them."[66]

In one case, Father Demo was the only connection between child and parents. A young woman wrote him requesting her baptismal certificate, but all she knew about herself was that Father Demo was instrumental in placing her in the children's home where she grew up. Father Demo checked his records, and supplied the girl with her birthday, baptism date, and alternative spellings of her parents' names. She thanked him, and added "I was told that you knew about my mother . . . I hope someday in the near future I will have an opportunity to see you so I can acquire the information I am seeking."[67]

Parents were especially apt to call in Father Demo when a daughter ran away from home. There were probably two reasons for this. One was that Italian parents worried about their sons, but they gave them more personal freedom, both because they were boys and because, in Italy, they travelled far in search of work. Girls were supervised more closely. Second, since girls sometimes ran away from home to get married, it made sense to enlist the parish priest, who eventually got a request for the girl's baptismal certificate that allowed the parents to relocate their offspring.

A letter we have already mentioned, written to persuade a runaway girl to return home, is a good example of Father Demo's tact with his young parishioners. Rather than sermonizing on the obedience owed parents, Father Demo told her "your parents, your brother and your little sister are dying to see you and embrace you again." He recognized the girl might have her own side of the story to tell, and promised that if she thought she faced any problems at home, "they can be removed easily, for you may also count upon me for help." He reiterated his offer when he signed his name: "As soon as you receive this letter do me the favor to answer me freely and without delay. Inform me of your intentions for I mean to help you where I can."

Like the Asilo Scalabrini, the youth ministry took Father Demo out of the Italian Catholic community of Greenwich Village and into the larger world. He left a box full of correspondence with Catholic and secular charities regarding children's problems.[68] He made donations to charities especially concerned with children.[69] Working with children also took him into the larger world in another way. In order to reach the youngsters effectively, he had to keep up with American culture.

The subtle changes Pompei's youth ministry made in the entire parish become clear in a 1921 sermon given to honor Father Demo. The sermon was in Italian, until the preacher began describing the youth apostolate. Then, only English words would do, and Father Demo was praised for incorporating *"il Christmas Tree, il Moving Pictures, il Day Nursery"* into parish life. Little by little, the rise of a new generation changed Pompei from a parish focused on the Italian immigrant ministry into a part the larger American community in Greenwich Village.

NOTES

[1] Leary to Demo, 28 August 1908, CMS Box 1, Folder 9. *See also Souvenir Journal, Grand Bazaar.*

[2] Bernadette McCauley, "Philanthropy and Social Mobility: Ladies' Auxiliary Societies in New York City's Catholic Hospitals, 1906–1929," Paper delivered at "American Catholicism in the Twentieth Century" conference, University of Notre Dame, 2 November 1990.

[3] Meeting minutes, 8 October 1911, CMS Box 18, Folder 205, page 17.

[4] Charles Zerbarini to Demo, 4 May 1929, CMS Box 21, Folder 247.

[5] Flyer advertising *Il Pescatore di Balene*, 24–25 October 1915, Box 12, Folder 144.

[6] Ferrante to Demo, 7 June 1917, CMS Box 7, Folder 61.

[7] Balance sheet, 24–25 October 1915, CMS Box 18, Folder 212.

[8] Filippo Isola to Rev.mo Padre Provinciale, 26 April 1916, CMS Box 2, Folder 17.

[9] H.G. MacAdam to "Superintendent, Asilo Scalabrini," 20 June 1918, and to "The Person-in Charge," 25 February 1924, both in CMS Box 18, Folder 217.

[10] Ethyll M. Dooley to Demo, 24 January 1922, CMS Box 18, Folder 216.

[11] 2927 Third Avenue to Demo, 2 December 1924, CMS Box 18, Folder 212.

[12] Bryan J. McEntegart to Julia Rosetti, 19 November 1926, CMS Box 18, Folder 216.

[13] Mrs. Arthur M. Dodge, circular, 17 February 1927, CMS Box 5, Folder 37.

[14] Gertrude King, circular, 23 January 1925, CMS Box 5, Folder 33.

[15] Rosenwaike, 203.

[16] Rima D. Apple, *Mothers and Medicine: A Social History of Infant Feeding, 1890-1950* (Madison: The University of Wisconsin Press, 1987).

[17] Mary F. Maguire to Demo, 11 December 1902, CMS Box 10, Folder 129; and Margaret M. Hannay to Demo, 19 April 1910, Box 1, Folder 11.

[18] Sister M. Agatha to Demo, 14 January 1917, CMS Box 3, Folder 19.

[19] L. Outerbridge to Demo, 8 April 1924, CMS Box 5, Folder 30.

[20] M.M. [or W.W.] Dmikie, R.N., to Demo, 23 April 1923, CMS Box 4, Folder 29, and 25 Jones to Demo, Box 5, Folder 34.

[21] Philadelphia to Father G. Moretto, 6 October 1926, CMS Box 5, Folder 36.

[22] Copy of speech in CMS Box 11, Folder 134.

[23] Webster Grove, Missouri, to Demo, 15 December 1925, CMS Box 5, Folder 34; and Francis M. Verrilli, Esq., to Demo, 23 September 1926, Box 5, Folder 36.

[24] J.F. Navoni, M.D., to Demo, undated, CMS Box 3, Folder 23.

[25] For a family that could not afford to keep children at home, *see* 23 Bedford to Demo, 31 March 1915, CMS Box 2, Folder 16. For a single mother boarding her child, *see* Eugene Tedeschi to Demo 31 January 1916, Box 2, Folder 17.

[26] *E.g.*, Samuel Ludlow to Demo, 12 January 1923, CMS Box 29, Catholic Guardian Society Folder.

[27] *E.g.*, J.B. Pitcher to Demo, 15 March 1916, CMS Box 2, Folder 17.

[28] *E.g.*, John J. Rongetti to Demo, 2 October 1916, CMS Box 2, Folder 18.

[29] Babylon, New York, to Demo, undated, CMS Box 3, Folder 24.

[30] M.R. Burns to Demo, Watertown, New York, 16 November 1923, CMS Box 4, Folder 30.

[31] *E.g.*, 540 W. Broadway to Demo, 17 February 1918, CMS Box 3, Folder 21.

[32] To Michael Cosenza, no place, no date, OLP Papers before 1975, Cosenza Folder.

[33] Michael A. Cosenza, *Our Lady of Pompei in Greenwich Village* (New York: OLP, 1967) 8; *New York Times,* 28 July 1913, 7:6; Coney Island to Demo, 22 July 1913, CMS Box 2, Folder 16; post card, ca. 27 July 1913, Box 2, Folder 14; and funeral speech in Box 11, Folder 134.

[34] South Harwich, Massachusetts, to Zanoni, 15 January 1985, OLP Papers 1980–1985, January 1985 Folder.

[35] Flyer 6–7 May 1914, CMS Box 12, Folder 144.

[36] CMS Box 1, Folder 12.

[37] (New York) *Il Progresso Italo-Americano*, 23 December 1923.

[38] *E.g.*, 558 Morris Park Avenue to Demo, 7 April 1914, CMS Box 2, Folder 15.

[39] *Il Corriere d'America*, 27 April 1925, p. 9.

[40] Ware, 312.

[41] 34 Morton to Demo, 23 August 1913, CMS Box 2, Folder 14.

[42] St. Luigi Gonzaga Society meeting minutes, CMS Box 26, Folder 300.

[43] Demo to Giuseppe Sorrentino, S.J., 6 November 1914, CMS Box 7, Folder 80.

[44] Daniel Burke, circular letter, CMS Box 13, Folder 162.

[45] *Ibid.*, CMS Box 13, Folder 162.

[46] Demo to Editor, *Catholic News,* 4 April 1921, CMS Box 13, Folder 162.

[47] [Ralph Stella], OLP Scrapbook, OLP Scrapbooks II.

[48] Holy Name meeting minutes, 9 March 1925, CMS Box 13, Folder 162.

[49] Demo to Sorrentino, 6 November 1914, CMS Box 7, Folder 80.

[50] To Demo, 26 March 1915, CMS Box 2, Folder 16.

[51] To Demo, 31 January 1909, CMS Box 1, Folder 10.

[52] *Circolo Gioventù Femminile* meeting minutes, 10 December 1912, CMS Box 27, Folder 301.

[53] *Circolo Gioventù Femminile* meeting minutes, 6 January 1913, CMS Box 27, Folder 301.

[54] New York Federal Writers' Project, *The Italians of New York* (New York: Random House, 1938; reprinted, New York: Arno, 1969), 194.

[55] John M. Berry and Frances Panchok, "Church and Theatre," *U.S. Catholic Historian* VI:2–3 (Spring/Summer 1987), 151–179.

[56] Demo to Washington, D.C., before 14 January 1919, CMS Box 3, Folder 23.

[57] The flyers are in CMS Box 12, Folder 144.

[58] Committee on Athletics and Cooperation of Girls Club Work meeting minutes, 12 December [1924?], CMS Box 5, Folder 32; and Irene Casey to Demo, 15 January 1926, Box 5, Folder 35.

[59] J.L. Redmond to Demo, 29 January 1917, CMS Box 3, Folder 19.

[60] Alice Conway to Demo, 5 March 1921, CMS Box 3, Folder 26.

[61] *OLP Parish Bulletin* XXIV:5 (May 1963, 8).

[62] *Village Bells* (Spring 1983), 1–2, and Catholic New York, 14 February 1985.

[63] Gravina, Bari, to Demo, 15 August and 30 September 1921, CMS Box 3, Folder 26; 30 May 1922, Box 4, Folder 27; 27 May and 21 June 1923, Box 4, Folder 29; 6 May 1925, Box 5, Folder 33; and 7 July 1926, Box 5, Folder 36.

[64] St. Louis to Demo, 13 October 1909, Box 1, Folder 10; St. Louis to Demo, 7 and 18 February and 14 March 1910, Box 1, Folder 11; Brooklyn to Demo, 20 March 1914, and New London, Connecticut to Demo, 15 June 1914, Box 2, Folder 15; 22 E. 45th to Demo, 30 October 1915, Box 2, Folder 16; Buffalo to Demo, "Thursday 22" 1917, Box 3, Folder 24; to Demo, 14 March 1918, Box 3, Folder 21; to Demo, 29 October 1918, Box 3, Folder 22; Pinehurst, North Carolina, to Demo, 1 May 1919, Box 3, Folder 21; 22 E. 45th to Demo 17 April 1919, Box 3, Folder 23; Tryon, North Carolina, to Demo, 12 November 1919, Box 3, Folder 23; 22 E. 45th, 16 April 1920, Box 3, Folder 24; Naples to Demo, 10 June 1922, Box 4, Folder 27; to Demo, 14 April 1924, Box 5, Folder 31; New Rochelle to Demo, 8 April 1926, Box 5, Folder 35; Demo to New Rochelle, 15 October 1926, Box 5, Folder 36; Saint Louis to Demo, undated, Box 3, Folder 24; and 349 E. 41st to Demo, undated, Box 6, Folder 44.

[65] Troy, New York, to Demo, 24 July 1914, CMS Box 2, Folder 15.

[66] Randall's Island to Demo, 27 March 1925, CMS Box 5, Folder 33.

[67] Peekskill to Demo, 4 May and 9 June 1918, CMS Box 3, Folder 21.

[68] CMS, Box 10

[69] *E.g.*, Mother Cleophas to Demo, Westchester, 12 October 1917, CMS Box 3, Folder 23.

5

A Citizen of Greenwich Village

In Pompei's early history, we saw how Greenwich Village's Italian Catholics banded together partly to be able to use a familiar language and follow familiar customs, and also because other Americans, and other Catholics, excluded the Italians from their communities. Italian Catholics eventually became part of the larger Catholic community, and institutions in the larger society eventually accepted Catholics, but how did these things occur? Books on the subject make it seem as though this happened only after World War II and Vatican II. Interfaith cooperation started at the top, among theologians, and only slowly trickled down to the laity.

At Pompei, though, well before the Italians were supposed to have assimilated, and well before Vatican II, the parish was already the center of a series of concentric circles that reached out to include other neighborhood agencies. Father Demo corresponded with other Italian parishes, non-Italian parishes, Village social services, and New York City social services. Pompei's relationships with its New York neighbors had two turning points: World War I, and the incorporation of Catholic Charities.

When Pompei was founded, there were already several Italian Catholic parishes in the Archdiocese of New York, all of them on Manhattan, and most of them southeast of Greenwich Village. Archbishop Corrigan, who had brought the Scalabrinians into New York, authorized several more Italian parishes before his death in 1902. Cardinal Farley followed Archbishop Corrigan's precedent, and continued authorizing Italian parishes. When Cardinal Farley died in 1918, his successor, Patrick Joseph Hayes (Cardinal Hayes after 1924), followed the same policy until his death in 1938. Pompei was part of this community of Italian Catholic parishes. Father Demo received invitations to other Italian parishes' special events , and solicitations regarding their collections.[1]

There were other Catholic institutions for Italians besides parishes. Saint Anthony of Padua opened New York's first Italian parochial school in 1874. The Scalabrinians staffed the New York branch of the Saint Raphael Society for the Protection of Italian Immigrants until 1923. Mother Cabrini and the Missionaries of the Sacred Heart came to New York to open an orphanage for

Italian Catholic girls. The Scalabrinians also opened Columbus hospital. The hospital soon ran into financial difficulties, and in 1892 Mother Cabrini assumed responsibility for it. Several parishes besides Pompei had day care centers, and a couple of parishes ran summer camps where city children went for country vacations. Father Demo patronized Italian Catholic charities, sending parish youngsters to summer camp, and donating money to other Italian parishes.[2] He supplied Columbus Hospital with a priest to give spiritual talks to the staff, and recommended its fund raisers to his parishioners.[3] There were other non-Catholic Italian organizations in New York City, but Father Demo did not have much correspondence with them.

Italians and their pastors outside New York City contacted Pompei with their needs. When a West Newfoundland pastor wanted a character reference on a city slicker who married one of his parish girls, he wrote Father Demo to investigate.[4] When an Italian grandmother who had been away from the sacraments for many years finally consented to see a priest, a friend asked if she could bring Father Demo to Clifton, New Jersey, to see the old woman.[5]

Priests in the non-Italian parishes on Manhattan referred to Father Demo Italians living in their parish boundaries. For example, one priest sent Father Demo three children for Confirmation.[6] His parish followed the American custom of having one person sponsor all the Confirmation candidates. The children's mother wanted to follow the Italian custom of giving each child its own sponsor, chosen from the family's friends and kin. So, the pastor sent the family to Pompei where the children could be confirmed as the mother wished.

By the early 1920s, the Archdiocese of New York had over two hundred separate Catholic benevolent organizations. Some were institutions with buildings in which they cared for people: asylums, hospitals, foundling homes, orphanages, etc. Others provided non-residential care: Saint Vincent de Paul gave people material assistance in their own homes, and there were Catholic foster home and Catholic parole-work societies. Each establishment raised its own money and did its own public relations to let people know what help was available. There were two possible ways that Pompei's parishioners could get into this Catholic charitable system.

One way was via a reference letter from Father Demo. In the novel *The Last Hurrah,* the main character, the Irish-American mayor of a large city, takes the reader through a typical day at his office. In the morning, the mayor is "at home" for his constituents. Citizens of every description come to tell him their problems. The mayor listens to each person, figures out what he can do for them, and makes arrangements. Judging from his correspondence, Father Demo's office must have been like that.

A second way for Pompei's parishioners to get into a Catholic welfare agency was to come to the agency's attention without first going through Father Demo.

This seems to have happened most often when a person got into trouble with the law. Volunteers who visited the city's jails found out which inmates were Catholic, and which needed special language services, and notified the appropriate pastors.[7] Volunteers working with young people notified Father Demo whenever they thought youngsters needed special attention.[8]

Having numerous independent Catholic charities had its advantages and disadvantages. The system was flexible enough to permit a new charity to be established when a new need was identified. It allowed needy Catholics to be cared for by people who spoke their own language and understood their customs. However, unless every pastor was as knowledgeable as Father Demo, it was hard to steer people toward appropriate sources of help. Without a central fund raising agency, soundly financed philanthropies survived while equally worthy and necessary philanthropies failed. With each parish raising money for its own Saint Vincent de Paul Society, middle-class or wealthy parishes had sufficient funds but few poor parishioners to aid, while working-class parishes had plenty of people to aid but not enough funds. As Protestant and secular philanthropies developed new charities, the Catholics appeared old-fashioned and insufficiently helpful.[9]

The Protestant-secular-Catholic rivalry was most important to New York's Catholic leadership. New York's Catholic bishops suspected, not without reason, that non-Catholic agencies used charity to lure Catholics from their faith. As Cardinal Hayes explained: "Recent experiences in the Charity world force on us the conviction of how organized and united are those not of spirit and faith against our doctrine . . . The first thing is to know and study the spirit and methods of the opposition."[10] A prominent Catholic layman and journalist put it more bluntly: Catholics should adopt "the tactics of the enemy."[11]

Quotes such as these make one think that Catholics never dealt with non-Catholic social services. Father Demo, though, was on civil terms with most of the Village's public institutions and private agencies. He had parishioners in the care of these organizations, and they weren't any less Catholic for the experience.

For example, antagonism between New York Catholics and public schools went back to the establishment of the city's public school system in 1842.[12] Father Demo's own experience with New York's public school was different. Many Greenwich Village public school personnel were Catholic, and, like modern workers who attend churches near their work place for daily Mass or prayers, were quasi-parishioners at Pompei.[13] They took an interest in their pupils' religious education, and notified Father Demo if they encountered children they thought needed catechetical instruction.[14]

Father Demo did his part to ensure professional relationships with Village educators. Beginning in 1913, he served, at his request, on the Advisory Board of the School and Civic League.[15] He donated a ten dollar gold piece as the reward in an annual Demo Prize for Character at the local boys' school.[16] He presented another ten dollars as an award for "general excellence" at the local girls' school.[17] Village educators reciprocated. Principals invited Father Demo to parents' meetings and to graduations.[18] They released Catholic children for Mass on holy days of obligation.[19] When the city implemented release time for religious education, the local elementary school principal called on Father Demo to explain the system.[20] It's not clear whether the opening of Pompei's parochial school altered Father Demo's relationships with area public schools, because he died before the school had its first graduating class.

Decent relations with their pupils' pastor made the educators' work easier. Principals referred to Father Demo children whose parents were unavailable for school conferences.[21] When the children circulated a rumor that May 1 was a holy day on which home work was forbidden, the principal rectified the situation with a note to Father Demo.[22] Knowing school officials made Father Demo's job easier as well, because he contacted them to obtain working papers for parishioners' children.[23]

There is no well-publicized history of prejudice against immigrants at the New York Public Library. However, historians have not thought of Italian immigrants as library patrons, because so many of them could not read. Father Demo's parishioners, though, regularly used him as a reference so that they could get library cards.[24] Father Demo helped the librarian at the Hudson Park branch identify Italian-language books to order for the library's collection.[25]

Father Demo worked with several private charitable agencies in the Village. Founded in 1853, the Children's Aid Society was one of New York's oldest philanthropies. Like the public schools, it had a history of troubled relations with Catholicism, especially where Italians were concerned.[26] At least one worker at the Sullivan Street Children's Aid facility knew of the history of conflict between Children's Aid and Catholics, for she made a point of reassuring Father Demo that she was not usurping his authority, but supplementing it with Children's Aid's own Christian uplift.[27] Relations with Children's Aid during Father Demo's time were cordial. Whenever Children's Aid needed someone to teach a course, it sent the job announcement to Pompei to see if any parish women were interested.[28] For his part, Father Demo read Christmas stories for Children's Aid's annual party.[29]

Another welfare agency with which Father Demo dealt was the Charity Organization Society, which was founded in 1882 by Josephine Shaw Lowell. COS did not give out money. It collected information on the types of services needed, and on the people requesting services so that only the truly needy were helped, and only enough help was given to return the needy to self-sufficiency. Catholics eventually adopted COS methods, but at first were suspicious of a charity that wasn't as open-handed as the Good Samaritan or the father of the Prodigal Son. John Boyle O'Reilly, editor of Boston's Catholic *Pilot,* summed up Catholics' views when he wrote that the COS acted "In the name of a cautious, statistical Christ."[30]

Protestant and Catholic leaders differed on how best to help the poor, but when Father Demo saw a source of aid for his parishioners, he took advantage of it. He supported COS, and once offered to assist in its fund raising campaign.[31] He referred parishioners to the COS district office at 47 and at 59 Morton Street. COS often referred his parishioners back to him, because he gave them money to tide them over until appropriate referrals could be made.[32] COS did pay rent for people waiting for applications to be processed, and there are numerous letters indicating that when the applicants were parishioners, COS and Father Demo each paid half the rent.[33]

Reference checks were supposed to see if the poor were the "worthy poor." Judging from the correspondence, COS and Father Demo agreed on standards for worthiness, with one predictable exception. COS social workers found Catholics' attitude toward divorce and remarriage frustrating. They were baffled by people who were separated from a first spouse, and who even took a second spouse in a civil ceremony or in a common-law arrangement, but who remained Catholic rather than join a denomination which permitted divorce and remarriage.[34]

One new social service institution popular at the turn of the century was the "settlement house," in which American-born, college-educated young men and women "settled" in urban ethnic neighborhoods, studying their needs and offering them assistance. Mary Kingsbury Simkhovitch founded the Village's most important settlement, Greenwich House, in 1901. Mrs. Simkhovitch found Catholics thought this new charity was, like the older ones, out to entice people away from their faith. To convince them otherwise, she asked prominent Catholics to serve on Greenwich House's board of directors.[35]

Father Demo had extensive and varied contacts with Greenwich House. Social workers there consulted him when they wanted information about the neighborhood.[36] Mrs. Simkhovitch invited him to all sorts of meetings: conferences to propose zoning plans, discussions of publicly-funded improvement projects, lunches to talk about church-state relations, and committees to improve settlement management.[37] Father Demo responded to these solicitations. Asked to join the Greenwich Village Improvement Society, he noted that he sent in his dollar.[38]

Perhaps the most dramatic example of cooperation between Pompei and Greenwich House came at the memorial Mass for the victims of the Triangle Shirtwaist Factory Fire in 1911, described in a preceding chapter. Usually, activities at Greenwich House were of a more pleasant nature. Greenwich

House was involved in the performing and creative arts, and invited Father Demo to drama club meetings, art exhibit committee meetings, displays of pottery made by settlement house students, Old Home Week festivities, and children's pageants.[39] Its social workers were on good enough terms with Father Demo that they asked for favors, such as requesting he publicize their music school or lend them Pompei's slide projector for an evening entertainment.[40]

The event which accelerated Father Demo's contact with the world beyond Pompei was World War I. On August 1, 1914, the chancery sent a circular requesting archdiocesan congregations say special prayers to ward off the coming of war.[41] But it was too late. The Allies, England, France, and Russia, and the Central Powers, Germany and Austria-Hungary, were on the way to war. Italy joined the Allies in 1915; the United States joined the same alliance in 1917. The war was hard on the Italian people. The Italian-Austrian border became a battlefield. Breadwinners were drafted into the army, leaving needy family members behind. The Italian war effort was not of the same caliber as the English or French, or even the enemy war effort and Italy felt inferior as a result.

New York's Italian Catholics mobilized to help the Italians back home. In the fall of 1915, the chancery official in charge of the Italian national parishes, Monsignor Gherardo Ferrante, called a meeting of New York's Italian clergy. The meeting established a Committee of New York Italian Clergy for the Families of Italian Soldiers, charged with raising funds and dispensing charity to the dependents of men who returned to Italy to fight. Father Demo was the committee's treasurer.[42] On February 7–8, 1916, Pompei's benefit performances of *La Cieca Di Sorrento* [The Blind Woman of Sorrento] raised $230.45 for poor families of Italian soldiers.[43] Father Demo extended aid to individual Italian soldiers, such as the man who wrote asking for help locating his immigrant sister.[44]

Americans still hoped the United States could stay out of war. When in 1915 Cardinal Farley departed from local custom and authorized parishes to hold a midnight Mass at Christmas he asked that people pray for world peace.[45] Father Demo began receiving letters from interfaith committees (usually Protestants and Catholics) asking him to help keep the United States out of war.[46] The war, though, seemed far away. Pompei was busy with its twenty-fifth anniversary, marking the occasion with anniversary observances and by making special events out of the annual round of missions and feast day celebrations.[47]

In April, the United States about-faced and marched off to war. Father Demo compiled a list of seventy-seven parishioners in the military. All of them were men (women didn't join the armed forces until World War II) and all but one had an Italian surname. A handful served in the war zone itself, but one parishioner got to see Anniston, Alaska, when he was stationed there during the war.[48] Father Demo thought three or four parishioners lost their lives in the war but post-war changes in the Village prevented an accurate count.[49]

Greenwich House rallied the Village to support the war. By May, the settlement had organized a parade from Sheridan Square to Washington Square, and located Civil War veterans for the reviewing stand.[50] The United Organizations of Greenwich Village invited Father Demo to the reviewing stand of its Flag Day "monster" parade and mass meeting.[51] In 1918, Father Demo gave a blessing at a flag-raising service, and, in another example of the interfaith activity the war fostered, shared the platform with the Reverend E.H. Schlueter of Saint Luke-in-the-Fields Protestant Episcopal Church on Hudson Street.[52]

Soon after the United States entered the war, local charities began emphasizing the patriotic importance of their services. The United Catholic Works sold tickets to its 1918 benefit concert by depicting its philanthropy as benefitting people threatened by the war: "Thousands of husbands, fathers, and stalwart sons have answered our country's call. We must be mindful of those they have been obliged to leave, who need our help and sheltering care."[53] The New York Society for the Suppression of Vice explained that reporting immorality was a patriotic duty that ultimately protected soldiers and sailors in transit through the harbor.[54]

Italians in the United States took the position that since the United States and Italy fought on the same side, they shared the same goals. In 1918, an Italian American organization drafted a telegram, in Italian, quoting approvingly President Wilson's famous call to make the world safe for democracy, and assuring the president of Italian American support.[55] The idea was to have numerous Italian organizations send the same telegram to the White House on Independence Day 1918. However, probably figuring that President Wilson spoke no Italian, Father Demo helpfully translated the telegram into English—and ended up thanking the president for making "Democracy safe for Mankind."[56] Presumably, the error got fixed before the telegram went to the White House. Father Demo reported to his parishioners that Pompei got a nice thank-you letter from President Wilson's secretary, Joseph M. Tumulty.[57]

The federal government itself was already planning ways for people to support the war effort. The war time agency with which Pompei had the most correspondence was the Food Administration. The Food Administration's director was Herbert Hoover, whose activities in this office added to his reputation and later won him the presidency. Hoover's job was to make sure that both the civilians and the military had the food they needed. One of the ways Hoover accomplished his goal was by calling for food conservation. If civilian demand for food went down, then it would be easier to divert food to the military. Also, conserving food was a daily activity that allowed people to show their support for the war.

Hoover used churches to campaign for food conservation. In a circular letter asking ministers to preach a special sermon on "Food Conservation Sunday," Hoover explained why he wanted the clergy's cooperation: "The women of America have never failed to answer such a call as comes to them now. The saving of food is within their sphere . . . the outcome of the world war is in the hands of women no less than in the hands of men."[58] However, there was as yet no radio or television to reach women at home, nor could Pompei's female parishioners be expected to be able to read billboard posters or even to understand English. Nor, perhaps, could one expect poor, working class, ethnic Americans to pay much attention to the federal government, which was far less involved in everyday life than it would be later. The people needed to be reached by those they already accepted as their leaders.

Federal officials sent Father Demo more information on Food Conservation Sunday, including pledges for housewives to sign.[59] Usually, though, the federal government did not deal with parishes directly. Instead, it relied on the archdiocese to encourage parish food conservation. When it came to his attention that nothing was being done to advertise food conservation among the Italians, the first District Director of the Bureau of Conservation wrote the chancery official in charge of minority-language Catholics, and that official circulated the letter among the Italian clergy.[60] The federal government also relied on Greenwich House, and Greenwich House relied on Father Demo. Greenwich House's assistant director and chair of a district food council invited area retailers to food conservation meetings, and asked Father Demo to say a few words to them: "I hope very much that you will be present because with the food shortage becoming more and more serious we are going to need the cooperation of all those agencies which reach the women of the poorer classes."[61]

The reference to the poorer classes raises a question. Would not poor people already be limiting food purchases? How much more could they really do to help the war effort in this way? A possible answer to these questions may be found in Pompei's announcements. In June 1918, a chancery official wrote Father Demo about an upcoming Italian Day, the purpose of which was to encourage saving food. Father Demo was to announce this event to his parishioners.[62] Father Demo's announcement, translated into English, read: "the mayor of New York and the cardinal recommend that everyone cooperate in every possible way . . . in these times of great communal sacrifice." [63] Father Demo probably figured his parishioners could not save any more food than they were already doing.

On the other hand, Father Demo took an active role in the Treasury Department's programs. He sold Liberty Loan bonds and savings stamps to his parishioners.[64] Italian immigrants needed to save money, to buy homes or businesses in the United States, to bring over relatives from Italy, or to return to Italy themselves. Their needs, and the need the United States government had for cash with which to fight the war, came together to make the war bond program popular at Pompei.

When the United States entered World War I, the American Catholic hierarchy mobilized along with the rest of the population. In 1917, the bishops created a National Catholic War Council. This was soon renamed the National Catholic War Conference, because the word "council" sounded too much like a legislative body for the canon lawyers at the Vatican. The Knights of Columbus provided the personnel and administrative skills for nation-wide collections to fund military chaplains and recreation services for Catholics in arms.[65] The 1917 collection was organized quickly and the collection was modest. In July, Father Demo offered to take up a Catholic War Relief Fund collection in his parish.[66] In August, the Knights thanked him for the $28 collected.[67]

The next year, the Catholics tried harder. March 17, 1918, which combined Sunday with Saint Patrick's Day and was sure to bring in the Irish Catholics, was set aside as collection day. The Knights again sponsored the collection, but this time archdiocesan officials fell all over themselves to assure a good turn out. Pompei received at least a half dozen memorandums regarding administrative meetings, pledge cards, and other collection supplies.[68] The chancery set an optimistically high target for Pompei's contribution to the campaign, $8,000.[69] The parishioners gave $2,285, 28% of their quota, but much more than in 1917.[70]

When World War I ended, Italian-Americans still had their responsibilities to those in Italy who suffered during the war. Pompei honored parishioners returning from the armed forces with free admission to one of its fund raising programs for any one in military uniform.[71] The Italian Red Cross and others continued to raise money on behalf of Italians civilian and military casualties.[72] In 1921, Father Demo participated in a New York service held simultaneously with a Roman service entombing Italy's Unknown Soldier.[73]

The war had a far-reaching impact on Catholics in the United States. After the war, the National Catholic War Conference converted itself into the National Catholic Welfare Council. It is the ancestor of the U.S. Catholic Conference. Ultimately, the N.C.W.C.'s Bureau of Immigration replaced organizations such as the Saint Raphael Society in caring for immigrants on Ellis Island.

Before World War I, Cardinal Farley had begun bringing together New York's Catholic charities under an umbrella organization called United Catholic Works. World War I and Cardinal Farley's death interrupted the plans. After the war, the organizational process started again, and, in 1922, Catholic

Charities was incorporated. According to public relations articles, Catholic Charities was supposed to coordinate New York Catholics' efforts to do good.[74] Rather than have each agency raise its own funds, Catholic Charities conducted one annual campaign, and from this collection gave some funds to each agency. Also, rather than have each agency conduct its own public relations, or depend on pastors to channel parishioners towards the best sources of help, Catholic Charities had its own referral service.

Catholic Charities made two changes in Pompei's service to the poor. The first was in fund raising. Like the other parishes, Pompei participated in the annual Catholic Charities fund drive.[75] A committee canvassed the parishioners, solicited pledges, and forward money and pledges to Catholic Charities headquarters. There, Catholic Charities compiled, and published, lists of how each parish did, comparing parishes to each other and to the parishes' own past records. The comparisons weren't always meaningful. There was no way to compare parishes in wealthier neighborhoods with those in poorer ones; it should come as no surprise that Pompei consistently gave less than the archdiocesan cathedral. Ethnic parishes such as Pompei already had a history of giving primarily to charities within the ethnic group, so usually national parishes staffed by religious order clergy gave less than territorial parishes staffed by archdiocesan clergy. In 1926 the city condemned Pompei's old church, and the parish had to divert funds towards constructing a new one.[76]

Second, once Catholic Charities opened its referral service, Father Demo relinquished his job as an intake social worker. Instead of referring parishioners to a welfare agency himself, he referred them to Catholic Charities, explained what the problem was, and Catholic Charities was supposed to take care of the rest.[77] This was a new system, and not everyone trusted it. The Italian Catholics, who had encountered discrimination in the past, especially needed reassurance. Once Father Demo sent a family to Catholic Charities and, when nothing happened, sent a second letter and an explanation. "This people are under the impression that you do not care at all to act in their favor therefore this new recommendation."[78]

Father Demo's correspondence with Catholic Charities reveals as much about Catholic Charities as it does about Pompei. Like the Protestant and secular organizations on which it was modelled, Catholic Charities was a clearing house attempting to prevent duplication and waste. Its agents contacted pastors to keep them updated on their parishioners' cases.[79] Catholic Charities sent cases back to Father Demo when the people involved could use Italian Catholic institutions, thus saving Catholic Charities resources for those ineligible for Italian care.[80]

Like most early twentieth century welfare agencies, Catholic Charities thought its mission was to support the family, and to support the family members in their accustomed roles. Men were supposed to be breadwinners, and Catholic Charities tried to find jobs for the heads of households.[81] If the male head of the household couldn't work, it might take the entire rest of the family to replace the lost income. In one case that came to Father Demo's attention, when the head of the household took sick, Catholic Charities expected the entire rest of the family to pitch in. His mother agreed to stay at home and care for him, his wife and seventeen-year-old found jobs and the couple's fifteen-year-old planned to drop out of school to add to the family's earnings.[82]

Also, like other early twentieth century agencies, Catholic Charities had religious standards for those whom it helped. Families had to be practicing Catholics to qualify for aid. Catholic Charities kept pastors such as Father Demo busy verifying that potential clients had indeed been married according to Catholic standards.[83] In at least two cases that came to Father Demo's attention, Catholic Charities' efforts to help people halted temporarily until the people were properly baptized.[84]

Besides Catholic Charities, one other archdiocesan initiative brought Pompei into contact with the larger world. Pompei already had shown some interest in workers' welfare; it started a day care center for working mothers, and cooperated with the Women's Trade Union League after the Triangle Shirtwaist Factory Fire. Cardinal Hayes supported efforts to organize workers into unions. At least twice, he sent circulars to pastors asking them to support improved wages for police, fire fighters, and postal workers.[85] One could not separate church from work in the early twentieth century, not when there were so many Catholics among the working class, and so much needed to be done to protect workers from exploitation.

There were limits to Father Demo's participation in the world beyond Pompei. Despite an appeal that pleaded "the timid, the weak, and the youth of our city *should be able to look to you*" to end Mayor Jimmy Walker's corrupt administration by voting for Fiorello LaGuardia, Father Demo did nothing more than send his personal wishes for LaGuardia's success.[86] He was not a U.S. citizen, and never involved himself in politics except through his cooperation with Greenwich House.

There was one reform movement which might have caused Father Demo some hardship. The Eighteenth Amendment to the Constitution prohibited the manufacture, transportation, sale, and consumption of all alcoholic beverages. Wine was an integral part of Italian culture, and drunkenness was not an issue at Pompei: Father Demo received few letters concerning problem drinkers. However, from 1920 to 1933, drinking was a federal crime. According to one of Father Demo's correspondents, the law was almost unenforceable. "There is considerable wine [here] but hidden in cellars and other places."[87]

Before World War I, Father Demo was the messenger from his parish to the other institutions in Greenwich Village. In the 1920s, as American-bred Italians grew up, they took some of the responsibility for relations between Pompei and Village social service agencies. When the Knights of Columbus took up a collection for a new building, twenty-seven Pompei men and women helped with the drive, eight joined the Knights, and four contributed the top figure toward the campaign.[88] When the coordinator of the local girls' basketball league wrote Pompei about the upcoming basketball season, she wrote to "Mr. Michelini," probably August or Leon.[89] When the National Council of Catholic Women wanted Pompei to send a representative to a meeting, Father Demo forwarded two names, including that of Emilia Razzetti, who had been involved in Pompei's girls' activities. As this generation matured, they were both parishioners of Pompei and citizens of Greenwich Village, and they helped make Pompei a significant part of Village community life.

There were also limits to the friendships that developed among Village agencies. On November 21, 1921, Pompei observed Father Demo's twenty-fifth anniversary as a priest (and his twenty-second year in the Village) with a huge silver jubilee celebration. Head usher and trustee John A. Perazzo led the parish in planning a special Mass and luncheon. Monsignor Michael J. Lavelle, the chancery liaison with ethnic Catholics, celebrated Mass. Father Francesco Canonico Castellano, assigned to the papacy's diplomatic corps in Washington, preached the sermon. The party was a *parish* affair, with no participation on the part of anyone from any of the agencies with which Father Demo regularly corresponded. Father Demo never won any local awards. Forty years later, when Father Mario Albanesi was at Pompei, things would be different.

The silver anniversary sermon was published in 1923, in a large brochure accompanied by photographs of Father Demo, and of the exterior and interior of the Bleecker Street church. These were last look at the old church. By the time they were published, events were in motion that forced Pompei to make one last move to a new location.

NOTES

[1] For an event, *see* John Dolan. P.S.M., to Demo, 5 July 1904, CMS Box 2, Folder 5. For donations, see Giuseppe A. Caffuzzi, 28 November 1930, Box 6, Folder 40 (Italian).

[2] For camp, *see* J[oseph] M. Congedo to Demo, 24 July 1923, CMS Box 4. Folder 30. For donation, *see* Sister M. Matilde Marazzi to Demo, 8 May 1926, Box 5. Folder 35.

[3] For sending clergy, *see* Mother Mary Josephine, M.S.C., to Demo, 12 December 1923, CMS Box 4, Folder 29. For recommending Columbus Hospital events, *see* Pacifico C. Rossi to Demo, 81-83 Centre Street, 24 May 1924, Box 5, Folder 31.

[4] Francis Cacciola to Demo, Bar Harbor, Placentia Bay, West Newfoundland, 26 September 1913. CMS Box 2, Folder 15.

[5] To Demo, 644 East 235th, 14 December 1926, CMS Box 5, Folder 36.

[6] Frank Corri to Demo, Jersey City, New Jersey, 22 May 1913, CMS Box 2, Folder 14.

[7] D.P. Conway to Demo, 12 May 1910; and Anna Cornetta to Demo, 15 June, 17 June, 29 July and 30 December 1910, Box 1, Folder 11; Cornetta to Demo, no date and 19 January 1911; and D[ennis] J. Gerrity to Demo, 2 September 1911, CMS Box 1, Folder 12.

[8] Theresa M. Hide to Demo, 30 April 1910, CMS Box 1, Folder 11.

[9] Louise C. Spaziano to Demo, 4 October 1922, CMS Box 4, Folder 28. The letter is reporting a tussle in which the Roman Catholic Orphan Asylum received custody of an Italian Catholic boy from the Baptist Judson Memorial Health Center. However, this was more than a Protestant-Catholic quarrel; it signified differing opinions in child-care methods. The orphanage put the boy in an institution; Judson wanted to put him in family foster care.

[10] Hayes, circular letter, 31 October 1917, CMS Box 3, Folder 20.

[11] Thomas F. Meehan, "Evangelizing the Italians." The Messenger XXXIX (1903), p. 32.

[12] Diane Ravitch, *The Great School Wars: New York City, 1805–1973: A History of the Public Schools as Battlefield of Social Change* (New York: Basic Books, 1974), 3–76.

[13] *E.g.*, 490 Hudson to Demo, 25 June 1924, CMS Box 5, Folder 31.

[14] *E.g.*, P.S. 95 to Demo, 6 December 1918, CMS Box 3, Folder 22.

[15] *E.g.*, Mary F. Maguire to Demo, 12 December 1912, CMS Box 1, Folder 12.

[16] Harold Peyser to Demo, 4 June 1925, CMS Box 5, Folder 33.

[17] Demo to Loretta Rochester, 17 June 1925, CMS Box 5, Folder 33.

[18] For parents' meeting, *see* Maguire to Demo, 13 February 1907, CMS Box 1, Folder 8. For graduation, *see* Katherine Bevier, 16 June 1916, Box 2, Folder 17.

[19] Maguire to Demo, 21 February 1912, CMS Box 2, Folder 13.

[20] *E.g.*, Maguire to Demo. 8 June 1915, CMS Box 2, Folder 16.

[21] Peyser to Demo, 16 June 1926. CMS Box 5, Folder 35.

[22] Maguire to Demo, 1 May 1913, CMS Box 2, Folder 14.

[23] *E.g.*, Katherine Bevier to Demo, 12 May 1914. CMS Box 2, Folder 15.

[24] *E.g.*, M.A. Leonard to Demo, 19 March 1912, CMS Box 2, Folder 13. *See also* Frederick Goodell to Demo, 15 August 1915, Box 2, Folder 16. These are from two different branches of the public library.

[25] Anna B[illegible] to Demo, 25 October 1910, CMS Box 1, Folder 11.

[26] Charles Loring Brace, *The Dangerous Classes of New York and Twenty Years' Work among Them* (New York: Wynkoop and Hallenbeck, 1880; reprinted, Montclair, New Jersey: Patterson Smith, 1978), p. 198–199.

[27] M.S. Collins to Demo, ca. 14 November 1918, CMS Box 3, Folder 21.

[28] *E.g,* Augustus E. Califano to Demo, 14 October 1920, CMS Box 3, Folder 26.

[29] M.S. Collins to Demo, 6 December 1915, CMS Box 2, Folder 16.

[30] Robert H. Bremner, *From the Depths: The Discovery of Poverty in the United States* (New York: New York University Press, 1956), p. 53.

[31] Hudnut to Demo, 9 March 1926, CMS Box 5, Folder 35.

[32] M. Barrows to Demo, 22 May 1924, CMS Box 5, Folder 31.

[33] *E.g.*, Hudnut to Demo, 25 March 1925, CMS Box 5, Folder 31.

[34] Cornelia Ougheltree to Demo, 14 May 1928, CMS Box 5, Folder 38, and Hudnut to Demo, 7 July 1925, Box 5, Folder 34.

[35] Mary Kingsbury Simkhovitch, *Neighborhood.* 162.

[36] *E.g.*, Mary Carpenter to Demo, 9 March 1916, CMS Box 2, Folder 17.

[37] For limiting Village construction, *see* Simkhovitch to Demo, 2 February 1916, CMS Box 2, Folder 17. For meeting with "prominent residents," *see* Simkhovitch to Demo, 14 December 1921, Box 3, Folder 26. For lunch, *see* Simkhovitch to Demo, 21 March 1925, Box 5, Folder 33. For steering committee, *see* Simkhovitch to Demo, undated, Box 3, Folder 25.

[38] William Spinney to Demo, undated, CMS Box 2, Folder 16.

[39] For drama, *see* Helen Murphy to Demo, no date, CMS Box 6, Folder 44. For art exhibit committee, *see* Simkhovitch to Demo, 27 March 1922, Box 4, Folder 27. For pottery display, *see* Edith King to Demo, 16 April but no year, Box 3, Folder 33. For Old Home Week, *see* Simkhovitch to Demo, 13 May 1926, Box 5, Folder 35. For children's pageant, *see* Simkhovitch to Demo, 11 May 1916, Box 2, Folder 17.

[40] For music school, *see* Margaret W. Camman to Demo, 1 December 1923, Box 4, Folder 30. For slide lantern, *see* Lillian Front to Demo, 27 November 1929, Box 6. Folder 39.

[41] Joseph J. Mooney, circular letter, 1 August 1914, CMS Box 8, Folder 89.

[42] Circular letter, December 1915, CMS Italian-Americans and Religion Collection, Series I, Box 3, Archives of the Diocese of Brooklyn Miscellaneous Folder.

[43] Brochure in CMS Box 12, Folder 144. The $230.45 comes from subtracting Father Demo's expenses of $69.65 from the gross of $300.10.

[44] Via Gran S. Bernado #1 Milan to Demo, 7 September 1916, CMS Box 2, Folder 18 (Italian).

[45] John Cardinal Farley, circular letter, 14 December 1915, CMS Box 8, Folder 90.

[46] For Peace Sunday, *see* Hamilton Holt to Demo, 10 May 1916, CMS Box 2, Folder 17. For anti-German protest, *see* William H. Owen, Jr., circular letter, 22 January 1917, Box 3, Folder 19. For Bryan meeting *see* Frederick Lynch, circular letter, 26 January 1917, *ibid.*

[47] OLP Scrapbook has prayer cards which are souvenirs from the Holy Rosary feast day and annual mission held during the *Giubileo d'Argento.*

[48] List dated 29 September 1918, CMS Box 16, Folder 195.

[49] John J. Dunn, circular letter, 26 September 1920, CMS Box 8, Folder 95.

[50] Leroy Peterson, circular letter, 14 May 1917, CMS Box 8, Folder 95.

[51] John F.X. O'Connor to Demo, 12 June 1917, CMS Box 3, Folder 20.

[52] James J. Dover to Demo, 23 September 1918, CMS Box 3, Folder 22.

[53] Vincent de Paul McGean, circular letter, ca. 13 January 1918, CMS Box 3, Folder 21.

[54] Cleveland F. Pratt, circular letters, 17 September 1918, CMS Box 3, Folder 22.

[55] Eduardo Marcuzzi, circular letter, 29 June 1918, CMS Box 3, Folder 22 (Italian).

[56] Undated draft, CMS Box 3, Folder 22.

[57] Sunday announcements, 14 July 1918, CMS Box 29, Folder 316 (Italian).

[58] Herbert Hoover, circular letter, Washington, D.C., 18 June 1917, CMS Box 3, Folder 20.

[59] Charles S. Wilson, circular letter, 27 June 1917, *ibid.*

[60] F. E. Breithut to Michael Joseph Lavelle, 17 January 1918, CMS Box 3, Folder 21; and Lavelle, circular letter, 18 January 1918, *ibid.*

[61] Mabel F. Spinney to Demo, 11 April 1918, *ibid.*

[62] Gherardo Ferrante to Demo, 15 June 1918, CMS Box 3, Folder 22.

[63] Sunday announcements, 16 June 1918. CMS Box 29, Folder 316 (Italian).

[64] For bonds, *see* Ernest Iselin to Demo, 10 and 18 October 1918, CMS Box 3, Folder 22. For stamps, *see* Milton W. Lipper to Demo, Washington, D.C., 14 February 1918, CMS Box 3, Folder 21.

[65] Christopher J. Kauffman, *Faith and Fraternalism: The History of the Knights of Columbus, 1881-1982* (New York: Harper and Row, 1982), 192-224.

[66] Edward A. Arnold to Demo, 24 July 1917, CMS Box 3, Folder 20.

[67] William P. Larkin to Demo, 14 August 1917, *ibid.*

[68] CMS Box 14, Folder 168.

[69] John J. Dunn to Demo, 21 February 1918, *ibid.*

[70] *New York American Sun*, 31 March, 1918.

[71] Program, 28–29 January 1919, CMS Box 12, Folder 144.

[72] Gherardo Ferrante to Demo, 19 December 1918, CMS Box 3, Folder 22.

[73] *Il Carroccio* XIII (November 1921), 635–636.

[74] Patrick J. Hayes, "The Unification of Catholic Charities," *Catholic World* CXVII (May 1923), 145–153.

[75] John J. Dunn, circular letter, 8 March 1920, CMS Box 8, Folder 95.

[76] Catholic Charities published annual reports listing how each parish performed for the year of the report and the year before.

[77] Demo to Catholic Charities, 19 September 1929, CMS Box 6, Folder 39.

[78] Demo to Catholic Charities, 23 July 1926, CMS Box 5, Folder 36.

[79] *E.g.*, John Philip Bramer to Demo, 14 December 1925, CMS Box 5, Folder 34.

[80] Catherine Hart to Demo, 18 June 1932, CMS Box 6, Folder 42

[81] Bramer to Demo, 28 January 1926, CMS Box 5, Folder 35.

[82] Alice B. Claus to Demo, 22 October 1930, CMS Box 6, Folder 40.

[83] *E.g.*, Minnie Costello to Demo, Yonkers, 22 May 1925, CMS Box 5.

[84] *E.g.*, M.H. Lagrille to Demo, 1 June 1926, CMS Box 5, Folder 35.

[85] Hayes, circulars, 28 May 1920 in CMS Box 8, Folder 95; and 20 October 1923, Box 9, Folder 98.

[86] Arthur Little to Demo, 16 October 1929, CMS Box 5, Folder 39.

[87] Buffalo to Demo, 19 March 1920, CMS Box 3, Folder 24. Since Father Demo was a pastor, he could get wine for religious purposes. and he did receive letters asking him to divert some of it for non-religious use. *See* 417 Broome to Demo, 6 July 1920 and 3 August 1920, Box 3, Folder 25.

[88] John L. Podesta to William P. Larkin, 23 December 1921, OLP Box 3, Folder 26. The contributors were Dominick De Vivo, Leon Michelini, Victor E. Podesta and John J. Repetti. The Knights were John J. Podesta, Messrs Michelini, De Vivo, Victor E. Podesta and Repetti, plus Charles Basso, Julius Laneri, and Amerigo Roscelli. The helpers were Lucia Agresta, Aurelia Armellino, Francis Avellino, Emma Brignole, Laura Calamari, Anthony Camisa, Ida and Louis Cardinale, Rossetta Ferno, Joseph Fontana, Amerigo Levan, Florence Lucca, Teresa Lunardini, Albina Mariani, Julia and Nina Paretti, Joseph Peragallo, Paul V. Peroni, May Pollito, Stephen Puccetti, Adele and Mary Raffo, Emma and Louise Razzetti, Alfred and Charles Rosotti, and Ralph Stella.

[89] Helen Thompson to Mr. Michelini, 19 January 1925, CMS Box 5, Folder 33.

Dedicating Pompei's present church at Carmine and Bleeker Streets, October 7, 1928. Carrying the holy water is Joseph Pernicone, later New York's first Sicilian-born auxiliary bishop. Next to him are Vincent Jannuzzi, pastor of Saint Joseph's on Catherine Street, Patrick Cardinal Hayes, and John Marchegiani, Pompei's Pastor from 1933 to 1937. Behind are Giovanni Battista Peruzzi, Sr., and Fr. Anthony Demo.

Sedente sul Soglio di Pietro
Il Sommo Pontefice Pio XI

Essendo Arcivescovo di New York
Sua Eminenza il Cardinale Patrick J. Hayes

Reggendo la Pia Societa' Scalabriniana Istituita sotto la protezione di San Carlo Borromeo
Sua Eminenza il Cardinale Gaetano de Lai

Essendo Rettore della Parrocchia (fondata nel 1892)
Il Reverendo Padre Antonio Demo

Regnando in Italia
Sua Maesta' Vittorio Emanuele III

Governando
Sua Eccellenza Benito Mussolini

Essendo Presidente degli Stati Uniti d'America
Hon. Calvin Coolidge

Governatore dello Stato di New York
Hon. Alfred E. Smith

Sindaco della Citta di New York
Hon. James J. Walker

A gloria di Dio, Ottimo e Massimo

Ad onore della Beata Maria Sempre Vergine
Cui questa Chiesa sotto il nome di Madonna di Pompei s'intitola
A lustro della fede cattolica,
Ad onore dell' Italia che ci ha geniti,
Ad onore dell' America, che ci ha adottati,
Auspicante un popolo fedele, numeroso, festante,
Oggi III Ottobre 1926
Questa Pietra Angolare solennemente benedisse e pose il

Rev. Monsig. Michael J. Lavelle deputato rappresentante Sua Eminenza
il Cardinale P. J. Hayes.

This greeting was placed inside Pompei's present church's cornerstone, which was laid October 3, 1926. A translation apperars in the text. The handwriting on the side is Fr. Demo's.

6

The Last New Church, 1921–1928

World War I temporarily halted immigration. After the war, trans-Atlantic steamers again filled up with immigrants, leaving their war-torn homelands. Early in the 1920s, the United States Congress took steps to halt immigration permanently. In 1921, and again in 1924 and 1927, Congress passed laws assigning each nation a quota of immigrants. Ostensibly the quotas were created by taking a percentage of each national group already represented in the United States. Actually, the percentages were rigged to exclude as many immigrants as possible, especially those from southern and eastern Europe. Italy, which between 1900 and 1914 sent a hundred thousand immigrants a year to the United States, got a quota of under 5,000. The quota laws remained in effect until 1965.

Father Demo protested these laws, knowing what they portended for Pompei.[1] In a 1924 letter to his superior, Demo explained that the Scalabrinians had to be sure to teach missionaries English before they were sent to the United States, explaining, in Italian, "the old immigration is closed, and with the passage of a few years our language will be a historical memory and nothing more."[2]

Despite the end of immigration, the future must have looked bright at Pompei, because in 1922 Father Demo made an expensive proposal to the Diocesan Council, a body of clergy who advised the archbishop on diocesan affairs. He requested permission to purchase property between Bleecker and Hancock Streets, a lot overlooking the rear of Pompei's Asilo Scalabrini. The lot had an old three-story house with shops on its ground floor, and a dilapidated stable. Father Demo wanted to tear down the two buildings and put up a parochial school.[3]

The archdiocesan bureaucracy moved slowly. The Secretary to the Diocesan Council did not acknowledge Father Demo's letter until September 14, 1922, at which point Archbishop Hayes appointed a committee to study the feasibility of a school.[4] Less than a month later, Father Demo got word that a new committee had been created, consisting of Monsignor Lavelle of Saint Patrick's Cathedral and Monsignor Daniel Burke of Saint Philip Neri in Bedford Park. Both were liaisons between the chancery and the Italian community. Father

Demo was to schedule a meeting with these two to discuss his proposal.[5] Meanwhile, Archbishop Hayes inquired among friendly brokers to find out how much money Father Demo should offer for the plot. He told Father Demo not to go over $42,000.[6] Official permission to buy finally came November 2, 1922.[7]

While waiting for the chancery to grant permission to buy, Father Demo continued with his parish activities. In 1923, he hit upon an activity that had everything. Between 1923 and 1932, Passion Plays provided Christian education, expanded devotional opportunities, drew on Pompei's experience with drama, gave individuals a chance to show off their talents, brought the parishioners together to work as a group, and raised funds.

Pompei had a Passion Play once before, when Father Pio Parolin organized one to benefit the Asilo Scalabrini.[8] The 1923 Passion Play called on people who had acted in Pompei dramas throughout the 1910s. Luigi Raybaut directed the Passion Play and played Judas, Luigi Laneri played "the Christus," Antoinette Scagni played the Blessed Mother, and Concetta Mollica played Saint John. The Holy Name Society men took the male crowd roles, and played apostles, Pharisees, scribes, and soldiers. Sunday School teachers took the female crowd roles.[9]

The Passion Play had nine scenes: Jesus' entrance into Jerusalem, the Last Supper, the meeting between Judas and Caiphus, Jesus in the Garden of Gethsemane, Jesus before Pilate, Judas hanging himself, Jesus on the road to Calvary, the crucifixion itself, and the resurrection and ascension. Judging from other Passion Plays and from later photographs, the scenes were literally scenes, or tableaux, with a minimum of action. There was some dialogue, in English and Italian. And there was music by *maestri* Fontana and Carbone. Whoever designed the programs must have thought attending a Passion Play would be a novelty for the audience, for the program included etiquettes tips. The audience was to sit down, give dignified and religious attention to the play, and not to applaud. The first run must have been at least a modest success in terms of how well the players themselves enjoyed it, the attendance, and the income it generated, because Pompei went on to make it an annual event.

However, there was a new and serious problem with the school plans. On December 16, 1923, Father Demo informed Archbishop Hayes that the lot's owner wanted an exorbitant price, so Pompei couldn't buy the property it wanted. Not only that, but the city was digging a vehicular tunnel to link New Jersey with New York. Sixth Avenue was to be extended from West Third Street south to Canal Street to hold the tunnel traffic. Father Demo asked two questions. Should Pompei wait to see what the city's plans were before embarking on any new "Parochial enterprises?" And, shouldn't Pompei begin buying property for a new church in Greenwich Village?[10] Father Demo's letter is the first mention in Pompei's records of the Holland Tunnel, the construction of which forced the parish to do some construction of its own.

One event at the end of that year was also full of meaning for the future. On December 27, 1923, Italy's King Victor Emmanuel III bestowed upon Father Demo the title *Cavaliere dell'Ordine della Corona d'Italia,* a medal in the shape of a Maltese cross, suspended from a ribbon.[11] Father Demo may not have known the story behind his medal. In October 1922, Benito Mussolini became prime minister of Italy, and installed a new kind of dictatorship, which he called fascism. Mussolini called the Italian immigrant communities in the United States and elsewhere "colonies," although they hardly bore the same relation to Italy that Hong Kong bore to Great Britain. Mussolini hoped to extend Italy's power and influence outside its own borders, and one way to do so was to strengthen ties between the Italian homeland and the Italians living abroad. To this end, Mussolini urged King Victor Emmanuel to award decorations to local leaders in Italian immigrant neighborhoods, and to other people whose support Mussolini wished to cultivate.

During 1924, while waiting to hear about the city's plans for its tunnel, Father Demo held another Passion Play. This time he saved the receipts.[12] The Passion Play was an expensive production. The actors' labor was free, but bills for lumber, printing, and the like added up to $728.05. Ticket sales, though, amounted to $1,499.10, a profit of $771.05.

Late that year, New York City announced a plan for changing Greenwich Village's horse-and buggy street pattern to accommodate automobile traffic.[13] The plan extended Sixth Avenue beyond its old terminal at Minetta Lane and Carmine Street. New Sixth Avenue cut diagonally through the Village, which already had more diagonal streets than the rest of the city (all of them going diagonally the *other way* from the new avenue). Crossing or passing Bleecker, West Houston, Bedford, King, Prince, Charlton, Vandam, MacDougal, Spring, Clarke, Broome, Watts, Grand, and Sullivan, the elongated Sixth Avenue emptied into Canal Street, which was widened so that Laight Street, immediately to Canal's south, nearly disappeared. The new Sixth Avenue obliterated Hancock and Congress Streets, destroyed the homes of some ten thousand people, and demolished businesses that had spent years building up clientele. Pompei stood squarely in the path of this "progress."

Real estate agents pressured Pompei to liquidate its assets while they still had value and to commit itself to a new location while places were still available. "You are undoubtedly aware of the plan contemplated by the city for the extension of Sixth Avenue which will affect your property . . . . As these procedures are long and drawn out, would you rather avoid this by selling at a reasonable price at this time and would you then be in a position to purchase or lease something else in the immediate neighborhood?"[14]

Now that Pompei had to move, projects such as the Passion Play assumed added urgency. It was not yet clear how much money the parish would need. Plus, as Father Demo explained to one city official, congregational morale was at stake.[15] The Bleecker Street church was a tangible sign of the community. If the church was endangered, Pompei parish had to have other signs of its community life, such as parish activities. Pompei held its third annual Passion Play from March 22 through April 5, 1925, an eight-day run.[16] Probably because the parish had already made a substantial investment in costumes, props, and equipment, the expenses decreased to $542.50 despite the increased performances. Pompei netted $665.35

In buying the site for the new church, Father Demo was assisted by several lay men, some of whom had been attached to Pompei since before his arrival. Vincent Pepe, real estate broker, appraised Pompei's property so the parish would know what to expect from the city for compensation.[17] The Rosotti family, lithographers, printed ten thousand colored reproductions of the architect's drawings for the new church, and portraits of the current pope, Pius XI, to use in fund raising.[18] Charles Zerbarini, lawyer and sometime trustee, did the legal work. In late May 1925, Mr. Zerbarini opened negotiations for Pompei to purchase from a family named Norris a single large bloc of property.[19] The land consisted of contiguous lots from 2–10 Leroy Street, 236–248 Bleecker Street, and 17–25 Carmine Street. Pompei paid $65,000 down and took on a mortgage for $110,000 for the site.[20]

Although the property was a single unit owned by a single family, it was divided into lots with buildings on them. Each building was occupied by a business or a residential tenant. Rather than wait until they all expired, Pompei bought out the leases. Buying the leases was more expensive, but it saved time, and time was important because the city was moving a head with its plans.[21]

Now that Pompei had a lot, what kind of church to build? Pompei may have borrowed an idea from another Manhattan parish staffed by the Scalabrinians, Saint Joseph's at the corner of Monroe and Catherine Streets. In 1925, Saint Joseph's was created out of the old Scalabrinian chapel of Saint Joachim's, and moved into a new building that was a combination church, rectory, and parochial school. Pompei also decided to build a combination church, school, and convent plus a connected rectory.

Such a large and complex structure required more than an architect, and Father Demo found such a person in Matthew Del Gaudio. Mr. Del Gaudio had designed Saint Joseph's, and also the Church of the Sacred Hearts of Jesus and Mary, at 309–315 East 33rd Street. Both pastors who employed him believed he had saved them considerable money.[22] Mr. Del Gaudio offered to be the general contractor as well as the architect, and to find the sub-contractors for each phase of the construction.[23] Raising one large building, and having one person act as architect and contractor meant that Pompei paid a great deal of money all at once. However, it may have been less expensive in the long run, because all the work was coordinated. It also avoided having to repeat the process of asking the chancery for permission to build.

Father Demo and Mr. Del Gaudio submitted plans for archdiocesan approval. The architect's design called for a steel frame for the church complex. The walls hidden from public view would be of brick. The rectory facade, the church facade, and the wall along Bleecker Street would be of cut lime stone. The estimated cost was $589,400.[24] That was too much for Cardinal Hayes, who feared Pompei wouldn't be able to raise the necessary money. He authorized spending only $385,000. The savings were effected by using brick instead of cut stone for the rectory facade, and building only the basement level of the proposed school.[25]

Boosting parish morale in the face of the impending move and filling the parish bank account continued apace. In February, the Sunday School teachers produced three one-act plays for the benefit of the parish.[26] Two-hundred-ten people paid thirty cents a ticket to attend the performances, for a gross revenue of $63.00. Since the plays cost only $4.80 to produce, the profits were $58.20. The 1926 Passion Play netted another $876.45.[27] The Passion Play was the last big event at 210 Bleecker. In March, workers demolished the buildings on Pompei's new site.

Pompei's new church has become such a landmark that it is sad to think of the other, older, landmarks that were torn down so that it could be built. There are pictures of how Carmine Street looked before Pompei was erected. The best-known is probably a landscape painted in 1912 by American artist John Sloan. The painting is titled *Carmine Street Theatre*, for its focal point is a play house that stood where Pompei stands now. In a way, Pompei is already in the picture, for walking along the foreground of the painting is a nun, dressed like the Pallottines who took care of the children at the Asilo Scalabrini a block away.

In June, as workers laid foundations for Pompei's new church, the city formally condemned the old one.[28] Pompei received an eviction notice for its church, another for Asilo Scalabrini, and copies of two more notices intended for tenants who lived in parts of 8 Downing not occupied by Asilo Scalabrini. All tenants had to be out by August 31.[29] Pompei's ten thousand neighbors received their eviction notices the same day, giving the entire neighborhood only about a month to find new homes in an area which suddenly had many fewer houses.

The New York *World* quoted Father Demo on the situation. "For ten years the city has been talking about the extension but when it comes to moving thousands of poor people who have no place to go, only thirty days are allowed.

We are erecting a new church on the corner of Carmine Street, but it will not be ready for occupancy until next Easter. I am much worried, though, about my parishioners."[30] In the midst of trying to find a new home for Pompei, Father Demo took the time to find new homes for the more vulnerable members of his flock. On behalf of an elderly couple, he explained, "The house where they have been living for almost half a century is to be demolished in a short time and therefore they decided to enter a [senior citizens'] home."[31] The city fell behind schedule and did not evict all tenants by August, for on September 27, Father Demo wrote to the controller to try to buy even more time at the old church.[32] Nevertheless, Pompei was put on notice that it had to hurry.

The new building's cornerstone was laid October 3. Monsignor Lavelle represented Cardinal Hayes for the occasion. Photographs of the blessing appeared in numerous area newspapers. *Il Corriere d'America* carried a touching photograph of Monsignor Lavelle blessing the temporary altar in the church under construction, standing on a concrete floor with the bare walls all around him.[33]

In the cornerstone Pompei placed a sheet of paper listing the prominent leaders of the day at the time the cornerstone was laid: Patrick Cardinal Hayes, Archbishop of New York; Gaetano Cardinal de Lai, administrator of the Scalabrinians; Father Demo as Pompei's pastor; King Victor Emmanuel III of Italy; Italian Prime Minister Benito Mussolini; President Calvin Coolidge; Governor Al Smith; and Mayor Jimmy Walker. The paper ended with the inscription: *Ad onore della Beata Maria Sempre Vergine cui questa Chiesa sotto il nome de Madonna di Pompei s'intitola a lustro della fede cattolica, ad onore dell'Italia che ci ha geniti, ad onore dell'America, che chi ha adottati, Auspicante un popolo fidele, numeroso, festante.* This may be translated into English as "For the honor of the Blessed Mary, ever virgin, to whom, to add luster to the Catholic faith, this church is dedicated under the name of the Madonna of Pompei, for the honor of Italy which gave us birth, and for the honor of America which adopted us, a faithful, numerous, and festive people gives its best wishes."

Shortly thereafter, Luigi Barzini, the editor of the Italian-American newspaper *Il Corriere D'America* sent Pompei a circular letter soliciting contributions to honor a member of Italy's fascist government who was coming to New York on an official visit. (Mr. Barzini's letter doesn't say, but the official was probably military hero Italo Balbo). Father Demo explained he could not afford to contribute, but assured Barzini *"Il vecchio granatiere d'un tempo non potendo rispondere all' appello con dinaro, [illegible] col pensiero per onorare i prodi della patria d'origine,"* or "This old grenadier of long ago cannot answer the call for money [but he will] honor in his thoughts the heroes of the homeland."[34] Father Demo seems to have thought that fascism, which glorified military prowess, was a new, better, version of the liberal nationalist government in whose army he had served in the last century.

With the old church being torn down and the new one incomplete, there had to be a fund raising project more extensive than the annual Passion Play. On December 27, 1926, Father Demo signed a contract with the McKeown System, a public relations firm specializing in fund raising. This was a parish first. For expenses plus $4,000, the contract called for the McKeown company to supply a director and secretary for a fund raising campaign, and to do all the planning and the publicity.[35]

Mr. McKeown had already written out a detailed calendar for the proposed campaign.[36] The first project was to take a census, to see how many people were in the parish, and thus how widely the financial burden could be shared. The list of census captains contains many names of men with records of parish service: August and Leon Michelini, Alfred and Charles Rosotti, Victor E. Podesta, Charles Nobile, Dominick De Vive, George Fontana, Fred Verdiani, Frank and Mario Stella, Frank Castaldo, Paul Laneri, Paul Peroni, Fred Pasquale, Leo Cavagnaro, and Joseph Perrino.[37]

Each captain had a team of men and women. For example, Mr. Castaldo's team included Domenick Casino, Emma Scala, Catherine De Madini, Josephine Shizzoni, Clelia Ulova, Adeline Gotti, Ralph and Dante Stella, Eliusa Bertolotti, Cleana Senno, Jerry and Michael Cioffurio, Louise Segaline, and Sabastian Romanzo.[38] At that time, Ralph Stella was a younger man involved in the Junior Holy Name Society, and perhaps the others on the list were also younger people just beginning their parish service.

The census workers were invited to an information meeting on January 3, 1927, with refreshments and entertainment.[39] The parishioners had already been notified of the upcoming census via a circular letter sent out over Father Demo's signature.[40] The initial announcement was followed up in January with an English and Italian brochure, explaining the purpose of the census and asking for cooperation.[41]

During January, the census workers walked from house to house, climbed stairs, knocked on doors, found out if the residents were parishioners, and then took down their names. Every week the census workers met to tally results and enjoy refreshments. By the month's end, they had collected 25,000 names.[42] This figure was more than double that reported on a form Father Demo filled out for the United States Census of Religious Bodies in December 1926. At that time, Father Demo claimed he had only 12,000 parishioners, 5,000 men and 7,000 women, or 4,000 people under thirteen years of age and 8,000 over thirteen.[43] Father Demo knew he had 20,000 parishioners earlier in the 1920s, so it is not clear why he reported this figure. He may have estimated how many parishioners he lost in the widening of Sixth Avenue. If so, the parish census results would have come as a pleasant surprise. (The other possibility is that the census counted not just parishioners, but neighbors willing to contribute. If so, the extent of community support must have been gratifying).

Once Pompei knew from whom it could solicit donations, the next step was to have a huge fund raiser. Pompei chose an unusual fund raiser. Rather than a bazaar or a dramatic production, it sponsored a complimentary dinner for all the male heads of households in the parish. The prospective guests were identified from the census, and invitations sent out. An announcement encouraged "the good women of the parish to urge their men to attend this dinner. . . ."[44]

Mr. McKeown's public relations team made every effort to give the men a sense of ownership in the project of building the parish plant. The membership list of the organizing committee contained 104 names. Some of them, such as Charles Zerbarini, were parish trustees. Others, such as Fiorello La Guardia, were honorary members, whose names added luster to the whole project. Others, such as contractor George Fontana, had been faithful parishioners since the last huge fund raiser, the 1911 bazaar to finance the Asilo Scalabrini.[45]

Mr. McKeown also spared no expense, aware that the dinner was not just a fund raiser, but a fun time and a way to encourage parish unity. He booked the Pennsylvania Hotel, which is still standing, across from Madison Square Garden. He carefully attended to the seating arrangements so that friends could dine together. The menu included antipasto, minestrone, celery, arciofini, olives, filet of sole italienne with parsley potatoes, roast stuffed chicken (one-half chicken per diner) with butter beans and salad, ice cream, cake, coffee, cigars, and cigarettes. The featured speaker was the Honorable John J. Freschi, a New York State judge active in the movement to make Columbus Day a legal holiday.[46] The affair was advertised as a testimonial to Father Demo.

On the night of February 11, almost everything went according to plan. Judge Freschi had to cancel at the last moment but Monsignor Lavelle filled in for him, and Father Demo also said a few words. During dinner, the fund raising captains assigned to each table took pledges, and, when the evening was over Pompei had commitments for $40,000 in donations, a huge sum by Italian parish standards.[47]

But it was not enough. Father Demo explained to his parishioners that the next step in raising money was to "adopt American methods. All our religious and social service institutions throughout America are financed by the deferred payment plan," whereby each donor paid a small amount per month for a number of months, thus turning many small donations into large ones.[48]

Organizing the deferred payment plan meant rounding up the volunteers for a second parish visitation. The people who took the census must have volunteered for this second canvass, for in his circular letter to them, Father Demo began by thanking them for their census work. "Now comes our real task. The Italian-Americans of this neighborhood will presently be called upon to show our Diocesan Authorities their interest in the new parochial plant . . . . So we are going to have a campaign. Not a collection, but a campaign for membership in our Builders' Society." Once again, workers were invited to a meeting at which there would be refreshments, entertainment, and the distribution of information packets.[49]

Father Demo had already started explaining the Builders' Society to the parishioners. Every wage earner in the parish was eligible for membership. All one had to do was make an initial donation of five dollars and then set aside ten cents per day or three dollars per month for the next two years. One made one's donations by placing them in an account at a neighborhood bank, which kept a record of all contributions.

The announcement stressed the importance of membership in the Builders' Society for wage-earning teen-agers living at home. It wasn't enough, Father Demo said, for teen-agers to say that their families gave to the church. Teen-agers themselves would benefit from the meeting and recreation rooms that the new plant would include. They themselves would attend the new church in their adult lives, marry in it, and raise their own children in it.[50] Including the young wage-earner may have reflected how much the parish needed the money, and therefore how widely it had to cast the net for contributions. It was also consistent with Father Demo's interest in the religious lives of young people.

Mr. McKeown arranged for a prominent Catholic to start the donation campaign. Cardinal Hayes sent his best wishes and five hundred dollars toward the building fund.[51] On March 3, 1927, Father Demo wrote to thank the cardinal and to apprise him of the state of the fund raising. Pledges made during the Pennsylvania Hotel dinner were put at $42,035, and Builders' Society pledges at $105,200.[52]

During that Lent, Pompei was still between buildings, and so for the second year in a row missed its Passion Play. By April, the construction crew finished the new church's basement, and on May 1 there was a procession carrying the Blessed Sacrament from the old church and placing it in the tabernacle in the new. Father Demo said the first Mass in the new building in honor of the old one. Pompei celebrated Christmas midnight Mass in the unfinished main sanctuary of its new church.

Construction continued throughout the first eight months of 1928, so for a third year, the Passion Play was not held. The new church was ready for dedication October 7, 1928.[53] Cardinal Hayes himself came, and a roster of clergy active in the Italian community: Monsignor Lavelle; Monsignor Burke; Scalabrinian Provincial Leonardo Quaglia; and Father Vincent Jannuzzi, pastor of Pompei's sister parish of Saint Joachim.

The ceremonies began with a procession, which was headed up by a color guard bearing American, Italian, and Vatican flags. Cardinal Hayes blessed the church's interior, walked in procession around the perimeter of Pompei's property showering holy water on the walls for the blessing of the exterior, and returned to the sanctuary for the Mass. *Maestro* Fontana composed a Mass for the day and presided over the organ; soloist Anna Carbone LaPadula and a choir of twenty-five young women sang. Father Giacomo Gamberra, the senior Scalabrinian missionary in the United States, preached in Italian, reviewing the history of the parish.

After Mass, Cardinal Hayes spoke briefly to the parishioners:

> I cannot tell you the depth of the emotion I felt when dedicating this church as I thought of the goodness of your people and the zeal of your pastor. And I want here today to express publicly and officially my deep congratulations for what you have done in this parish. The church itself, as you see, is most majestic. You need only to enter the door to have your thoughts directed heavenward. This ranks among the noblest and most beautiful of all the churches in the archdiocese and that is saying a great deal. It speaks of the advance our Italian Catholic people have made here. Your fathers came to America as poor immigrants, like most of us. I as Archbishop have learned to depend much on you, my Italian people. You have a glorious ancestry both in blood and in faith. What a glorious land you have come from! We have a right to expect from you that you will bring with you a warm-hearted Catholic faith.

Like the cornerstone laying, this was a well-documented and well-photographed affair. Parishioners participated through their parish societies: a photograph of the congregation at Mass shows adult men, in their dark suits, seated on the left side of the church, and what seems to be the Children of Mary, in white veils, on the right. The neighborhood council of the Knights of Columbus stood in a row across the front o the sanctuary, and at the moment of the consecration of the Eucharist, they raised their ceremonial swords.[54]

The new church contained some of the furnishings of the old one. The life-size crucifix from the old church was placed in a "memorial shrine," a niche to the right of the entrance of the new church.[55] The Corpus Christi was brought to the new church and was for many years used at the Good Friday services.[56] The painting of Our Lady of Pompei was also brought over to the new church and installed in the new altar.

The old organ, though, didn't make the trip. An organ technician informed Father Demo that it would cost $2,800 just to move the organ one block, and another $1,500 to renovate it for its new location.[57] Pompei purchased a new organ from the Kilgren Company, the same firm that had installed an organ for Saint Patrick's Cathedral. Monsignor Lavelle returned to Pompei to bless the organ April 18, 1929, and to attend an inaugural concert featuring a choir of parish volunteers and its two long-time organists, *maestri* Fontana and La Padula.[58]

Once settled in its new home, Pompei resumed the parish activities that combined finances and fun. The fifth Passion Play ran from March 10–26, with evening performances Sunday, Tuesday, and Thursday nights, and Sunday matinees. By now, it probably seemed to the audience as though most of the parishioners were in the cast: the family men from the Saint Joseph's society joined the male crowd parts, and the Sunday School teachers, the Pie Donne, and the Young Ladies Club joined the female chorus. With tickets priced at fifty and seventy-five cents, Pompei made $1,912.50.[59]

Not only were affairs at Pompei settled, affairs in Italy were being stabilized, too. In 1929, the papacy and the Italian government signed documents known as the Lateran Treaties. The Italian government recognized that Vatican City constituted an independent state, and paid an indemnity for lands formerly belonging to the papacy which in the nineteenth century had been conquered for united Italy. Vatican City in turn recognized that Italy constituted a separate country and that its government had its own legitimate interests.

Before the year was out, Mussolini was stretching the Italian government's "legitimate interests" to the point where Pope Pius XI complained, in his encyclical *Non Abbiamo Bisogno*, that the fascists were resurrecting the "pagan worship of the state."[60] However, Pius's protests against Mussolini had to be vaguely worded; he was uncertain whether Mussolini would honor the Lateran Treaties he had signed. The American hierarchy, concerned with the depression at home and with a revolution in nearby Mexico, did not emphasize opposition to fascism.

In 1929, Father Demo let the Associazione Nazionale Combattenti Italiani, an organization for veterans of Italy's armed forces, hold its annual requiem for deceased members at Pompei. The way the organization dated its thank you letter gave a clue to its fascist sympathies: the year is given as "VII," the Roman numeral for the seventh year of fascist rule.[61] But no one objected to Father Demo hosting this troupe. Everyone thought the Lateran Treaties had solved the Vatican's differences with the Italian government for good, and that the future held no further problems.

NOTES

[1] *Il Corriere del Bronx*, 24 January 1924.

[2] Demo to Pacifico Chenuil, 4 July 1924, CMS Box 7, Folder 58.

[3] Demo to Diocesan Consultors, 13 June 1922, AANY, OLP Folder, Microfilm Reel #10.

[4] Secretary to the Diocesan Council to Demo, 14 September 1922, *ibid*.

[5] Secretary of the Diocesan Council to Demo, 6 October 1922, *ibid.*

[6] Michael Joseph Lavelle to Secretary to the Diocesan Council, 18 October 1922, *ibid.*

[7] Secretary of the Diocesan Council to Demo, 2 November 1922, *ibid.*

[8] Program, undated [1912–4?], CMS Box 12, Folder 143.

[9] Program, 19–22 March 1923, CMS Box 12, Folder 143.

[10] Demo to Hayes, 16 December 1923, CMS Box 18, Folder 205.

[11] The certificate is in CMS Box 11, Folder 133.

[12] Program, 9–15 April 1924, CMS Box 12, Folder 143; and New York *Daily News*, 21 March 1931.

[13] New York *Sun*, 19 December 1924, CMS Box 23, Folder 274. Map in CMS Box 21, Folder 243.

[14] Van Vliet and Place to Charles Zerbarini, 5 May 1925, CMS Box 21, Folder 242.

[15] Demo to Charles W. Berry, 27 September 1926, CMS Box 21, Folder 243.

[16] Program, 9–15 April 1924, CMS Box 12, Folder 143.

[17] Vincent Pepe to Demo, 26 January 1926, CMS Box 21, Folder 243.

[18] To Cosenza, North Bergen New Jersey, 29 May 1967, OLP Papers before 1975, Cosenza Folder.

[19] *New York Times,* 31 May 1925. CMS Box 23, Folder 274.

[20] Zerbarini to Demo, 26 May 1925, CMS Box 21, 242.

[21] Demo to Berry, 27 September 1926, CMS Box 21, 243.

[22] Vincent M. Jannuzzi to Thomas G. Carroll, 29 April 1926; and Joseph Congedo to Carroll, 3 May 1926, both in AANY OLP Folder, microfilm reel #10.

[23] M[atthew] W. Del Gaudio to Carroll, 26 April 1926, *ibid.*

[24] Undated proposal (probably 26 April 1926), *ibid.*

[25] Carroll to Demo, 8 May 1926, *ibid.*

[26] Ticket dated 22 February 1926, CMS Box 12, Folder 144.

[27] Program, 1926, CMS Box 12, Folder 143.

[28] OLP Scrapbook.

[29] Eviction notices, undated, CMS Box 21 Folder 243.

[30] New York *World*, 30 July 1926, p. 6, CMS Box 17, Folder 203.

[31] Demo to Robert L. Harrison, 23 March 1926, CMS Box 5, Folder 35.

[32] Demo to Berry, 27 September 1926, CMS Box 21, Folder 243.

[33] *Il Corriere d'America,* 17 October 1926, CMS Box 17, Folder 203.

[34] Demo to Luigi Barzini, 19 November 1926, CMS Box 5, Folder 35.

[35] The contract, dated 27 December 1926, is in CMS Box 20, Folder 228.

[36] The calendar, undated but beginning with 13 December 1926, is in CMS Box 20, Folder 229.

[37] Circular letter to census captains from Demo, 20 December 1926, *ibid.*

[38] Sheet of lined paper dated December 1926, *ibid.*

[39] Circular to census workers from Demo, 29 December 1926, CMS Box 20, Folder 228.

[40] Circular from Demo, 20 December 1926 (Italian), CMS Box 20, Folder 229.

[41] Brochure dated January 1927, CMS Box 22, Folder 271.

[42] Typed sheet dated January 1927, CMS Box 20, Folder 229.

[43] Circular from Thomas G. Carroll, 10 December 1926, CMS Box 9, Folder 109.

[44] Announcement dated 6 February 1927, CMS Box 20, Folder 230.

[45] George Fontana or G. Fontana appears in both the *Souvenir Journal, Grand Bazaar*, and on the building committee list printed in *Il Corriere d'America,* 2 February 1927, p. 17, CMS Box 17, Folder 203.

[46] Federal Writers' Project, *The Italians of New York*, 137.

[47] Announcement 13 February 1927, CMS Box 20, Folder 230.

[48] *Ibid.*

[49] Circular from Demo, 16 February 1927, *ibid.*

[50] Announcement, 23 January 1927, *ibid.*

[51] Hayes to Demo, 24 January 1927, AANY OLP Folder, Microfilm Reel #10.

[52] Demo to Hayes, 3 March 1927, CMS Box 20, Folder 231.

[53] *New York Times*, 8 October 1928, 30:7.

[54] *Bollettino Della Sera*, 8 October 1928, p. 1, CMS Box 17, Folder 203.

[55] *Village Bells, (Summer 1981), 2.*

[56] Interview 0002.

[57] Wilfrid Lavallee to Demo, 21 September 1926, Box 21, Folder 243.

[58] Program, 28 April 1929, CMS Box 12, Folder 144.

[59] Program 12–26 March 1929, CMS Box 12, Folder 143.

[60] *Catholic Action: Encyclical Letter of His Holiness, Pope Pius XI* (Washington, D.C.: National Catholic Welfare Conference, 1931), 22.

[61] Catanzaro Rosario to Demo, 14 October 1929, CMS Box 6, Folder 39.

7

The End of an Era, 1929–1936

Altogether, Pompei's parish plant cost about $1,170,000.[1] The funds for the new plant came from a variety of sources. New York City paid $265,045.27 for the property condemned at Bleecker and Downing Streets.[2] The city's payment covered about 22% of the cost of buying the land and building the new church. The $42,035 pledged at the Pennsylvania Hotel dinner and the $105,200 promised through the Builders' Society amounted to $147,235, or a little over 12% of the cost. Pompei cleaned out its savings account of $100,000 to get another 8% of the cost. About 42% of the cost of putting up the new building was paid for with funds on hand.

The other 58% of the cost was covered by borrowing. On June 14, 1929, trustee and lawyer Charles Zerbarini wrote Father Demo that Pompei had a secured a mortgage of $450,000 at 5% interest. Interest payments were due each June 10 and December 10, and the principal was due on June 10, 1934.[3] This was in addition to the $110,000 mortgage for the land. Pompei was now over a half-million dollars in debt.

Four months later, the stock market crashed. The people and businesses that invested funds on Wall Street lost their money, and thus had nothing to lend. Without the big loans available through Wall Street transactions, basic industries, such as the Hudson River shipping trade which employed many Greenwich Village men, shut down operations and laid off workers. When those laid-off workers spent all their savings and all the unemployment compensation to which some of them were due, they stopped spending money for vacations, recreation, shoes, clothing, even stopped paying their mortgages, rent, and food bills. This put the small retailers serving consumers out of business. When retailers stopped selling, the industries producing for the consumer market, such as the garment industry in New York City, suffered. All this took a year or so, and so it is no surprise that Pompei did not at first notice economic difficulties lying ahead.

Father Demo did make an extra effort to publicize the sixth Passion Play. The 1930 advertisement carried a column headed "What some prominent authorities think of our past performances." Endorsements came from chancery official Monsignor Lavelle; Father Giuseppe Cafuzzi, pastor of Our Lady of

Mount Carmel in Belmont; the past chairman of the New York Knights of Columbus; and the past vice-president of the Catholic Actors Guild. The advertisement also included subway and elevated railway directions to the parish.[4] The Passion Play was in Italian, but the story was familiar enough that even those who did not speak the language could follow it, and Father Demo tried to attract a wider audience by printing the program in English. As an indication that even the crowd roles were played by people carefully chosen and rehearsed, the names of all the soldiers, Scribes, Pharisees, Sanhedrin members, crowd members, and the choir were listed in the program.[5]

The sixth season, which ran from March 23 to April 15, was a big success. People wrote from as far away as Kingston, New York, inquiring about tickets.[6] One person apparently found it a very compelling performance, for her letter to Father Demo is full of details indicating she paid close attention. (She thought Luigi Laneri made a fine Christ, but it was obvious to her that the person playing Saint John was a girl.)[7] Pompei spent $1,027.35 for the Passion Play and received $3,152.70, for a profit of $2,125.35.[8]

The money was all the more welcome because that fall Pompei opened its long-delayed parochial school. On July 12, 1930, Father Demo signed a contract with the provincial superior of the sisters chosen to staff the school and the relocated day care center, the Missionary Zelatrices of the Sacred Heart.[9] The Zelatrices were founded in Italy in 1894, and had historic ties to the Scalabrinians. Bishop Scalabrini had been one of the congregation's early mentors and Zelatrices already staffed the school at Saint Joseph's on Monroe Street.

The part of the plant housing the parochial school and the Asilo Scalabrini was ready for occupancy by late August 1930. Caroline Ware, a scholar at Greenwich House, toured the premises with Father Demo:

> Occupying a conspicuous corner, standing above neighboring houses and tenements in its Renaissance dignity, and ringing out over the neighborhood every evening its fine chimes, this new church was the pride of the priest and of its people. In showing visitors over the edifice, however, it was not the architectual beauty of its style to which the priest called attention, but the extensive equipment and the immaculateness of the school, the roof playground, the gymnasium, the boys' and girls' clubrooms, the stage for dramatic affairs, the hall for dances and wedding receptions, and, most important of all, the tiled showers equipped with the latest and finest American plumbing.[10]

There were two other elements of modernity at Pompei which are so widely accepted today that it is worth making special mention of them. First, despite calls to make Italian parochial schools the bearers of Italian nationalism as well as the Catholic faith, Pompei's curriculum was not very different from that of other parochial schools in the area. It did not teach the Italian language, history, or culture. Second, one can still walk around New York's older parochial schools, such as Holy Cross on 42nd Street, or even public schools, such as P.S. #1 on Henry Street, and see the separate entrances for boys and girls. Pompei was always coeducational.

The parochial school and the day care center were blessed August 31, 1930, after which parents registered their youngsters for admission to the two institutions.[11] One sister recalled that by its second year of operation, the school had two hundred children in each grade and one hundred in the kindergarten.[12] Even with these numbers the school was less than full, for two reasons. Since the convent wasn't built yet, the top floor of classrooms was given over to the Zelatrices' use. Also, Pompei followed archdiocesan custom and started with just the beginning grades. As the students progressed, Pompei added grades until it reached the eighth. During the 1930s, Pompei had "closing exercises," an assembly in which each grade contributed a performance; the first graduation came in the spring of 1939.[13]

Sisters teaching in the 1930s often had just finished the twelfth grade and their novitiate before returning to the classroom. At Pompei, though, the Zelatrices took advantage of New York's Catholic colleges to further their education, and one of Father Demo's successors assured parents that the "Nuns are continuously studying and even during the summer attend classes at Fordham University to major in some particular field of science."[14] As it turned out, for the first sisters, pedagogy was only part of their ministry. One recalled: "Those were hard times, when the sisters took time out from their teaching to feed the hungry of the neighborhood. There was a lot of poverty then, even among the families of the school children."[15]

With the school, the church, and the debt to consider, parish fund raisers naturally grew more anxious. The advertisement for Pompei Dramatic Society's production of *La Nemica* explained that the profits were going to benefit the new church building. "Our wonderful Pastor, Father Demo, is looking forward to the pleasure of seeing you at the play, sure of always being remembered by his old friends."[16] In December of 1930, the parish presented another drama, *Il Padrone delle Ferrier*, and a musical program.[17] In February 1931 came another drama, *Una Causa Celebre,* and a musical program.[18]

Father Demo redoubled the Passion Play publicity. Advertisements for the seventh Passion Play carried an expanded section of endorsements, including Father Parenti of the Scalabrinians' Church of the Holy Ghost in Providence, Rhode Island; the past State Deputy of the Knights of Columbus; the Commissioner of Highways; and the District Superintendent of the Board of Education.[19] Father Demo saved the letter in which he thanked the people for allowing him to use their names and carefully assured them: "The expression used under your name in our publicity campaign, would be, I am sure, your own sentiment, had you witnessed a performance of this Passion Play beforehand."[20]

Father Demo need not have worried. The 1931 Passion Play netted Pompei $1,676.94.[21]

Part of the Passion Play revenues for 1931 were generated by the sale of a souvenir booklet which is important because the booklet contains a rare photograph of the present church before it was decorated. The windows were clear rather than stained glass, the ceiling was painted white rather than with frescoes, and the wall behind the altar wasn't gilded. The painting of Our Lady of Pompei on the altar didn't have its rounded upper corners yet.[22] The altar only looked like it was marble; it was really plaster. The columns also only looked like marble. They were really steel girders coated with an ingenious mixture of marble chips and plaster called scagliola. This is what the new building looked like throughout Father Demo's stay there. He couldn't afford to pay the debts, maintain a schedule of worship services, keep up the social programs, and decorate the church.

Despite the hard times, Father Demo still had his parishioners' confidence. In 1931, Father Demo went to Italy for a few months. Pompei threw a big celebration on his return. Trustee John A. Perazzo formed a committee of parish men. The Holy Name Society, the Daughters of Mary, the Our Lady of Pompei Boys Club, and a regional society, the *Cittadini Napoletani e della Campania* rounded up their members. The parishioners gathered in the auditorium for a banquet and to hear Father Demo describe his trip. According to the newspaper reports, Father Demo brought his parishioners up to date on affairs in Italy:

Osservato in Italia che per opera dell'uomo inviatole dalla Divina Provvidenza, Benito Mussolini, ha fatto e continua a fare grandi progressi, che non è piu divisa in fazioni inquiete, che è disciplinata e dove si gode perfetto ordine, rispetto per tutti, e si ha un governo che veramente può chiamarsi governo.

I observe in Italy that by the work of the man sent by Divine Providence, Benito Mussolini, there has been made and continues to be made grand progress, that no longer are there divisions into turbulent factions, that there is discipline and duty leading to the enjoyment of perfect order and respect for all, and there is a government which can truly be called a government.[23]

The parishioners' support of Father Demo is more touching when it is set alongside other incidents in the 1930s. Most parishioners could not have known the developments that began unfolding shortly before Father Demo left for his 1931 trip. These events led to a personal crisis for Father Demo, and a serious turning point in Pompei's history.

Shortly before Father Demo left for Italy, it became apparent that Pompei was having grave difficulty meeting ordinary expenses. During the time the Christian Brothers conducted Pompei's catechism classes, Pompei guaranteed Mass would be said at the Brothers' chapel. Pompei's clergy didn't themselves say the Masses, either because the chapel was across town or because not all of Pompei's clergy spoke English. Instead, Father Demo paid another priest a stipend to say the Masses. In November 1930, when the Zelatrices became available to teach catechism, the arrangement ended. However, Pompei still owed the priest money. Father Demo admitted to archdiocesan authorities that he had bargained with the priest to accept $90 rather than the $240 that was due him. Instead, the priest took his case to the chancery, and Father Demo paid the additional $150.[24]

Father Demo could not afford the unfavorable attention unpaid bills got him. Pressure was already building from several sources. After Bishop Scalabrini's death in 1905, the Scalabrinians entered a period of confusion leading to a Vatican investigation and reorganization. Thus, Father Demo's superiors were anxious that he and the other missionaries not do anything Vatican officials might find scandalous.

Father John Marchegiani, Father Demo's immediate superior, was especially worried. Father Marchegiani was born at Gubbio, in Perugia, on September 3, 1880, and ordained there March 8, 1903. He joined the Scalabrinians April 27, 1920, emigrated to the United States, and served in a parish in Utica, New York, from 1921 to 1933. He became provincial in 1932, about the time Pompei's financial difficulties became serious.[25] In his efforts to do his job conscientiously, he was extremely cautious with his subordinates, since a misstep on their part could lead to trouble for the provincial office.

An additional complication was that while Father Marchegiani was responsible to his Scalabrinian superiors, those superiors based their judgement of his performance at least partly on information coming from the Archdiocese of New York. The Great Depression affected the whole archdiocese: Catholic Charities' 1931 annual report noted that many people who had formerly given to this cause were now coming to request aid from it. Cardinal Hayes looked to the pastors under him to conduct their affairs in such a way as to preserve the archdiocese's reputation for prudence.

A final factor to consider in studying Pompei during the Depression was that there were documents in Father Demo's files indicating that he had been questioned about parish finances before. In 1924, he wrote a letter to his superiors at Piacenza defending himself against an accusation that he was siphoning parish funds to his relatives. He explained that the only money he gave his relatives came from presents given to him personally for his twenty-fifth anniversary as a priest, some of which he gave to his widowed father to help him purchase a home.[26] That might sound a little unusual in an age when the elderly in the United States have the benefits of a generation of economic growth and old age pensions. The elderly in Italy after World War I had no such benefits.

An immigrant son who had some good fortune in the United States naturally shared it with his father.

In 1931, there had been an exchange of correspondence between Father Demo and his provincial superior regarding a financial report which revealed Pompei had very few liquid assets. The superior's letter contained a line probably intended as a warning to Father Demo: it might be necessary to name a new pastor who would do away with old methods and have the best moral and financial interests of the Scalabrinians at heart. Father Demo responded by pointing out that after all, Pompei's financial problems stemmed from an economic situation beyond the parish's control, and which, while temporary, wouldn't right itself soon.[27] As individual events, the 1931 and 1924 incidents were unimportant. Taken together, they form a pattern. Someone who knew nothing about Father Demo except those letters might conclude that Pompei's problems stemmed not from the widening of Sixth Avenue, not from the Depression, but from Father Demo's conduct of parish affairs.

During 1932, Pompei's financial situation worsened. The parish held fund raisers at a frantic pace, and the more fund raisers, the less each earned. Earnings are not available for the 1932 Passion Play, although, judging from the newspaper reports, it was as popular as ever: the stage manager had to come out after every act to remind the audience not to applaud during the religious drama.[28] In April, Pompei put on a performance of *Le Due Orfanelle,* which netted $180.36.[29] A December performance of *Figli di Nessuna* brought in a disappointing $43.85.[30]

The final crisis came in 1933. Father Demo missed a voluntary repayment on the principal on Pompei's mortgage, and an obligatory payment on the interest. Central Hanover Bank notified the archdiocesan chancery. Since a religious community was involved, the chancery notified the provincial superior, Father Marchegiani. From there matters went to the cardinal secretary in Rome responsible for the Scalabrinians. In August 1933 Father Marchegiani became Pompei's administrator. On October 28, Father Demo left for Rome.[31]

A second burden also fell in 1933. Father Demo's father, Pietro Demo, died at home at Bassano del Grappa, near Venice, March 19, 1933. Pietro had been born at Bassano June 29, 1840; he was ninety-two at the time of his death.[32] He had been widowed nearly fourteen years: Father Demo had made a trip home in 1919, and his mother passed away the day after he left his parents' household to return to the states.[33] When he returned from Italy in 1931, Father Demo remarked at the pleasure he had taken in seeing his *novantenne genitore,* his ninety-year-old parent. Father Demo did not reach Italy in time for his father's death or burial.

Father Demo remained in Italy for almost two years. His superiors apparently hoped to keep him there permanently; he himself asked to return to the parish that had been his home for over thirty years. When he returned to Pompei in 1935, it was in the capacity of pastor emeritus and superintendent of the parochial school. It is a minor mystery as to how he got along with Father Marchegiani, for, as we shall see in the next chapter, Father Marchegiani was not just there to fill in for Father Demo; he was an active pastor in his own right. Perhaps Father Demo approved of what Father Marchegiani was doing, and did not wish to interfere. Perhaps he was content to let Father Marchegiani handle the parish's major administrative duties, while he himself concentrated on the work that had long interested him the most, helping people get the charitable services they needed, and taking care of children and youths.

Even if Father Demo accepted his new position, it seems to have been a hard blow. When he returned from his "visit" to Italy, he had lost much of his spirit, his energy, and his coloring.[34] An undated newspaper clipping, perhaps from 1935, describes Father Demo, now gray, presiding over the congregation in Pompei's basement chapel during the Low Mass at midnight on Christmas.[35]

On December 1, 1935, Father Demo was in the gymnasium moving a heavy piano with some other men when his hand slipped and the piano fell on his foot. The resulting fracture sent the sixty-five-year-old to bed, where he spent Christmas 1935 and New Year's Day 1936. On the evening of Thursday, January 2, 1936, while he was conversing with a lay friend who had come to keep him company, Father Demo suddenly stopped talking. He had suffered a heart attack. His visitor called for assistance. Father Manlio T. Ciufoletti, a curate, came in time to administer the last rites.[36]

G.B. Perazzo, long-time undertaker, parishioner, and parish leader, prepared Father Demo's body for burial. The remains were laid out in the church so that friends could pay their last respects. Among those making a final visit was Mayor Fiorello LaGuardia. On Monday, January 6, after the evening devotional services, the church was crowded for the chanting of the Office of the Dead. The funeral was Tuesday, January 7, at 10:30 a.m. All the parish societies were asked to participate, Scalabrinians came from all over the province, and Auxiliary Bishop Stephen J. Donahue and Monsignor Michael Lavelle were probably the best known of the secular clergy. Father Marchegiani said the Mass, and Provincial Superior Nazareno Prosperizi gave the sermon.

There is some disagreement as to who pronounced the final blessing. The newspapers thought it was Monsignor Lavelle, but Father Sassi, writing soon after the event, thought it was Ernesto Coppo.[37] In 1936, Coppo was a bishop in the missionary territory of Australia, and just happened to be in New York for the funeral. Twenty-five years earlier he had been a colleague who shared with Father Demo the work of saying Mass for the victims of the Triangle Shirtwaist Fire.

NOTES

[1] Sassi, 68.

[2] Zerbarini to Demo, 8 June 1929, CMS Box 21, Folder 245.

[3] Zerbarini to Demo, 14 June 1929, CMS Box 21, Folder 245.

[4] Circular, CMS Box 12, Folder 143.

[5] Program in *ibid.*

[6] Kingston, New York, to Demo, 25 March 1930, CMS Box 6, Folder 40.

[7] Miss Convert to Demo, 31 March 1930, CMS Box 6, Folder 40.

[8] Balance sheet in CMS Box 12, Folder 143.

[9] Contract between Demo and Sister Celestine Regio, M.Z.S.H., 12 July 1930, CMS Box 18, Folder 218.

[10] Ware, 314.

[11] Announcement 2 August 1930, CMS, Box 12, Folder 144.

[12] To Thomas [Carlesimo], 4 April 1981, OLP Papers 1980-1987, January 1984 Folder.

[13] Program, 21 June 1933, CMS Box 12, Folder 144.

[14] OLP Scrapbook.

[15] Program for a Missionary Zelatrice's fiftieth anniversary, OLP Scrapbook.

[16] Circular 13 September 1930, CMS Box 12, Folder 144.

[17] Circular in CMS Box 12, Folder 144.

[18] Circular in CMS Box 12, Folder 144.

[19] Advertisement in CMS Box 12, Folder 143.

[20] Demo, circular letter, 4 March 1931, CMS Box 6, Folder 41.

[21] Balance Sheet, CMS Box 12, Folder 143.

[22] Souvenir booklet in CMS Box 12, Folder 143.

[23] *Il Progresso Italo-Americano,* 6 November 1931.

[24] Papers in CMS Box 7, Folder 54.

[25] Mario Francesconi, C.S., to Zanoni, Rome, 12 July 1989, OLP Village Bells Material Box.

[26] Demo to Francesco Tirondola, 24 November 1924, CMS Box 7, Folder 82.

[27] Leonardo Quaglia to Demo, 16 February 1921, with reply 17 February 1931, CMS Box 7, Folder 74.

[28] OLP Scrapbook.

[29] *Le Due Orfanelle*, balance sheet in CMS Box 12, Folder 144.

[30] *Figli di Nessuna*, balance sheet in CMS Box 12, Folder 144.

[31] *Village Bells* (Summer 1986), pages 2–3.

[32] OLP Scrapbook.

[33] Pozzaleone, Italy, to Demo, 20 February 1919, CMS 3, Folder 23.

[34] Sassi, 75.

[35] OLP Scrapbook.

[36] OLP has among its papers a photocopy from pages 16 and 17 of some sort of Scalabrinian newsletter which seems to be the fullest early account of events.

[37] Announcement, CMS Box 31, Folder 328; *New York Times*, 4 January 1936, 15:2; Sassi, 75–76, OLP Scrapbook; and *Village Bells* (Winter 1986), 4.

8

Non Arma, Non Duces, Sed Virgo Maria Rosarii Fecit Nos Victores, 1934–1946

Neither Father Marchegiani nor his successor, Father Ugo Cavicchi, saved records with Father Demo's thoroughness and zeal. Still, from the records that do exist, from interviews and letters, and from what we know of the period's history, we can guess that the time from the middle 1930s to the middle 1940s was a period of transition at Pompei in two ways. The American-born and -raised Italians to whom Father Demo devoted so much attention reached adulthood, and were in a position to shape parish life to some degree. "To some degree," because there was a limit on what the parishioners could do given the state of the economy during the Great Depression and World War II. Pompei itself may not have been a wealthy parish, but, until the 1929 crash, it at least had the advantage of living within a burgeoning economy. Then, Pompei suffered the double burden of being a struggling parish in a struggling economy. Father Marchegiani moved from Pompei's administrator to its pastor on November 1, 1934. He resigned his position as provincial superior in 1935, distressed that he was not doing enough to improve the Scalabrinian parishes' fortunes during the Depression. He remained at Pompei until 1937. In 1940, Father Marchegiani resigned from the Scalabrinian community but not from the priesthood. Instead, he returned to his home town and died as the pastor of a parish in Gubbio. The steps Father Marchegiani took in an effort to stabilize Pompei's financial situation set precedents for later. The next time Pompei faced economic recession and debt was between 1967 and 1981, and the parish followed the same steps in its search for financial security.

The first step was to reduce expenses. Father Marchegiani renegotiated the loan with Central Hanover Bank to decrease the interest on the debt from 5% to 4%, or from about $25,000 to about $20,000 annually.[1] He issued organist *maestro* Fontana a new contract and had him pare down the choir.[2] He suspended the annual Passion Play and other dramatic events which had brought in money but which were also costly to produce.

The second step was to squeeze more revenue from existing sources. Father Marchegiani reorganized the sodalities and thus increased the income from dues.[3] Usually, when Catholics have a baptism, wedding, funeral, or special Mass, they give the officiating priest a "stole fee" as gift. Under Father Marchegiani, the clergy transferred half their stole fees into the parish fund.[4]

The third, most complicated, and most fruitful step was one Pompei had discovered long ago. It was to realize that every fund raiser is also a parish activity. Pompei had to concentrate on good liturgies, meaningful devotions, useful charity, and entertaining parish get-togethers. If Pompei built a solid community, then the funds would follow.

For example, during the Depression parishioners were attracted by an evening of fun which didn't cost too much and which held out the possibility of winning cash or prizes. Accordingly, Father Marchegiani held the first of what later became a parish institution. One of the Sunday announcements for February 14, 1937, read *Domani sera, dopo la funzione, nel nostro Basamento si darà principio al giorno del Bingo a beneficio della nostra scuola.*[5] In a photograph of Pompei taken in 1937 one can make out a sign over the entrance to Father Demo Hall: BINGO GAMES.[6] Even after the economy recovered, bingo continued to be popular. It was a relatively inexpensive fund raiser to sponsor, and working at the games, or playing them, brought the parishioners together for some community time.

Father Marchegiani found another way to combine community building and fund raising, a method that has since become very common. Rather than think of the parish as one big project funded by one general account, he thought of it as many little projects, each sponsored by individuals, families, or parish societies. For example, in order to decorate the church, Father Marchegiani kept a notebook with separate entries for each stained glass window and each picture other than the main mural above the altar. The names of the donors of some of the stained glass windows were placed beneath the windows, but all the windows, and all the smaller paintings, were paid for by sponsors.[7] Sometimes a parish can tie a community to a church by emphasizing the church as the place where people gather for worship and social events. Father Marchegiani tied the community to Pompei by stressing the physical features of the church itself. It had a beautiful mural, it had elaborate decorations, and the parishioners had watched the funds go from their own hands to this stained glass window or that painting.

Thanks to careful budgeting, Pompei resumed work on its unfurnished parish plant. In July 1934, the parish purchased a sounding board. In the days before electronic amplification, sounding boards were placed above pulpits to direct the sound of the homily out toward the congregation rather than letting it float uselessly to the ceiling.[8] In October 1934, the plaster altar which had been installed when Pompei was built was replaced with a Carrara and Regalito marble altar made by the DaPrato Statuary Company.[9]

Father Marchegiani's biggest project was installing the mural over the altar. Father Marchegiani himself conceived the mural's design. The artists hired for the work were themselves Italian immigrants. Antonio D'Ambrosio was born in Campagnia, Salerno, in 1900. He and his wife emigrated to the Bronx in 1924, where Antonio began working with his brother, a painter who did church restoration. Antonio then opened his own firm, and employed his own children on painting jobs.[10]

Since this was the church of the Madonna of the Rosary, the mural included important events in the history of rosary devotion. The mural's most prominent part showed the Madonna, with the Child Jesus on her lap, giving a rosary to Saint Dominic and Saint Catherine of Siena. In the lower right of the mural went the Battle of Lepanto, a 1571 struggle between Christian and Moslem navies. The Christians attributed their triumph in that battle to the Madonna of the Rosary, hence the Latin phrase carved below the mural: *Non Arma, Non Duces, Sed Virgo Maria Rosorii Fecit Nos Victores* ("Neither arms nor leaders but the Virgin Mary of the Rosary made us victors.")

If the mural could be detached from the ceiling and placed somewhere else, one would still know it was Pompei's mural by the section in the lower center, which connected the medieval history of the rosary to the twentieth-century New York City parish. Standing at the left was Saint Charles Borromeo, patron of the Scalabrinian order. In the middle went representative figures of religious communities of sisters, brothers, and priests. All around were figures of the laity, representing immigrants who relied on the help of the Church. In the background on the right went Pompei's campanile or bell tower.

The remaining space was taken up by a scene of purgatory, in the lower left corner, and by angels in flight throughout the picture. Altogether, the mural covered 1680 square feet. It seems that the mural was done by November 1937, when Father Marchegiani was transferred to Rome.

Father Marchegiani's successor was Father Ugo Cavicchi. Father Cavicchi was born February 23, 1901, at Passignano sul Transimeno, Perugia. He was ordained March 20, 1926 and sent to the American missions. He had served in Italian parishes in Illinois and in Wisconsin before he was assigned to Pompei. He arrived at Pompei November 25, 1937, Thanksgiving Day and also the day the Scalabrinians celebrated the fiftieth anniversary of their foundation. In 1946, Father Cavicchi was reassigned to other missionary work.[11] He died April 15, 1984.

The economy was still sluggish when Father Cavicchi became pastor, and there were still many parishioners feeling the effects of the Depression. Father Demo had dispensed parish charity himself and Father Marchegiani had tried to recruit people from Pompei's sodalities into a group to coordinate social work. It was under Father Cavicchi that Pompei took another step in Americanization and organized a Saint Vincent de Paul Society. The Saint Vincent de Paul Society consisted of parish laymen. It received money from various sources within the parish, and disbursed the money within the parish. Whenever parochial school children with threadbare clothing, broken shoes, or skimpy lunches came to the attention of the parochial school teaching sisters, the sisters informed the Saint Vincent de Paul Society, and the men went into action.[12]

Pompei's parish budget continued to show the ill effects of the Depression. The parish was still in debt, and the interest had risen to 6% interest. Those may sound like favorable terms, but, adjusted for inflation, they were akin to a two-million-dollar mortgage at 11% interest. A solution to the debt problem came not from the parishioners, but from the archdiocese. Cardinal Hayes died in 1938, and in 1939, Francis Joseph Spellman (Cardinal Spellman after 1946) was appointed his successor. Archbishop Spellman immediately went to work on the debt that burdened not only Pompei but numerous other parishes. On August 23, 1939, he announced a system whereby parishes could renegotiate their loans with the archdiocese. Father Cavicchi took advantage of the offer and reduced Pompei's interest rate to 3%.[13]

Father Cavicchi was the first pastor to use the printed word to foster a sense of community. In May 1940, Pompei parishioners received the inaugural issue of what has since become a staple of parish life: the parish bulletin. The first bulletin was a monthly magazine. It was published by a commercial company which did this sort of work for numerous parishes, but the magazine was tailored to the individual parish. In Pompei's case, the cover carried a sketch of the parish. The first page had the parish schedule. Most of the other pages were devoted to a listing of who had contributed and how much they gave to last month's collection. Interspersed with the collection statistics were short articles on parish events. The commercial company had a supply of filler, undated material on devotional or inspirational topics, that took up the left over spaces at the ends of columns.

The first bulletin, published in May 1940, provides a snapshot of parish activities at the time.[14] Pompei had seven Sunday Masses: 6:00, 7:00, 8:00, 9:00, 10:00, 11:00, and 12:20. The 9:00 was for children and the 11:00 was a High, or sung, Mass. Pompei had begun its schedule of "perpetual novenas," weekly devotions instead of the traditional nine special days of prayers. Monday was the novena for the Miraculous Medal, a devotion which was just beginning to be promoted in the United States. Tuesday was the day traditionally devoted to Saint Anthony of Padua, Wednesday was for Saint Rita of Cascia, Thursday for Saint Theresa of the Little Flower, Friday was the exposition of the Blessed Sacrament, Saturday was Our Lady of Pompei, and Sunday evening there were vespers.

There was an impressive roster of societies: two for the Holy Rosary, Sacred Heart, Saint Rita, Children of Mary, Saint Theresa (little girls), Mothers' Club, Saint Joseph, Holy Name, Junior Holy Name, Saint John Berchmans (altar boys), Saint Aloysius, Our Lady of Pompei alumni, Saint Vincent de Paul, Confraternity of Christian Doctrine (or C.C.D., for catechism outside of parochial school), Passion Players' Dramatics, Boy Scouts, Girl Scouts, and separate Christian Youth Organizations (C.Y.O.) for teen-age boys and girls. Pompei may not have been quite so busy a parish as this list suggests; the Passion Players, for example, hadn't put on a performance in years.

Under Father Cavicchi, the artists working on the church's interior executed the plans for the nave. High on the wall on the left side of the nave went paintings of the five Joyful Mysteries of the rosary: the Annunciation; the visit between Mary and Elizabeth, the Nativity, presenting the Infant Jesus in the temple, and finding the Boy Jesus teaching the elders in the temple. Opposite these, on the right wall, went the five Sorrowful Mysteries: Jesus' agony in the garden, the scourging, the crowning with thorns, the road to Calvary, and the crucifixion. In the oval medallion along the ceiling went the five Glorious Mysteries: the Resurrection, the Ascension, Pentecost, the Assumption of Mary into heaven, and her Coronation.

Four more paintings went on walls in the rear of the church. On the left of the entrance, where the connection with the rectory made a stained glass window impossible, went a painting of Saint Margaret Mary, promoter of the adoration of the Sacred Heart of Jesus. On the back wall of the choir loft went a chorus of angels. On the left choir loft wall went Saint Cecilia, patroness of church music. On the right choir loft wall went King David, traditionally credited with composing the Psalms.

Father Cavicchi arranged for the installation of the stained glass windows. On the church's Bleecker Street side went a series of windows depicting the sacraments: Baptism and Confirmation, the Eucharist and Penance, Extreme Unction and Ordination, and Marriage. Since there were seven sacraments but eight window panels, a scene depicting the profession of religious vows went under the marriage section. Other windows testified to the Italian presence at Pompei. In one window, Leo XIII directed the missionary Mother Cabrini to the Americas. Next to that went a window of Saint Anthony. Other windows showed saints who were familiar sights in many churches: Saints Peter and Paul near the entrance to the church, and evangelists Saints John and Luke near the altar.

On the church's rectory side was a second series of windows based on the beatitudes. Each beatitude was accompanied by an appropriate illustration. Saint Francis of Assisi (*ca.* 1181–1226), known as *il poverello*, adorned the section dedicated to the poor in spirit. Saint Stephen whose martyrdom was described in the Acts of the Apostles, was chosen to represent the meek who inherit the earth. Saint Rita of Cascia (1381–1457), who refused to avenge her murdered husband's death, represented those who mourned. The blessing of those who hunger and thirst for justice was illustrated with a scene from the life of Saint Ambrose of Milan (ca. 340–397) in which the saint brought the emperor himself to do penance for a massacre he had ordered. Saint John Gualbert (1073–1193), who spared the life of the man who had murdered his brother, represented the blessing of the merciful. The mystical marriage of Saint Catherine of Siena illustrated the blessing of the pure in heart. The beheading of John the Baptist accompanied the blessing of those persecuted for righteousness sake. Only one beatitude was not accompanied by a scene from the lives of the saints. The blessing of the peacemakers was illustrated by a panel praising the freedom the Catholic Church enjoyed in the United States, an appropriate choice in the late 1930s, when Catholicism was threatened by dictatorships in several countries.

Two windows near the Beatitudes had special meaning to the parish, a stained glass portrait of Our Lady of Pompei, and a depiction of the commissioning of the first Scalabrinian Missionaries. Two other windows, portraying the evangelists Saints Matthew and Mark, were companions to the windows on the Bleecker Street side.

Throughout the stained glass windows were touches that made the windows unique to Pompei. There were many other martyrs that could have been used to illustrate the blessing of those persecuted for righteousness sake. The martyr chosen, Saint John the Baptist, was the namesake of the man in whose memory the window was donated. A young Zelatrice assigned to the parochial school posed for the window honoring those who entered religious life.[15] The priest in the window honoring marriage may have been modelled after a photograph of Father Demo. He is taller than the other people in the group, and has Father Demo's eyebrows, his hair line, and the expression he usually assumed for cameras.

There was less of a system about the other elements of Pompei's decoration. Father Cavicchi added the two side altars, one with a picture of the Blessed Mother and the other with a picture of Jesus rescuing those in purgatory. (These were reminiscent of the side altars in the Bleecker Street church, with their pictures of the Assumption and the Crucifiction.) He also added the baptistry, and, after World War II and her canonization, a shrine to Mother Frances Cabrini.[16] Pompei's communion of saints was eclectic, but favored those associated with the Italian American community. For example, in about 1948, one parish family donated the picture of Saint John Bosco (1815–1888), founder of the Salesians and contributor, through his religious order, to New York's Italian Catholic ministry.[17] Most of Father Cavicchi's work was done by May 7, 1939, when the parish held a celebratory service. There was a solemn novena conducted by Father F. Pambianco, O.S.A., then a feast day Mass attended by Father Francesco Tirondolo, a Scalabrinian official on a visit to the United States.

There was one element of Pompei's appearance only New York City could supply. On June 1, 1941, the city named the lot across from the church "Father Demo Square." The area was dedicated in a ceremony organized by G.B. Perazzo, and involved numerous Village, Italian, and parish societies. Anna Carbone LaPadula led the audience in singing the national anthem, and several city authorities spoke. Then a parade, led by Washington Square Post 1212 of the American Legion, marched to Washington Square Park for a flag ceremony and back to Pompei for a memorial Mass.[18] The city paved Father Demo Square with bricks and furnished it with street lamps, trash cans, and park benches. Like churches in Italy, Pompei faced a piazza. In this communal open space people could escape from small apartments, catch a breath of air, sit, chat, and watch other people.

The phrase *non arma non duces* probably went on Pompei's wall for no other reason than its association with the Battle of Lepanto. It was, though, appropriate for the world in 1937 as well. The events leading to World War II were already underway. As with World War I, two enormous alliances were forming in opposition to each other. Germany, Italy, and Japan constituted the Axis. England, France, the Soviet Union, the Republic of China and the United States were usually referred to as the Allies. The Second World War began September 1939. Italy joined the war June 1940, the United States in December 1941. The war in Europe ended May 1945, in the Far East in August 1945.

Pompei's records for this war are sparse, but one can assume the war meant some hardship for Italian immigrants. Many Americans, not just Italians, approved of Mussolini's early career (he seemed to be an improvement over his anti-clerical predecessors), and only gradually became disillusioned with the direction fascist Italy was taking. The American Italians' situation was complicated by Mussolini's actions. During the 1930s, Italy increased its efforts to turn Italian immigrant communities into "colonies" for an Italian empire. One obstacle to this plan was the rapidity with which Italian children assimilated to the country where they were raised. The key to keeping the youngsters Italian was to have Italian schools. The closest thing to Italian schools in New York were Italian parochial schools. So, about 1934, Italy began inquiring about New York's Italian parochial schools, trying to find out how much needed to be done to make their curriculums serve the Italian government's ends.

Father Marchegiani firmly repulsed the Italian government's efforts to influence Pompei's parochial school. Instead of answering the government's inquiries, he wrote the chancery:[19]

I beg to inform you that the Italian consulate of this City (134 East 70th Street) has requested me, with several letters, to give some information regarding this Parish School of Our Lady of Pompei. Considering that our Parish School is under the direct control of the Archdiocese of New York and of the State, I did refuse to give any information in this matter. At the same time I had considered always as a great danger for the Catholic Schools of this country to let any stranger nation interfere with.

That was the end of the potential for fascist interference at Pompei.

The day after Pearl Harbor President Franklin Delano Roosevelt signed an executive order under which people from countries against which the United States was fighting automatically became enemy aliens. The executive order included many Italian immigrants who, for various reasons, never became naturalized citizens, although they had been law-abiding residents for years. The enemy alien status of non-naturalized Italian immigrants was revoked on Columbus Day 1942.[20]

In 1943 Mussolini's own government lost confidence in him, and he fled to northeastern Italy. Although Italy was a co-belligerent on the Allies' side, the country remained a battlefield for the rest of the war, turning into refugees people whose families had lived in the same towns for centuries. Father Demo's protégé, Father Joseph Pernicone, helped direct collection of clothing among New York's Italian Catholics for those suffering in Italy.[21]

The archdiocese counted twelve hundred men and women from Pompei in the United States armed forces during World War II.[22] Pompei's clergy thought they had 12,000 parishioners, which would mean 10% of the entire parish population was in uniform.[23] Thirty men and one woman lost their lives in the war.[24] One casualty, Fred Massoni, wrote a last letter to his parents and left it to be delivered in the event of his death. He was killed in action, the letter was sent home, and it was read not only by his parents but from the pulpit during Mass.[25]

In World War II radios and publishing replaced pulpit announcements, and rationing replaced voluntary conservation, so Father Cavicchi was not called upon to fill the roles Father Demo had filled. Pompei concentrated on pastoral ministry during the war. Father Cavicchi played another, more pastoral role. He notified families when relatives died in the armed forces.[26] The names of parishioners in the services were inscribed in the memorial shrine near the crucifix from the old church so that civilian parishioners could pray for them.[27]

Pompei's fiftieth anniversary as a parish fell in 1942. The parish held a Pontifical Mass of Thanksgiving with auxiliary Bishop Francis McIntyre representing Cardinal Spellman. Scalabrinians and archdiocesan clergy added to the length of the procession and the dignity of the ceremony. Singers from the Rossini Opera Company added to the strength and abilities of the choir. However, the war cast a shadow on the celebration, since so many young parishioners were away, and so many of the ones who remained at home were worried about them.[28] The war delayed full publication of the first parish history since 1911. Father Constantino Sassi, a Scalabrinian missionary assigned to the parish as an assistant, wrote the manuscript. The parish bulletin serialized the chapters during the anniversary year of 1942. The book was typeset in Italy and published after the war in 1946.

Since the earliest events were fast fading from living memory, Father Sassi concentrated his work on that time period. He organized his story around the institutional history of Pompei. Once he covered the parish's foundation, Father Sassi emphasized administrative history, introducing each pastor and his accomplishments. Father Sassi also wrote from the parishioners'-eye view. He recounted the Italian customs of the earliest parishioners, and described American customs as they must have appeared to Italian immigrants unfamiliar with them. His theme was the transformation of the Italian ways in the face of the American experience:

> *Coll' andare del tempo tutto cambia; anche le parrocchie sono suggette a mutamenti e variazioni. Le colonie italiane, dopo mezzo secolo di vita americana, si son trasformate. Lo spirito e gli usi americani sono penetrati negli individui e nelle famiglie, e della patria d'origine è rimasto soltanto un ricordo.*

> With the passage of time everything changes, even parishes are subject to change and variation. The Italian colony, after a half century of American life, has been transformed. The American spirit and customs have penetrated into individuals and into families, and of the country of origin there remains only a memory.[29]

On the other hand, Pompei did publish its history in Italian, so it wasn't so thoroughly Americanized as it would later be. But Father Sassi pointed to one change which had crept up on Pompei almost unnoticed: the waning of the immigrant generation and the growth of a second generation, raised to adulthood on American soil. There is no one event, no one moment where the first generation ended and the second began; indeed, Pompei still has parishioners who are first-generation Italian immigrants. However, changes were creeping into parish life, and, one by one, these changes added up to a revolution.

The most noticeable change was the increasing use of English. Father Marchegiani began writing English translations of some Sunday pulpit announcements the first Sunday of Advent, 1933.[30] In 1937, he had printed up for the parishioners' devotional reading a brief biography of Bishop Scalabrini, also in English.[31] Father Cavicchi wrote announcements in Italian and English, and did not just translate from one language to another, but took into account how Italian- and English-speaking people thought of their relationship to Pompei. In a 1945 appeal for funds, he stressed the importance of devotion for the Italians: *Non vogliate abbandonare la chiesa adesso che la guerra è finita quasi che non abbiate più bisogno dell'aiuto di Dio.* ("Don't abandon the Church now that the war is over on the theory that you no longer need the help of God.") He stressed service and parish citizenship for the Americans: "This is a little drop in the comparison to the large sum that we need, yet this church has always been supported and paid for partly by the small offerings which you, our devoted parishioners, have given."[32]

In 1940, all Masses were in Latin, but the 6:00, 7:00, 8:00, and 11:00, including the High Mass, had Italian sermons, and the 9:00 (or children's), 10:00, and 12:20 Masses had English sermons. Monday night's devotion to the Miraculous Medal had an English sermon, Friday night's exposition of the Blessed Sacrament and Sunday's vespers had Italian sermons, and it is worth pointing out that the Miraculous Medal, introduced in 1937, was the newer and more American devotion of the three.[33] Even parish societies were drawn along linguistic lines: the Holy Rosary Society had English and Italian branches. Saint Joseph was for Italian family men, and, although some parishioners participated in Italian Holy Name Society activities, the Holy Name was for English-speaking family men.[34] After World War II Father Cavicchi asked some young men to join the Saint Vincent de Paul Society so as to have some men fluent in English. One of the new men spoke no Italian at all.[35]

The older one was, the more likely one was to speak Italian and to practice the traditional devotions. One young woman recalled that her family had two parishes, one for each generation. She attended parochial school in another parish, but her mother, who didn't understand English, attended Pompei.[36]

The future lay with the English-speaking and with the young. Father Cavicchi knew this when he purchased four lots, with houses, along Leroy Street for about $10,000 each. With the deflated prices at the Depression, even a struggling parish could not pass up the opportunity to invest in real estate. Now that the parish had its parochial school, it was beginning to dream of a high school as well. Father Cavicchi could not have known then that his real estate purchases would indeed be useful to the parish, but not in the way he intended.

NOTES

[1] Francis A. McIntyre to Marchegiani, 8 October 1935, CMS Box 7, Folder 83.

[2] Marchegiani to "Ill.mo Signore," 13 Janaury 1934, Box 7, Folder 83.

[3] Marchegiani to Hayes, 2 April 1935, Box 9, Folder 105.

[4] *Village Bells* (Spring 1984), 2.

[5] Sunday announcement, February 14, 1937, CMS Box 31, Folder 328.

[6] Federal Writers' Project, *The Italians of New York*, photograph facing page 83.

[7] The records are in CMS Box 22, Folder 264.

[8] Sunday announcement, Box 31, Folder 326.

[9] Unidentified clipping, 7 October 1934, OLP Scrapbook.

[10] *Shrine Church of Our Lady of Pompei Rededication* (New York: OLP, 1985), 14.

[11] *Village Bells* (Spring 1984), 1–3.

[12] *Village Bells* (Spring and Summer 1988), 3–4 and 4 respectively.

[13] *Village Bells* (Spring 1984), 3. *See also* Robert I. Gannon, S.J., *The Cardinal Spellman Story* (Garden City, New York: Doubleday, 1962), 249–252.

[14] CMS Box 32, Folder 330.

[15] St.Louis Missouri to Zanoni, 6 July 1981, OLP Papers 1980–1987, June 1981 Folder.

[16] *Our Lady of Pompei Shrine Church,* 8.

[17] To Zanoni, n.d., OLP Papers 1988, January 1988 Folder.

[18] OLP Scrapbook.

[19] Marchegiani to Thomas Carroll, 25 April 1934, CMS Box 9, Folder 104.

[20] John Morton Blum, *V was for Victory: Politics and American Culture during World War II* (New York: Harcourt Brace Jovanovich, 1976), 151–154.

[21] Interview with Most Reverend Joseph M. Pernicone, Bronx, 12 August 1983.

[22] (New York) *Catholic News,* 8 July 1944.

[23] Sassi, p. 79.

[24] Cosenza, 20.

[25] Communication 0008.

[26] Cosenza, 21.

[27] *Village Bells* (Summer 1981), 2.

[28] OLP Scrapbook, and Cosenza, 23–24.

[29] Sassi, p. 82.

[30] CMS Box 31, Folder 326.

[31] Manlio Ciufoletti, *John Baptist Scalabrini: Bishop of Piacenza, Apostle of Italian Immigrants* (n.p., 1937).

[32] Cavicchi, circular, 13 October 1945, OLP Memorabilia 1985–1988.

[33] Sunday announcement, 17th Sunday after Pentecost, 1937, CMS Box 31, Folder 329.

[34] Ribbon, 7 February 1937, OLP Scrapbook.

[35] Interview 0005.

[36] 18 E. 31st St., Brooklyn, to Pastor, undated, OLP Papers 1980–1987, January 1984 Folder.

Scene from the production of *If you Knew Caesar*, 1961. It was an activity of the Fathers' Club.

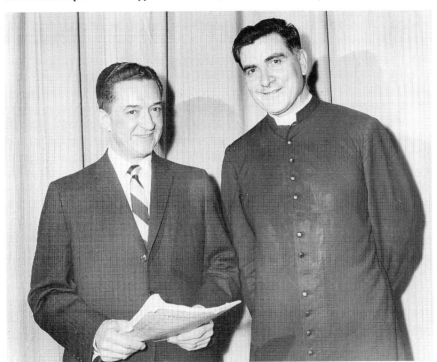

During Fr. Mario Albanesi's pastorate, 1952 to 1964, Pompei concentrated on supporting families on raising school-age children. Fr. Albanesi and John Corrado, first president of the Fathers' Club.

9

"The Village is Our Home Town,"
1947–1964

The period after World War II saw the emergence of a new middle class in the United States, one that for the first time included significant numbers of Catholics with roots in late nineteenth- and early twentieth-century immigration. For about twenty years after World War II, Our Lady of Pompei was a middle class parish. Parishioners who were school age or young married people in those years tend to recall them as a pleasant period in Pompei's history. It was not, though, a good time without effort. If Pompei enjoyed prosperous years, it was because pastors and parishioners worked hard for them.

How can one say Pompei was "middle class?" First, parishioners went further with their education. World War II and Korean War veterans benefited from low-cost educational loans offered through the G.I. Bill.[1] Among teen-agers, even those who wanted to go to work completed high school before doing so.[2] Second, parishioners' occupations changed. Advanced education allowed them to take more prestigious and better-paying white collar jobs. Pompei's newsletter, *The Village Bells*, ran several biographies of parishioners that prove this point, such as the one describing a grammar school graduate and civil servant whose son went on to college and a professional career.[3] Many of the older women profiled in *The Village Bells* labored in the garment trade, but the new generation of women seldom went into the garment trade, and when they did, it was as buyers and supervisors rather than laborers.[4]

There were three ways in which Pompei's parishioners differed from the usual profile of the middle class. First, the middle class was noted for its "baby boom," but Pompei's birth rate declined. Its records showed 113 baptisms in 1953, and 89 in 1963. Second, middle class neighborhoods didn't have labels such as "Little Italy," but Pompei was still an Italian parish. (Pompei may have been more "Italian" than it was in the 1890s, when its congregation was mostly Genoese in origin; by the 1950s it had parishioners whose families had migrated from all across the peninsula.) Third, and most important, middle class people usually lived in suburbs, but Pompei's parishioners remained in the city.

Why did they stay? They could easily afford to move; parishioners bought real estate on Long Island or in New Jersey, as investments and vacation homes.[5] They knew the risk of tying their personal welfare to New York's economic fortunes. The small businesses which had supported Pompei's parish leaders for a generation were being squeezed by national chain stores and by boutiques catering to the new beatnik culture. The Village's Italian population was declining. The housing stock was unsuitable for middle class living. They understood the dangers of raising youngsters in the city. Greenwich Village shared the nationwide concern over juvenile delinquency, and parishioners were aware of a drug problem, including the use of heroin.[6]

Pompei's parishioners stayed because they saw city life as an advantage they wanted their children to have.[7] If they were going to raise children in the city, though, parents wanted not only a sound family life, but also good community institutions to assist in their children's education and moral training. Families and Pompei developed a symbiotic relationship, each institution strengthening the other.

The first pastor of Pompei's middle-class years was Father Joseph Bernardi. Father Bernardi was born May 18, 1903, in Vincenza, Italy. He was ordained a Scalabrinian priest July 8, 1928, and came to the United States that year. Until 1947, he was pastor at Santa Maria Addolorata, Chicago; then he was transferred to Pompei.

One of Father Bernardi's longest-lasting actions as pastor was little noticed at the time. In 1947, he hired Mr. John N. Nicholls as parish organist and choir master. Mr. Nicholls left in 1953, but returned in 1964. He served as organist, cantor, and, sometimes choir master until his death in 1976.[8]

Father Bernardi's best-remembered activity at Pompei reflects the parochial school's importance in parish life at the time. Since 1930, the Zelatrices had been living in converted class rooms on the school's top floor. Father Bernardi erected two floors above the school and built a proper convent. By the time it was completed, in 1951, Father Bernardi's health was failing to such an extent that he was reassigned to a smaller parish. He died at Pergine, Trento, 25 January 1959.[9]

The man who is remembered as *the* pastor of Pompei's prosperous years was Father Mario Albanesi. Father Albanesi was born at Castelsangiovanni, Piacenza, Italy, May 11, 1915. He was ordained June 29, 1938, and came to the United States the same year. He served in several Scalabrinian parishes, and, just prior to coming to Pompei, was pastor of Father Bernardi's old church, Santa Maria Addolorata. Father Albanesi was at Pompei from 1952 to 1964, and went on to work in several other Scalabrinian parishes until his death August 17, 1984, at the young age of sixty-nine.[10]

Father Albanesi was wise enough to look beyond the post-war economic boom and to see that prosperity contained dangers. The more educated his parishioners were and the better their job opportunities, the more likely they were to leave the Village in search of more suitable housing. As parishioners left the Village, holes opened up in community life. Businesses owned by large corporations or by non-parishioners took the shops left by parishioners who retired from business or who went to work elsewhere. Young people and artists rented the apartments and lofts parishioners and businesses left behind. These changes weren't bad in themselves. Parishioners probably enjoyed supermarkets as much as anyone, and, as had happened when an earlier generation of bohemians came to eat at Italian restaurants and snack at Italian coffee shops, the Italians and the beatniks had a certain compatibility. The danger was that Pompei would lose its identity as parishioners moved away. The solution was to strengthen community life.

For a church, the first step in strengthening community life was to provide church services. Parish bulletins from Father Albanesi's pastorate indicate that Pompei had a full and varied worship life. The schedule that appeared in the January 1961 monthly parish bulletin remained unchanged through January 1964. There were three Sunday Masses with sermons in Italian, at 7:00 a.m., 8:00 a.m., and 11:00 a.m. There were three other Masses with sermons in English, at 9:00 a.m., 10:00 a.m., and 12:20 p.m.[11] Parochial school children and their families were expected to attend the 9:00 a.m. Mass, but not in family units. The youngsters reported to their class rooms, where the Zelatrices took attendance, escorted their students to the church, and supervised their behavior during Mass.[12]

Music was an important element at Sunday worship, and Father Albanesi maintained two choirs. According to the contract organist *maestro* Nicholls signed when he returned to the parish in 1964, the adult choir sang at the 11:00 a.m. Mass.[13] Father Albanesi himself directed the children's choir, which sang at one Mass, and also gave performances outside of church. After Father Albanesi left, Father Dorino De Lazzer conducted the children's choir.

Church decoration was another important element of worship. During Father Albanesi's tenure, Pompei replaced the floors in the nave's main aisle and sanctuary with more luxurious, and longer-lasting, marble. The parish refurbished the side altars with new mosaics of the Blessed Mother and of purgatory.[14] In 1955, the parish got its present life-size statue of Saint Jude; at the time it was placed on the right side of the altar.[15] On April 28, 1963, as part of the celebration of Father Albanesi's silver anniversary, Pompei first heard its new recorded chimes.[16]

Devotions were a final important element in Catholic prayer. Some idea of the variety of pious practices at Pompei in the 1950s may be had by following

Father Pio Parolin through a typical day. Father Pio, who had been Father Demo's curate at the turn of the century, returned to Pompei fifty years later for a second term as an assistant. Nearing retirement, Father Pio spent his time in prayer. His description of his daily routine covers almost every devotional practice of the 1950s: a morning rosary, noon Mass, participation in the perpetual novena of the day, reading his breviary, and visiting the Blessed Sacrament. Devout Catholics went to Confession frequently, and Father Pio did his best to make the sacrament available to the parishioners, hearing confessions every morning before the daily Mass.

The monthly bulletin showed that Pompei's perpetual novena calendar had two changes from the first schedule printed in the first bulletin in 1940: the addition of an English-language devotion to Mother Cabrini on Monday night and a similar Italian devotion on Thursday. Parish missions were an annual event in Pompei's devotional life. Among Father Albanesi's letters is one to the Reverend Dominic Grande, C.P. It was written in 1955, and booked Father Grande, three years in advance, to preach a mission in 1958.[17] Father Grande preached missions at Pompei from the 1950s to the mid-1970s.

The roster of parish societies changed more extensively. Four societies still used Italian. Three, Saint Rita, Saint Joseph, and Holy Rosary, were sodalities. The fourth was a young people's spiritual and social action group that was popular in Italy, *Azione Cattolica Italiana*. Five organizations used English. One was a devotional organization, Holy Name. One was an older charity organization, Saint Vincent de Paul. Three emphasized socializing and parish service: the P.T.A., the Fathers' Club, and the C.Y.O.[18] Vatican II is supposed to have made sweeping changes in devotional and sodality life, but one can see change underway at Pompei well before Vatican II. Evening devotions appealed to older Italians, with only two evenings out of seven in English. Doing things for the parish through a society appealed to younger Americans, with most of the parish social and fund raising groups being English-speaking.

Pompei was the Scalabrinians' largest parish, and thus the one chosen to celebrate important Scalabrinian events. It was from Pompei that the first Scalabrinian missionaries departed to minister to Italian immigrants in Australia.[19] The best-documented liturgy was the Mass commemorating the fiftieth anniversary of Bishop Scalabrini's death, held June 20, 1955. Francis Cardinal Spellman presided over the liturgy; a local bakery brought his throne from Saint Patrick's Cathedral in its delivery truck.[20] Many chancery and Scalabrinian dignitaries were at the altar. Pompei's choir and the Scalabrinians' Saint Charles Seminary Schola Cantorum sang *Ecce Sacerdos Magnus*, the Mass of Saint Joan of Arc, several Gregorian chants, the *Ave Maria*, and one English-language hymn, "To Our Venerable Founder." Father Dominic Fiorentino, pastor of Saint Dominic's in the Bronx since 1924, and a colleague of Father Demo, preached. A professional photographer recorded the entire event: Cardinal Spellman and the clergy, all in distinctive vestments, parish women in their best dresses—and hats—greeting each other on the church steps, little altar boys swinging thurifers to raise clouds of incense, men from the Knights of Columbus lifting ceremonial swords at the moment of consecration, and rows of sisters in their various habits sitting in the front pews saying their prayers before Mass began.

Much of Pompei's community life revolved around children, specifically school-age children. Since the closing of the Asilo Scalabrini in 1944, Pompei's school became its main service for youngsters. It was also the largest item in Pompei's budget. Cardinal Spellman believed Catholic education was not a luxury for the few, but a necessity to be shared as widely as possible. To that end, parochial schools had low tuition for parishioners, though rates went up for non-parishioners. The archdiocese itself provided some aid, especially for building new schools and training teachers, and the parish raised money for ordinary expenses.[21]

Pompei's school was bursting at the seams.[22] It held double sessions to accommodate all the students, and ran several classes at each grade level. It was not only the size of the population that made Pompei school active. The Zelatrices took an dynamic approach to their students' learning. They used television to keep their students abreast of current affairs, such as the Mercury and Gemini space shots. The Zelatrices also planned a series of assemblies, with each grade responsible for the content of a particular assembly.

One Pompei student in particular became something of a local hero. Sabino Romano, a twelve-year-old altar boy, was coming out of Pompei one day in April 1961 when he saw a bus, without a driver, rolling slowing down Carmine Street right toward the parochial school pupils in front of the church. Sabino boarded the bus via a rear door, ran to the drivers' seat, and applied what his older friends had told him about driving. He pumped the brakes. When they failed to respond, he pulled on the steering wheel so as to force the bus to jump the curb and roll to a halt against the church steps.[23]

There were several parish organizations for school age children. Some, such as the altar boys or choir, performed a double service, keeping youngsters busy and using their labor, time, and talent to improve worship services. Others did not have the bonus of improving worship services, but they kept youngsters busy, introduced them to peers whom their parents considered suitable friends, and allowed parents and children to do things together. The scouting movement is an example of such an organization, and Pompei had Brownies, Cub Scouts, Girl Scouts, Boy Scouts, and Cadet Girl Scouts.

Father Albanesi revived Pompei's plans for a high school, but was unable to buy property to complete the lot Father Cavicchi had begun assembling.[24] Even though teen-agers went elsewhere for high school, they still had their recreation and social programs at Pompei. Under Father Albanesi, Pompei had a Maria Goretti Club, named for a recently-canonized saint (1890–1902) popular as a model for youth. Father Albanesi set aside for the club one of the buildings Father Cavicchi had purchased. The club house contained pool tables and other activities for young people. The club was for young men, but it also reached young women, because whenever the boys planned a dance, they issued formal invitations to the parish girls.[25]

Pompei's C.Y.O. dated from Father Cavicchi's tenure. By the early 1960s, it was a co-ed organization under whose auspices teens played sports, held dances, and, at Pompei, produced dramas. Under the direction of Michael Enserra, a professional actor, and Andrew Brizzolara, a high school student and later adult moderator, the C.Y.O. revived and modernized Pompei's Passion Play tradition, and produced annual performances from 1963 to 1965.[26]

Parents followed their youngsters into parish activities. The P.T.A. brought together women of the same age and at the same stage in their lives. Mothers also followed their youngsters into organizations by involving themselves in scouting. Only the Boy Scouts required that adult leaders be men. The Cub Scouts had den mothers, the Brownie, Girl Scout and Cadet troop leaders were women, and there were extra opportunities for mothers to get involved during the annual Girl Scout cookie sale. Parishioner Sue Cosenza might hold some sort of record: she was the Village's Girl Scout cookie chairwoman for thirty-seven years.[27]

Scholars have thought that Italian-American working-class women did not join organizations outside their own families until the 1970s, when they had extensive work experience.[28] At Pompei, though, women became involved in affairs outside the home *because* of their families. Home, parish, and parochial school were different aspects of the same family and community life. The list of P.T.A. presidents included Josephine Alessandrino, Lucy Cecere, Irene Checchia, Joan Checchia, Yolanda Corrado, Theresa De Curtis, Helen Di Geronimo, Pearl Messina, Lena Mosso, Eleanor Olgiati, Marie Percadoni, Lydia Pertusi, Romana Raffetto, Lena Romito, Marie Rusinyak, Dolly Russo, Molly Segalini, Sara Tofano, and Barbara Vernieri.[29] Some of these names appear again later in Pompei's history.

Pompei's P.T.A. was almost entirely women, and Father Albanesi wanted to encourage a similar level of male involvement. In 1956, a circular from parishioner Vincent Lojacono invited men with children in Pompei's school to join the new Fathers' Club.[30] The Fathers' Club resembled the P.T.A. in several ways. It brought together men of the same age and at the same point in their lives. The first year, Father Albanesi appointed as officers the husbands of the P.T.A. officers. Within two years, the Fathers' Club, ensconced in its own club rooms in a building the parish owned at 27 Carmine Street, was electing its own officers and planning its own projects. A single Fathers' Club meeting had as many as 250 men in attendance, and filled Pompei's auditorium. Its list of early presidents—Joseph Calistro, Bob Cardinale, Peter Cifuni, Jr., Tom Collins, John Corrado, Andy Di Franco, Nick Di Geronimo, Peter Gatto, Ed Mooney, Fred Nicomini, Joseph Repetti, and Denis Vernieri—include many names which reappear on lists of trustees and members of other parish organizations.

When their children graduated from parochial school, the mothers graduated from the P.T.A. The fathers, though, continued in the Fathers' Club, which planned activities for teen-agers as well as children. The Fathers' Club opened the parochial school gym three nights a week until ten o'clock, so the boys had somewhere to play. The club also sponsored Friday night dances.

The P.T.A. and the Fathers' Club were Pompei's two strongest organizations in the 1950s and 1960s. With these organizations, Father Albanesi could put into practice a principle Pompei first learned under Father Bandini. If the parish sponsored activities that strengthened community spiritual and social life, it would at the same time strengthen parish finances.

The most regular source of income under Father Albanesi was the Sunday collections. Father Albanesi inherited the custom of printing in the monthly bulletin who had donated how much. Such a record had the advantage of helping him keep track of those who were active parishioners and therefore eligible for in-parish tuition rates, but it was occasionally more trouble than it was worth. Father Albanesi had to remind parishioners they had to *choose* to be anonymous donors, he apologized for typographical errors that in one case turned a five dollar donation into a fifty cent one, he went over the timing of the publication with people who couldn't figure out why their monthly records didn't match the ones in the bulletin, and he answered mail from mothers who thought publishing children's donations made poor children feel inferior.[31]

Father Albanesi made bingo a regular Tuesday evening parish event.[32] At its height, bingo filled the parochial school auditorium and gymnasium, grossed as much as $1,000 a night, and involved parishioners of every age and sex. The Fathers' Club kept the games going. Parish women staffed the kitchen. Teen-age boys sold refreshments from carts, like vendors in ball parks. Teen-age girls were runners, who brought the winning bingo cards to be verified. Like modern state lotteries with their multiple ways to win, there were many variations on bingo, designed to add excitement to the evening. Chatting with friends while playing added to the fun.

Dinner dances were another popular affair in the 1950s and early 1960s, and Pompei held at least one a year. The dinner dances' income-producing potential was expanded by publishing "souvenir books" for the event. These were the size of small-town telephone books, and carried advertising from local businesses.

Such advertising was worth more than the local businesses paid, for it was a way businesses showed their neighborliness and patronage of an important community service. Families, too, took out advertisements as signs of support. A 1967 Sunday bulletin gave the price list for family advertisements. A family advertisement cost $5, marriage anniversary advertisements and those commemorating deceased family members cost $10.[33]

Another way to combine fun and finances was special fund raisers. For example, in 1960, Father Albanesi wanted Pompei to use its lunch room as a summer library, but the parish did not have the necessary books. The P.T.A. mothers went to work. They decided upon a card party as a fund raiser. They picked a date that promised to attract a crowd, for it was the same date as a Fathers' Club activity. The mothers canvassed local stores, soliciting donations of consumer items for prizes, selling tickets, and putting up posters. Additional prize items came from the various classes in the school, and from the Zelatrices. So many items were collected the P.T.A. gave gifts to all mothers attending the party. After the cards and distribution of prizes came the Fathers' Club event, then refreshments.[34]

The most important annual fund raiser was the Fathers' Club show.[35] When the Fathers' Club was first organized, Father Albanesi suggested it stage a program. The first performance, later referred to as "an unpretentious 'Minstrel Show,'" appeared in 1957. The Fathers' Club staged three more annual reviews built around themes: *New York's My Home* in 1958, *Rendezvous in Paris* in 1959, and *The Roaring Twenties* in 1960. Then, 1961, the Fathers' Club took a new approach, and planned a musical comedy which they called *If You Knew Caesar* and advertised as a spoof about the Roman Empire. According to the advertisement for the April show, "Just the thought of [one of the fathers] playing Cleopatra should be enough to make you buy a ticket."[36]

The cast for *If You Knew Caesar* totaled twenty-eight middle-aged men who played both male and female roles and sang and danced in chorus lines of "Roman Jug Girls" and "Egyptian Slave Girls." The program credited parishioners for writing, directing, scenery design, settings, musical direction, choreography, vocal direction, wardrobe, writing parodies of popular songs, production, tickets, and publicity. Area businesses donated leather goods, jewelry, fans and accessories, sneakers, and breast plates, and New York University lent loudspeakers. The volunteers were amateur in the sense of being unpaid, not untrained. One of the two men who wrote and directed *If You Knew Caesar* was Michael Enserra, a professional actor who appeared in a number of Broadway shows, films, television programs and television variety shows, and starred in a couple of commercials.[37]

The Fathers' Club included in the program a page of thanks "To the girls who helped with our revue." The page listing the committees shows who did what. The actors, stage crew, and door committee were men. The ushers, costume, make up, and wig committees were women. Both men and women served refreshments and staffed the coat room. One element that made the program so special was provided by a woman: Josephine Passannante composed the parodies of popular tunes.

If You Knew Caesar gave the Fathers' Club the revenue it needed for one of its biggest projects. In November 1961, the parish bulletin announced that, beginning in June 1962, the club would award scholarships to Pompei parochial school graduates going on to Catholic high schools.[38] The Fathers' Club held three more spectaculars. The sixth annual review, in 1962, was entitled *Easy Living*, and revolved around getting rich at the races. *Rufus*, in 1963, was a play on the country-bumpkin-in-the-city theme. The eighth and last, in April 1964, was entitled simply ?[39]

Father Albanesi did not save as many letters as Father Demo, but those he saved provide another way to measure Pompei's well-being during his tenure. Father Albanesi wrote a few letters recommending poor boys get reduced rates at summer camps, or referring elderly women to Catholic Charities, but he was not so constantly involved in family economic crises as Father Demo had been.[40] Instead of recommending children for orphanages, he recommended them for Eagle Scouts, first jobs, and professional schools.[41] His letters regarding neighborhood crimes all concern traffic tickets and minor accidents.[42] Father Albanesi's correspondence tells only part of the story. Pompei's Saint Vincent de Paul Society spent about $300 per month in 1963, so not every parishioner rose on the economic high tide.[43] Even if every parishioner was well-off, a poor neighborhood could weaken the strongest parish.

Concern for the Village on which parishioners depended for their well-being led Father Albanesi beyond his pastor's office and out into the community. When residents along Leroy Street wanted additional lighting to make their street safer, Father Albanesi forwarded their proposal to the appropriate city authorities.[44] He wrote municipal officials requesting enforcement of prohibitions against truck traffic along Bleecker, and suggested the city enlarge Downing Street Playground for the Village's increasing population of children.[45] When he received the Greenwich Village Brotherhood Award in 1963, he used his acceptance speech to call upon community leaders to preserve the neighborhood by increasing the availability of middle-class housing. According to the parish bulletin that reported the event, Father Albanesi's speech "was interrupted at this point by a standing round of applause."[46]

Father Demo had been the main tie between Pompei and other neighborhood organizations. By Father Albanesi's day, the parishioners helped link Village and parish. When the Greenwich Village Fresh Air Fund presented Pompei with money to send youngsters to summer camp, it was parishioner and fund member Pearl Michelini who forwarded the donation.[47] When Pompei's Boy Scout troop presented Anthony Dapolito with its first annual Certificate of Achievement, it cited numerous neighborhood accomplishments: vice-president of the Greenwich Village Fresh Air Fund, past president of the Greenwich Village Association, Chairman of the Borough President's Planning Board for four years, Chairman of the Fourth Precinct Police Athletic League, member of the Fathers' Club, member of the Progressive Era Association, and director of the Washington Square Outdoor Art Show.[48] Parishioner involvement in Village activities became important later, when it took all kinds of Village organizations working together to preserve community life.

The parishioners' greater prominence in Village life was consistent with the greater prominence of Catholics in public life in general. In 1960, John Fitzgerald Kennedy was elected president. Kennedy was only the second Catholic to be nominated for the presidency by a major party. The first, New York Democrat Alfred E. Smith, contended with anti-Catholicism during his campaign, and even Kennedy had to reassure non-Catholics that he would not let the pope take over the United States. Kennedy's victory was seen as a symbol that Catholics had won a fuller acceptance into American society. His assassination was traumatic. It happened on a day the children's choir met for rehearsal, and the children were so upset by Kennedy's death that Father Albanesi cancelled the practice.[49] The C.Y.O. had scheduled a dance that night; the dance was not held.[50] Pompei's Girl Scout troop wrote a column for the parish bulletin, lamenting the president's passing and saying that it was as if a personal friend had died.[51]

The Second Vatican Council was, like the Kennedy administration, an event which increased the attention accorded to Catholics. On January 29, 1959, John XXIII, who had been pope for less than a year, announced his intention to hold an ecumenical council, that is, a meeting of bishops of the Roman Catholic communion. This was the first since the Vatican Council of 1870–1871. Vatican II's first session met from October 11 to December 8, 1962. Pope John died June 3, 1963, but the council continued under his successor, Paul VI. Catholicism's bishops met for a second session from September 29 to December 4, 1963, and for a third and final session September 14 to November 21, 1964. The council's mission was summed up in an Italian word Vatican II made famous, *aggiornamento*, or updating.

Pompei's bulletin first mentioned the council in October 1962. It was in the column of the parish bulletin devoted to the *Azione Cattolica Italiana*. The story was headed *"Che Cos' è il Concilio Ecumenico?,"* and it explained what an ecumenical council was, and why Pope John XXIII had called one.[52] The first English-language story came in February 1964. The article read as though it were written to reassure Catholics who had heard vague rumors of revolution at the council. It explained that the council could authorize changes in canon law, which, was drawn up by an earthly procedure, but not changes in the more important natural law, which was part of creation itself, or in positive divine law, which was part of revelation. Thus really, as the article's title said, "The Church Never Changes."[53]

Vatican II produced sixteen constitutions and decrees which addressed theological issues. Pompei's bulletin occasionally ran articles exploring these abstract theological concerns. The October 1964 bulletin reprinted an article by John Cogley, then a well-known Catholic liberal. Cogley's article set forth, in positive terms, the new role Vatican II envisioned for the laity. The Church formulated moral standards, but that it was up to the laity to let Church leaders know where moral guidance was needed, and it was up to the laity to apply moral standards in the larger world.[54]

A November 1964 article elaborated another aspect of conciliar thinking, the distinction between private and public worship. Catholics were used to joining sodalities, or going to church to say the rosary, or participating in novenas with other Catholics, activities that were done in groups but which were actually private acts of worship, different from the liturgy. The article sympathized that "This idea is not too familiar to the ordinary Catholic parishioner." Still, it enjoined Catholics to distinguish between worship which the Church intended to be for individuals, or for people getting together as individuals, and worship intended to be what the Church as the People of God did as a corporate body for the public. If one understood the distinction between private and public worship, one would see that people who attended Mass, but who were indifferent or distracted, detracted from the communal nature of public worship.[55]

As the phrase about unfamiliar counciliar theology indicates, some of the Vatican council's discussion was remote from the average parishioners' life. Other Vatican II concerns complemented trends in Greenwich Village so well that it was hard to tell where Vatican II left off and local initiative began. An example of the overlap of Vatican II and Greenwich Village was the interfaith spirit present at Pompei in the early 1960s. In 1963, Father Albanesi won the Greenwich Village Brotherhood Award for his contribution to religious life not only at Pompei but in the neighborhood. That same year, when Father Albanesi celebrated the silver jubilee of his ordination, the Reverend Dr. Jesse W. Stitt of the Village Presbyterian Church and Rabbi Irving J. Block of the Brotherhood Synagogue, co-authored a congratulatory message.[56] Neither the Brotherhood Award nor the silver jubilee message mentioned that Father Albanesi was acting in the spirit of Vatican II; rather, he seemed to be acting in the spirit of a good neighbor. But the neighborhood interfaith spirit fit in well with one of the basic interests of Vatican II.

After twelve years at Pompei, Father Albanesi was transferred to the position of Master of Novices at the Scalabrinians' house in Cornwall, New York.[57] The parish said *Arrivederci, Caro Padre* Sunday, October 4, 1964, with a huge farewell dinner in the parish auditorium. It was, like many parish activities, an event that combined opportunities for individuals to use their personal talents, socializing, and fund raising. Parishioners organized the affair, and trustee Edward J. Fontana took a leading role in the after-dinner farewell ceremonies. Hundreds of people got the opportunity not only to say good-bye to Father Albanesi, but to see each other. The parishioners presented Father Albanesi with some parting gifts, a stereo and an onyx desk set. He in turn presented the Scalabrinians with a gift: a recently-deceased parishioner had left a sum of money to the Scalabrinians to start a seminary building fund. Father Albanesi also indirectly presented Pompei with a gift; numerous people made donations to the Fathers' Club scholarship fund in his name.

There is one essay, written shortly after Father Albanesi left, that sums up Pompei's spirit during his tenure. In 1967, as part of Pompei's diamond jubilee pastor Guido Caverzan, commissioned Mr. Michael A. Cosenza to write a parish history. This was the first since Father Constantino Sassi's 1942 book, and the first ever in English. Mr. Cosenza's manuscript began with a short section on "Why Italians Came," but, unlike previous historians, Mr. Cosenza was more interested in the Italians after they settled down. "We are second, third, and fourth generation descendents of those hardy pioneers who years ago left their own 'paese' to seek a better life for themselves and their families." For Mr. Cosenza's generation, "This [the Village] is our home-town!"[58] No suburbanite with a house and a yard could have been more proud.

NOTES

[1] Interviews 0003, 0004, 0005.

[2] Miriam Cohen, "Italian-American Women in New York City, 1900–1950: Work and School," in Milton Cantor and Bruce Laurie, eds., *Class, Sex, and the Woman Worker* (Westport, Connecticut: Greenwood Press, 1977), 120–143.

[3] *Village Bells* (Fall 1984), 3–4.

[4] Interview 0003.

[5] Interviews 0003 and 0004.

[6] "A Priest Campaigns against Delinquency," *Jubilee* (November, 1959), n.p. This is a Franciscan publication.

[7] Interviews 0003 and 0004.

[8] *Village Bells* (Fall, 1984), 1–2.

[9] *OLP Parish Bulletin* XX:2 (February 1959); 3 and *Village Bells* (Spring 1988), 1–2.

[10] *OLP Parish Bulletin* XXIV:4 (April 1963), 5; Albanesi's silver jubilee souvenir journal, in OLP Memorabilia before 1975, Albanesi Folder; *Village Bells* (Fall 1982), 1–2; and a prayer card issued at Albanesi's death, in OLP Memorabilia 1985–1988, 1985 Folder.

[11] *OLP Parish Bulletin* XXII:1 (January 1961), 4; and XXV:1 (January 1964), 3.

[12] Interviews 0004 and 0005.

[13] Contract in OLP Papers before 1975, 1960–1969 Folder.

[14] Souvenir from Albanesi's farewell, OLP Scrapbook.

[15] Personal communication ,18 June 1991.

[16] Cosenza, 25.

[17] Albanesi to Dominic Grande, C.P., 15 March 1955, OLP Papers before 1975, 1950–1959 Folder.

[18] Cosenza, 26.

[19] Program, 19 October 1952, in OLP Scrapbook.

[20] Mario Albanesi to Zito Bakery, n.d., OLP Papers before 1975, 1950–1959 Folder and program in OLP Scrapbook.

[21] Gannon, 303.

[22] Interview 0006.

[23] New York *Daily News*, 28 April 1961.

[24] Albanesi to Leonard J. Hunt, 7 June 1959, and Joseph J. Cella to Albanesi, 8 January 1960. Both in OLP Papers before 1975, 1950–1959 Folder.

[25] Interview 0004.

[26] Brochure in OLP Memorabilia before 1975, Caverzan Folder.

[27] *Village Bells* (Spring 1985), 3–4.

[28] Judith N. De Sena, "The Participation of Italian American Women in Community Organizations," in Dominic Candeloro, *et al., Italian Ethnics: Their Languages, Literature and Lives* (New York: American Italian Historical Association, 1990) 185–189.

[29] *Village Bells* [1981?]. Clipping in OLP Scrapbook.

[30] Vincent Lojacono, "An Open Letter to the Fathers of Our Parish," n.d., OLP Papers before 1975, 1950–1959 Folder.

[31] For anonymous donation, *see* Albanesi to 190 Bleecker, 5 March 1955. For typographical error, *see* Albanesi to 19 Greenwich, 21 March 1955. For timing of bulletins, *see* Albanesi, no place, 6 March 1955. For children's donations, *see* "A Mother" to Catholic School Board, 30 April 1955. All in OLP Papers before 1975, 1950–1959 Folder.

[32] Interviews, 0004 and 0005.

[33] Sunday Bulletin, 2 April 1967, in OLP Bulletins, Box I.

[34] *OLP Parish Bulletin* XXI:6 (June 1960), 3.

[35] For early history of Fathers' Club shows, *see* program for *If You Knew Caesar*, April 1961, OLP Memorabilia before 1975, Albanesi Folder.

[36] *OLP Parish Bulletin* XXII:3 (March 1961), 4.

[37] *Village Bells* (Winter/Spring 1982[?]), 4.

[38] *OLP Parish Bulletin* XXII:9 (November 1961), 4.

[39] Fathers' Club annual reviews from 1961 to 1964 are in OLP Memorabilia before 1964, Albanesi Folder.

[40] For camp, *see* Albanesi to Reverend Camp Director, Newton, New Jersey, 6 May 1955 and undated. For elderly, *see* Albanesi to Thomas J. Gradilone, 29 March 1955. Both in OLP Papers before 1975, 1950–1959 Folder.

[41] Willis Lindquist to Albanesi, 7 February 1955, OLP Papers before 1975, 1950–1959 Folder. For job recommendation, *see* George T. Fowler to Albanesi, 14 June 1955. For school recommendation, *see* Gertrude E. Ferdon to Albanesi, 1 March 1955. All in *ibid.*

[42] Albanesi to Honorable Chief Magistrate Murtagh, 10 June 1955; Albanesi to J. F. Porrino, 27 July 1955; and Albanesi to Anthony Schiaffino, 30 July 1955. All in *ibid.*

[43] *OLP Parish Bulletin* XXIV:5 and 9 (May and November 1963), 14 and 8.

[44] Albanesi to Department of Water Supply, Gas and Electricity, 18 August 1955, OLP Papers before 1975, 1950–1959 Folder.

[45] Albanesi to Commissioner Barnes, 1 February 1962, OLP Papers before 1975, 1960–1969 Folder, and "To Whom It May Concern," undated, *ibid.*, 1950–1959 Folder.

[46] *OLP Parish Bulletin* XXIV:2 (February 1963), 4, OLP Bulletins, Box I.

[47] Pearl Michelini to Albanesi, 9 July 1955, OLP Papers before 1975, 1950–1959 Folder.

[48] *OLP Parish Bulletin* XXV:1 (January 1964), 5.

[49] *Village Bells* (Fall 1984), 1–2.

[50] Interview 0006.

[51] *OLP Parish Bulletin* XXVI:1 (January 1964), 6.

[52] *OLP Parish Bulletin* XXIII:8 (October 1962), 14.

[53] *OLP Parish Bulletin* XXV:2 (February 1964), 12.

[54] *OLP Parish Bulletin* XXV:8 (October 1964), 13.

[55] *OLP Parish Bulletin* XXV:9 (November 1964), 6.

[56] Cosenza, 25.

[57] Program, 4 October 1964, OLP Scrapbook.

[58] Cosenza, 30.

10

Vatican II at Pompei, 1964–1970

On November 29. 1964, Our Lady of Pompei's parishioners joined Catholics throughout the world in adopting the first renovations called for by Vatican II. Not since the Council of Trent (which ended in 1563) had Catholics made such major alterations in Sunday Mass.

One noticeable change was using the vernacular, or contemporary languages, instead of Latin, at Mass. At Pompei, that meant translating into English and Italian the Scripture readings, Kyrie, Gloria, Creed, part of the offertory, Sanctus, the Lord's Prayer, the Lamb of God, the reception of Communion, and the dismissal. A second innovation was the positions of the priest and people during Mass. In the Tridentine rite, priest and people faced the same direction, toward an altar that stood against the sanctuary wall. In the revised rite, the altar was moved to the sanctuary's center, and the priest and people faced each other across it.[1]

There was a system for introducing the Vatican II changes to the laity. Whenever the Vatican approved a particular change, it sent new guidelines to the dioceses. In the Archdiocese of New York, chancery officials then forwarded explanatory circulars to every pastor, and sometimes other material as well: when the ritual for confession was updated, the chancery sent booklets outlining the new ritual and a pastoral letter from Cardinal Cooke to be read from the pulpit. The bulletin publishing company also contributed to the education of the laity. After 1965, the bulletin's front cover carried a short essay on some aspect of the liturgy or Scripture. Inside the bulletin were etiquette tips, such as "Since the renewal of the ceremonies of the Mass, everyone must try his best to SING during the Mass."[2]

By and large, the pastors took up the task of leading their parishioners through Vatican II. Giving such responsibility to pastors made stable pastoral leadership very important. It was just at this point, however, that Pompei experienced a rapid turnover among its pastors. By the 1990s, the only person on Pompei's staff who even approached Father Demo's record for parish service was Brother Michael La Mantia who, except for two short re-assignments, had served Pompei since 1969.[3]

128

Father Albanesi's successor was Father Anthony Dal Balcon. Father Dal Balcon was born September 13, 1922, and ordained June 29, 1949. His most recent assignment, from 1958 to 1964, was as chaplain of the Italian Catholic Federation of California, but he had been assigned to Pompei from 1955 to 1958, and to the Scalabrinian parish of Saint Joseph's in New York City from 1949 to 1955.[4]

During Father Dal Balcon's pastorate, several other facts made liturgical renewal reasonably easy to accept. The Vatican did not alter everything overnight. Not until Sunday, March 7, 1965, four months after the initial changes, was the doxology at the end of the eucharistic prayer put into the vernacular, and the prayer for peace added after the Lord's Prayer.[5] Almost five years later, on Sunday, February 8, 1970, Catholics began using a three-year cycle with three Scripture readings instead of the Epistle and Gospel.[6] Almost twelve years later, in Lent 1976, the Vatican published the revised rite of reconciliation, or confession, thus ending its *aggiornamento* of the sacraments.[7] One final change, the option of receiving communion in the hand, was introduced at Pompei on November 20, 1977.[8] For some people, this meant they no sooner got used to one new thing than another was introduced. For others, it meant a chance to get used to one new thing before another was introduced.

Nor were all changes unwelcome departures from beloved traditions. A parish bulletin for the week of March 21, 1965, noted that there was now a regular evening Mass, at 7:30 on Sunday nights. Along with late-day Masses which allowed Catholics to meet their Sunday obligation with greater ease came changes not mandated by Vatican II but which were also accepted as modern conveniences. For example, in 1965 Father Dal Balcon replaced the monthly magazine-style parish bulletin with a weekly flyer.[9]

Changing the Mass did not immediately change other aspects of spiritual life. Under Father Dal Balcon, Pompei continued its traditional interest in devotions and sodalities, built a new shrine to the Infant of Prague, established a parish chapter of the Legion of Mary, and added a Holy Hour on First Friday nights. As late as 1973, Pompei scheduled new devotions; the Saint Jude novena was instituted that year.[10] Nor did it change Pompei's social and economic life. Father Dal Balcon added a second bingo night, on Sunday. There was enough money in the parish budget to relocate the baptismal font and to install air conditioning in the church and auditorium.[11] Father Dal Balcon did not revive the plans for a high school, but he requested, unsuccessfully, permission to purchase an abandoned factory for a youth center.[12]

Nor did changing the Mass change Greenwich Village. The Vatican II reforms complemented other reforms in United States society at the same time. President Kennedy's successor, Lyndon B. Johnson, called for an *aggiornamento* of his own to make the United States a "Great Society." Legislation enacting specific programs was passed from 1964 to 1967. At least two of these laws were of importance to Pompei.

The 1964 Economic Opportunity Act included a Neighborhood Youth Corps, which assisted teen-agers in the transition from school to employment, mostly by finding them summer jobs. Pompei created summer jobs by employing youths as tutors and as assistants in the school office, in the school library, to the parish secretary, and to the pastor. Pompei was involved in this program from 1969 to 1972.[13]

The 1965 Immigration Act replaced the laws passed in the 1920s, ending the racial discrimination in immigration that had been particularly hard on southern and eastern Europeans, including Italians.[14] In some ways, the Immigration Act represented a victory for Italians. Like many other ethnic groups, the Italians had an organization concerned with American immigration law, the American Committee on Italian Migration. A.C.I.M. was founded in February 1952 and affiliated with the National Catholic Resettlement Council. It lobbied for immigration legislation reform and served as a traveler's aid and resettlement agency for Italian immigrants, and affiliated with the National Catholic Resettlement Council. Father Caesar Donanzan, C.S., A.C.I.M.'s executive secretary, lived at Pompei starting in 1953. A.C.I.M. had a chapter in New York and several of Pompei's parishioners were included in its membership.[15]

A little over two years after his arrival, January 20, 1967, Father Dal Balcon took the pet puppy the parochial school children gave him for a present and left for a new assignment as director of Villa Rosa, the Scalabrinians' senior citizens' home in Mitchelville, Maryland.[16] Father Guido Caverzan, his successor, arrived in the parish January 23, 1967. Father Caverzan was ordained in 1950 in Piacenza, and emigrated to the United States in 1951; prior to coming to Pompei, he had served in Scalabrinian parishes in New York and Connecticut. He arrived in the midst of preparations for Pompei's diamond jubilee, which the parish celebrated with a Mass of Thanksgiving said by Bishop Pernicone, a dinner dance at the Roosevelt Hotel, and the publication of Mr. Cosenza's history book mentioned in the last chapter.

During Father Caverzan's first two years in office, the same influences that had made Vatican II relatively easy to accept continued to affect developments at Pompei. Father Caverzan continued the process of adapting to Vatican II and updating the parish in ways not mandated by Vatican II but consistent with it. The March 19, 1967, bulletin was the first to include office hours, so people could run errands at the rectory in a businesslike way.[17] In August 1967, Pompei ended the customs of holding separate Masses at the side altars during Mass at the main altar, of starting First Friday Adoration before Mass, and of confessions during Sunday Masses, thus setting a new standard of participation at Mass.[18] In 1968, Pompei said its last 6:00 a.m. Sunday morning Mass, a remnant of when parishioners met their Sunday obligation before work. In 1969, the parish exchanged black for white vestments and began using the Paschal candle at funerals, redirecting the focus of funerals toward the promise of resurrection.[19] That same year Pompei gave up its 7:45 p.m. Rosary, Benediction, and Vespers, evening prayers descended from services instituted by Father Bandini.[20] On March 4, 1970, archdiocesan authorities granted permission to hold a Saturday vigil Mass.[21]

Once Pompei got used to the changes, there was no going back. In 1972, after six years with Masses in English and Italian, Pompei experimented with re-introducing one Latin Mass per Sunday for Lent. The experiment ended with Lent.[22]

To the laity, liturgical renewal was the most obvious aspect of Vatican II, but other changes also affected Pompei. The Vatican directed the religious orders to evaluate their work and, if necessary, adapt it to modern requirements. Pompei had two orders, the Scalabrinian clergy and the parochial school Missionary Zelatrices. The July 16, 1967, bulletin announced that the Zelatrices had taken a new name. When the order was founded, in 1894, the sisters created the word "zelatrice" because women's orders generally didn't use "apostle;" that esteemed title was for men.[23] After Vatican II, when the laity in general and women in particular took greater roles in Catholic life, the Zelatrices became the "Apostles of the Sacred Heart."[24]

Father Caverzan's most complex project was organizing a parish council. The phrase "parish council" does not occur in any Vatican II documents. However, in its *Decree on the Apostolate of the Laity*, the Vatican Council cited Pope Leo XIII, saying "The laity should accustom themselves to working in the parish in close union with their priests." Pompei's weekly bulletin quoted this statement when, on September 14, 1969, it announced plans to create a parish council.[25]

The bulletin devoted several weeks to explaining what a parish council was. There were actually three different groups involved. Parish council advised the pastor and consented to decisions made regarding parish welfare.[26] There was also a parish assembly, which was a forum for discussing issues facing the parish but not a decision-making body. Finally, all parish council members served on council committees dealing with particular facets of parish life, such as worship.[27]

After several weeks of explanations, the bulletin announced "In February, 1970, a Parish Council shall, finally, be established."[28] On February 15, trustee Edward J. Fontana appeared at all Masses to speak to the congregation regarding the new council.[29] On March 29, the bulletin announced the first parish council officers: President Thomas Checchia, Vice-President Vincent Cifuni, and Secretary Madeline Costa.[30] The Parish Council had already had its first meeting on March 18. The first Parish Assembly took place April 29.

When Father Caverzan notified Council members of their election, he told them: "A formidable task lies ahead of you. The parishioners have staked their hopes on your leadership to stir up a new Christ-like spirit in the parish, to secure a closer cooperation among all, and to heal the numerous social ills which are afflicting our community."[31] He told the first meeting of the Parish Assembly: "Your attendance and moral support at the Parish Assembly are of vital importance to help the Council come to grips with the manifold problems facing our community in the fields of religion, education, aid to the poor and aged, and assistance to the youth."[32]

Father Caverzan's calls to action reflected alterations in the social and economic structures that had formerly supported reform and renewal. Disagreement was mounting over President Johnson's "Great Society" programs and over his Vietnam War policies. In the midst of this controversy came what was called a "recession," but which felt more like a depression in Greenwich Village. The two most visible symptoms of recession were a flat economic growth rate and a steep inflation rate, and both were particularly acute in New York. Inflation increased an already high cost of living. Slow growth meant that old jobs disappeared, and new ones failed to open up.

The recession threatened Pompei from every side. Some people moved out because they lost their jobs. Other people moved out because they had jobs, and could afford better housing than was available in Greenwich Village. Every old business or family that moved out left another hole in what had been Pompei's support system.

Beginning in 1968, Father Caverzan took steps to improve Pompei's income in the face of dwindling numbers of parishioners and high inflation rates. Pompei raised its parochial school tuition in 1968. Even then, tuition was $50 per pupil while the actual expenses of running the parochial school for a year were estimated at $165 per pupil.[33] In 1970, archdiocesan officials announced a new policy of raising tuition to a point where the schools covered some expenses without working a hardship on the poor and on large families.[34]

Also Father Caverzan began placing in the bulletin appeals to increase the collection.[35] He illustrated the seriousness of the situation with weekly comparisons of income and expenditure.[36] In 1969, he supplemented the bulletin by hiring a financial consultant who specialized in organizing explanation campaigns to increase church contributions.[37] Between April 21 and May 23, 1969, the consultant distributed brochures on the theology of giving. Parishioners canvassed door to door, soliciting pledges. Collections and envelope use increased for about a year, then again lagged behind parish needs.[38] In the early 1970s, Pompei's lay leaders took a more prominent role in encouraging the laity to make the envelope and tuition payments promptly.[39]

Pompei's economic difficulties were related to population changes in Green-wich Village. The recession and the housing shortage in Greenwich Village did not simply reduce parish population. It reduced parish population in a pattern. The parishioners most likely to move were families with enough income to do so and with children whom they wished to raise elsewhere. The more such families moved out, the more the families that remained behind suffered, because there were fewer and fewer like-minded families to raise their young-sters together. Without suitable companions, it was more likely that the remaining teen-agers would get into trouble.

Father Caverzan introduced a "Folk Mass," to appeal to parish youths.[40] In 1969, Mr. John Pettinato began meeting teen-age boys and young men in the gym for basketball. The problem, though, could not be solved simply by provid-ing spiritual and social activities. The April 19, 1970, bulletin carried the first reference to a juvenile delinquency problem. At this point, the announcement was written as though the problem was restless parish youths, and parents were reminded to keep an eye on their teen-agers.[41]

By the time Father Caverzan left Pompei, the spirit which had sustained Catholic reform, both at Vatican II and in the Kennedy and Johnson presiden-cies, had given way to a less supportive climate. Two dates can help make the change clear. Pompei's November 5, 1967, Sunday bulletin reported that the New York State Catholic Committee had approved the state's proposed new constitution as appropriately reflecting Catholic ethics in the areas of commu-nity development, education, health, housing, human rights, labor, safety, and welfare, and called for parishioners to vote "aye" on an upcoming referendum.[42] Catholic moral teaching was politically popular in the 1960s. Then, in 1970, the State of New York legalized abortion, and Catholic moral teaching became politically *un*popular, and not only where abortion was concerned.[43] Sympathy for social and economic reform vanished, just when that the recession made some reforms more necessary.

Father Caverzan was reassigned to Saint Lazarus in East Boston, and on September 12, 1970, Father James Abbarno succeeded him as Pompei's pas-tor.[44] Father Abbarno was born August 1, 1928; he was Pompei's first American-born Italian pastor. He seems to hold the distinction of being the first pastor of southern Italian descent. He was ordained June 10, 1956, and prior to coming to Pompei, he had served in parishes in upstate New York, and had successfully led one parish's project to renovate its sanctuary in accordance with Vatican II. During his time at Pompei, he also served as vicar provincial for the Scalabrinian order, which took him away from the parish for several months during 1971.[45]

By the late 1960s and early 1970s, the Sunday bulletins indicate Pompei was of two minds regarding the changes the parish was living through. Sometimes, the bulletin took a welcoming attitude toward innovation. When *Jesus Christ Superstar* set the Passion to rock and roll, the bulletin reflected Pompei's own experience sponsoring Passion Plays: "All in all we think it's [sic] a good thing. It makes the humanity of Christ something youth can identify with and it might persuade some of them to go back and read the original book."[46]

However the changes of Vatican II, combined with the changes in Greenwich Village's economic and social structure, also proved wearying. A short poem in one bulletin closed with the lines: "I hope all the Changes/Are just about done/And they don't drop Bingo/Before I've won."[47] Levity aside, the changes were not done, and adapting to Vatican II, and to a new economy and a new neighborhood population, continued to dominate life at Pompei into the 1970s.

NOTES

[1] "Modernizing the Mass," *Time* (13 December 1963), 80.

[2] Weekly bulletin, 17 September 1967, OLP Bulletins I.

[3] *Village Bells* (Winter 1987), 1–2.

[4] *OLP Parish Bulletin* XXV:8 (October 1964), 4 and flyer in OLP Scrapbook.

[5] C. J. McNaspy, S.J., "More Changes at Mass," *America* (27 February 1965), 281.

[6] Weekly bulletin, 8 February 1970, ibid.

[7] Terence Cardinal Cooke to "Dear Friends in Christ," 1 February 1976, OLP Papers 1975–1980, Correspondence 1976 Folder.

[8] Weekly bulletin, 13 November 1977, OLP Bulletins I.

[9] Weekly bulletin, 21 March 1965, ibid.

[10] Weekly bulletin, 12 August 1973, ibid.

[11] Cosenza, 26.

[12] Leonard J. Hunt to Anthony Dal Balcon, 15 September 1966, OLP Papers 1975-1980, Correspondence 1975 Folder.

[13] Dorino De Lazzer to Marta Valle, 4 June 1971, to Ed Coker, 22 June 1971, and to Marta Valle, 1 June 1972, OLP Papers before 1975, 1971 and 1972 Folders.

[14] John Higham, *Send These to Me*, second edition (Baltimore: Johns Hopkins University Press, 1984), 64.

[15] Cosenza, 27, and Frank J. Cavaioli, "A Sociodemographic Analysis of Italian Americans and the Twilight of Ethnicity," in Candeloro, *et al.*, 191–200.

[16] Cosenza, 26–27.

[17] Weekly bulletin, 19 March 1967, OLP Bulletins I.

[18] Weekly bulletin, 27 August 1967, *ibid.*

[19] Weekly bulletin, 28 December 1969, *ibid.*

[20] Weekly bulletin, 23 March 1969, *ibid.*

[21] Leonard J. Hunt to Guido Caverzan, 4 March 1970, OLP Papers before 1975, 1970 Folder.

[22] Weekly bulletin, 27 February 1972, OLP Bulletins I.

[23] Mary Louise Sullivan, M.S.C., "Mother Cabrini: Missionary to Italian Immigrants," *U.S. Catholic Historian* VI:4 (Fall 1987), 265–279.

[24] Weekly bulletin, 16 July 1967, OLP Bulletins I.

[25] Weekly bulletin, 14 September 1969, *ibid.*

[26] Weekly bulletin, 21 September 1969, *ibid.*

[27] Weekly bulletin, 12 October 1969, *ibid.*

[28] Weekly bulletin, 28 December 1969, *ibid.*

[29] Weekly bulletin, 15 February 1970, *ibid.*

[30] Weekly bulletin, 29 March 1970, *ibid.*

[31] Caverzan, circular, 6 March 1970, OLP Papers before 1975, 1970 Folder.

[32] Weekly bulletin, 19 April 1970, OLP Bulletins I.

[33] Caverzan, circular, undated, OLP Papers before 1975, 1970 Folder.

[34] George A. Kelly, circular, 21 August 1970, OLP Bulletins I.

[35] Weekly bulletin, 18 February 1968, *ibid.*

[36] Weekly bulletin, 6 October 1968, *ibid.*

[37] Contract between OLP and Thomas P. McCarthy, 17 January 1969. OLP Papers before 1975, 1960–1969 Folder.

[38] Final Report, Sunday Increased Revenue Program, *ibid.*, and weekly bulletin, 10 May 1970, OLP Bulletins I.

[39] Vincent Cifuni to "Dear Parent," 1 November 1973, OLP Papers 1975–1980.

[40] Weekly bulletin, 20 October 1968, OLP Bulletins I.

[41] Weekly bulletin, 19 April 1970, *ibid.*

[42] Weekly bulletin, 5 November 1967, *ibid.*

[43] Weekly bulletin, 22 February 1970, *ibid.*

[44] Weekly bulletin, 6 September 1970, *ibid.*

[45] "Comprehensive Pastoral Report 1970–1972," in OLP Pastoral Report of parish, 1970–1979 Folder, and weekly bulletin, 14 September 1971 and 3 October 1971, OLP Bulletins I.

[46] Weekly bulletin, 4 July 1971, *ibid.*

[47] Weekly bulletin, 3 November 1968, *ibid.*

The elaborate 1937 mural of the Madonna of the Rosary, was replaced in 1974 with this simpler piece, photographed during the 1980 parochial school golden jubilee. The original design, was restored in 1985.

In 1973 Pompei held its first Festa Italiana, now an annual get-together and fundraiser. This photograph was taken from the plaza across from the church. It was dedicated to Fr. Demo's memory in 1941.

11

A Time of Struggle, 1970–1975

Economic problems double the difficulties of reform movements. Not only do they make reform seem expensive, but cost-cutting measures carried out in the name of "reform," sometimes do more harm than good. This was the problem facing Pompei in the early 1970s. Despite the economic difficulties, despite the temptation to reduce services to save money, Pompei had to find ways to grow and serve its community.

Some idea of the threat from cost-cutting "reforms" may be had by looking at two documents. The first is an article by Pompei assistant Father Dorino De Lazzer, which appeared in the Scalabrinians' provincial newsletter.[1] The article explored new ministries for Pompei: care of elderly immigrants, meeting Greenwich Village's growing drug problem, an apostolate to Spanish and Portuguese immigrants. Without saying so, the article was rehearsing the arguments for Pompei's continued existence—just in case someone suggested that Pompei had outlived its usefulness and should be closed or consolidated with other area parishes.

The second document was written to meet a real threat. Given the recession, Greenwich Village's declining child population, the scarcity of teaching sisters, and the general questioning of the value of Catholic education, it should come as no surprise that in 1974 the archdiocese contemplated consolidating Greenwich Village's parochial schools. When the archdiocesan superintendent of schools discussed this with Father Abbarno, he responded with a letter listing all the reasons why Pompei school should be kept open.[2]

With the Scalabrinians' and the parishioners' commitment, Pompei and its school stayed open. The next step was to keep Pompei a useful presence in a Village that no longer had a large Italian community. Instead of ethnic groups, Pompei was increasingly serving age groups.

The first age group was teen-agers. The parish programs that Pompei had relied on to reach youths were no longer enough, because there were no longer that many parishioners among Greenwich Village teen-agers. Father Abbarno dealt with area youth not only through the church but through the police department, requesting assistance in keeping Pompei's property free of young vandals.[3] In November 1971, vandalism led to Pompei's closing its church between its 12:15 and 5:00 p.m. Sunday Masses.[4]

Provoking as young people could be, Pompei developed programs for them. The December 12, 1971, bulletin carried the first reference to what has grown into the Greenwich Village Youth Council. On that day, Pompei took up a special collection to enable John Pettinato and Phyllis Herbert to open a Drug and Counseling Crisis Center in the rectory basement. The center opened January 23, 1972, under the name of Genesis.[5] Mr. Pettinato continued the athletic program he had been conducting since 1969, with donations from area businesses and Tiro a Segno.[6] When it came to adults in trouble with the law, and especially the illegal drug market operating almost openly in Greenwich Village, Pompei joined with its neighbors in collective action.[7]

A second group was Pompei's elderly. There were all kinds of senior citizens: men and women, English-speakers and Italian-speakers, with family and without, financially secure and financially insecure, even youthful seniors who held part-time jobs or cared for families, and older people who felt the burden of their years. There were sodalities and there was a Saint Vincent de Paul Society, but, as letters to Catholic Charities show, senior citizens required more systematic care.[8]

The first step in serving the elderly was to create different organizations to meet different needs. Adjustments were made to allow the sodalities to keep functioning. The sodalities dedicated to the Sacred Heart, the Rosary, and Saint Rita were put under the direction of a single moderator, Brother Michael La Mantia, who combined them into the Three Societies.[9] Father Abbarno took a second group of older women, who were more comfortable with the English language and who had previously been members of service-oriented organizations such as the P.T.A., and in 1971 created a Ladies' Guild for them.[10] Both the Three Societies and the Ladies' Guild practiced their own familiar devotional activities, engaged in social activities of their choice, and assisted in parish-wide events.

Efforts to provide physical assistance to seniors began with efforts to keep them well-fed. In the early 1970s, several people at Pompei noticed that many elderly neighbors could not shop or cook for themselves, and had trouble maintaining healthy eating habits when they always ate alone. In 1971, Brother Michael and parishioners Lucy Cecere and Anne Di Simone started a program called the Golden Age Club, which served nourishing lunches in Father Demo Hall on Wednesdays.[11] By 1973, the program was popular enough that it planned on two hundred guests for its Christmas party.[12]

As the lunch program became more firmly established Pompei's parish leaders contacted other area institutions, and investigated city services.[13] In 1974, a consortium of Greenwich Village organizations applied for, and received, a federal grant to fund a nutritional program for area senior citizens. The grant covered the preparation of hot lunches every Wednesday at Saint Vincent's Hospital. Volunteers served the meals at four "sites" in the Village area. In 1975, the four sites were organized into a non-profit agency called The Caring Community of Greenwich Village.

In 1973, Pompei had a stroke of luck in selling a piece of real estate it had been holding for the never-built high school. The sale paid off debts that had accumulated from several years in which expenses exceeded income.[14] A more durable source of income came from doing something that Pompei had done before: studying its community and finding an event that combined community building with fund raising. The event was the Festa Italiana.

Pompei had annual bazaars in the past, as well as social and fund raising events emphasizing its Italian connections.[15] Ethnic festivals proliferated in the early 1970s, and in 1972 the parish bulletin advertised an Italian Heritage Cultural Festival being held in Central Park.[16] For the Italians in America, ethnic awareness was a potentially troublesome issue. Ethnic pride helped combat the stereotype that all Italians had Mafia connections, but people who really had criminal records used "ethnic pride" as a protective device, claiming they weren't guilty of anything, they were just innocent victims of anti-Italian prejudice. An example of using ethnic pride as a protective device was the Italian American Civil Rights League, founded by Joseph Anthony Colombo. Mr. Colombo was shot just before the beginning of his 1971 Italian American Unity Day celebration—and police thought the shooting was caused by rivalries among underworld gangs.[17]

Pompei's plans took much of this background into account. Pompei would celebrate both Catholicism and ethnicity; hence a Festa Italiana coinciding with the feast of Our Lady of the Rosary. It would be a parish feast, with different parish societies taking charge of different aspects of the planning. It would attract visitors from beyond the parish, and so would be held in the streets near Pompei rather than the church basement, and would last several days.

There were risks. Pompei had to contend with powerful forces already operating in the city. New York had a calendar of festivals, including some nearby, some within a month of Pompei's proposed celebration, and some emphasizing Italian culture, so the parish faced stiff competition. Pompei would have to go through a maze of city regulations to hold its feast. Finally, a tourist attraction may be a nice place to visit, but it is not necessarily a nice place to live: how would the neighborhood cope with the extra visitors, traffic, noise, and litter?

If anyone at Pompei anticipated the amount of work required, that might have figured as a drawback, too. Father Abbarno was honorary chairman. Experienced parishioners took the leadership positions. Victor Coccozziello, who worked with the state gambling commission, an important agency for the festa, served as chairman, Joseph Repetti and Joseph Guallini as co-chairmen, Maria Rusinyak as secretary, Emile Perazzo as treasurer, and Ralph Tardi as business consultant. Michael Cosenza was public relations director. The Fathers' Club took charge of the games of chance, and senior citizens had special tables of hand-made items for sale.

The planners sent scores of letters between July and November 1973.[18] They asked municipal officials which city ordinances applied to the Festa and sent away for the necessary permits and licenses. They ordered medals, rented equipment and signs, and scheduled extra police protection and trash removal. They invited important dignitaries, and made plans to have them test the Ferris Wheel. They sent out press releases in English, Italian, and Spanish. And then, when the Festa Italiana was all over, they sent thank-you notes to the people who had been of assistance.

Every attempt was made to unite the parishioners behind the new venture and to attract visitors from beyond the parish. The highlight of the internal parish publicity was a series of Sunday bulletin spots featuring photos and endorsements from former pastors, which made the Festa Italiana sound like a parish reunion. The highlight of the external publicity was an appearance on a local television program called "Midday Live," for which parishioners borrowed traditional Italian costumes and prepared Italian dishes to share.

The Festa Italiana opened September 27 with a Mass celebrated by Bishop Pernicone, and the reading of a proclamation from Mayor John V. Lindsay. Then, visitors had their choice of activities. They strolled from the corner of Bleecker and Leroy east to Sixth Avenue and then south along Carmine Street to Bedford, eating Italian, Mexican, Japanese, Korean, or Thai food, drinking beer and soda, and purchasing novelties. They rode the Ferris Wheel and tilt-a-wheel and photographed their children on the kiddie ride. They played games of chance alongside the food booths or in the church basement. They visited the church to light candles and buy religious objects. The festa ran weekends from 2:00 p.m. to 12:00 a.m. and weekdays from 6:00 p.m. to 12:00 a.m. until October 7, the parish feast day, when it closed with feast day observances.

When the books were balanced, Pompei realized a little over $70,000 from all its efforts.[19] The Festa Italiana met the other main requirement for a parish fund raising event, in that it was a good social affair as well. A new parish tradition had begun.

The Festa Italiana's potential for keeping up the connection between Pompei and its former parishioners was enhanced by the renovation of the Memorial Shrine, which Father Abbarno and parishioner Joseph Repetti redesigned to commemorate living and deceased parishioners.[20] Individuals and families paid a small fee to have their loved ones remembered at monthly memorial Masses. Plaques with the peoples' names engraved thereon were placed near the crucifix from the demolished old church to remind all who stopped by to include these individuals in their prayers. The memorial concept proved so popular that Pompei's daily and Sunday Mass intentions were booked years in advance.

The first Festa Italiana's success offset a disappointment that same year, the end of Pompei's parish council. Since its beginning in 1970, parish council made several contributions to life at Pompei. Under its auspices, the English- and Italian-language missions of Father Albanesi's day were revived, and Council's Community Relations Committee studied ways to increase parish involvement in neighborhood affairs.[21] In the late 1960s and early 1970s, Pompei suffered a vandalism problem that was at first attributed to restless young people, and council was asked to develop plans for keeping parish youths busy and out of trouble.[22]

Parish Council also expanded the parish leadership pool in one significant way. Since its earliest days, Pompei had parallel organizations for men and women. Parish Council put men and women in the same organization. After the 1972 election, the officers were president Bob Nash, vice-president Victor Coccozziello, and secretary Maria Rusinyak.[23] The 1973 election gave Mrs. Rusinyak the presidency, with Mr. Coccozziello again as vice-president and Pearl Messina as secretary.[24]

Parish council, though, was an organization which required a larger number of parishioners than Pompei had available in the early 1970s. Opportunities for better jobs and housing elsewhere took away many dedicated people. When former parish council president Bob Nash departed for another job, parish council's newsletter listed his services to Pompei: Cub Scout and Girl Scout dinners, electrician for P.T.A. functions, parish council member and president, Youth Committee, Liturgy Committee, helper at Tuesday Night bingo, and member of the original Holy Name, the revived Holy Name, and the Fathers' Club.[25] When Edward Fontana moved out of the Village early in 1971, Pompei held a testimonial dinner to thank him for forty years' service to the parish, including being a trustee.[26]

Death took away other dedicated parishioners. When Thomas Checchia died November 5, 1973, Pompei's Sunday bulletin printed an obituary for him. Mr. Checchia had occupied several leadership positions in and around Pompei: trustee, member of parish council, president of the Fathers' Club, and officer of the local Knickerbocker Council of the Knights of Columbus. Mr. Checchia's long record obscured that he was only 48 years old at the time of his death.[27]

Pompei's experiment with a Parish Council ended November 9, 1973. The letter announcing the decision reads:

In the light of many events, including the more recent circumstances, I regret to inform you that the Parish Council will suspend all its functions and activities, immediately, at least until further notice. This very painful decision has been made after long and serious deliberation—and consultation with many Pastors in New York and elsewhere. I sincerely feel that this step will restore much of the harmony that I have always strove to create and maintain in the parish. In the spirit of full intent and participation in parish affairs, by all the laity, the Parish Assembly will be held as scheduled and I will chair the session personally.[28]

There is no other written records as to why Pompei's parish council was dissolved. There is, though, one interesting comment, in the minutes of a 1976 Parish Advisory Board meeting. Reflecting on Pompei's parish council experience, an Advisory Board member ventured the opinion that "The role of Trustee had been played down in recent years because of the forming of Parish Council."[29]

There is certainly enough evidence to back up that observation. Pompei's trustees were instrumental in instituting the parish council, and a trustee had been selected to address the congregation on the subject. Trustees and former trustees were elected to council, indicating they held the congregation's confidence as well as the pastor's.[30] Trustees and men eligible for trusteeship formed a Finance Committee which took an active role in advising Pompei's pastors regarding parish income and expenditures.[31]

The trustees are even more interesting because they are different from what one encounters in the few historical studies available on how parishes adapted to Vatican II.[32] Those few studies put forth the theory that before Vatican II, parishes had absolutely no lay leadership, and so Vatican II was like a revolution, with anarchy and chaos breaking out all over the place. Pompei, however, already had some lay leadership in the form of its trustees. Perhaps the difficulty was not that Pompei went from no lay leadership to too much, but that it already had one form of lay leadership, and then had another form placed on top of the first with no effort to integrate the two.

Father Abbarno organized a Parish Advisory Board to get the lay input parish council had provided, and Pompei's parishioners accepted that change. The next year, though, brought another example of the difficulty of integrating old and new. The first reference to Pompei's renovations appears 1973, when some of the statues and votive candles were moved to new locations in the church vestibule and the Memorial Shrine was refurbished.[33] In May 1974 Father Abbarno solicited advice from architectural and design firms.[34] One submitted a proposal which was shown to Pompei's Liturgy Committee, and a small model of the proposed renovations was placed in the rectory office for parishioners to see. The Liturgy Committee was hesitant, but in August 1974, renovations got underway.[35]

Renovations literally began at the top. In August 1974, a design firm replaced the mural of Our Lady of the Rosary.[36] Most of the mural's main figures were painted on canvas and attached to the ceiling. Workers stripped off the canvas, painted the ceiling deep blue, and installed a mural with just the Madonna of the Rosary, Saint Dominic and Saint Catherine of Siena: no Battle of Lepanto, no scene in purgatory, no representative figures in the foreground, no picture of Pompei's bell tower. All that was left of the old mural was a single cherub which fell to the floor while the canvas was being removed and which one of the clergy saved for a souvenir.[37]

The mural was intended as the first phase of a larger project. The next step was to contact the archdiocese for permission to renovate the sanctuary. A contractor was chosen, an estimate for the cost arrived at, the Parish Board consulted, and the sources of funding—donations and the proceeds from the Festa Italiana—identified.[38] Meanwhile, parishioners were invited to the blessing of the new mural Thursday, September 26, 1974, the Festa's opening day.[39]

It was about this time most parishioners realized how extensive the renovations were. There is nothing in the written record about the parishioners' immediate reaction to the new mural, but oral tradition agrees they were stunned. Their reaction may have been delayed by the need to get through the Festa Italiana. After the Festa, Father Abbarno slowed down the pace of renovations. During four consecutive Sundays in October and November 1974 he delivered a series of sermons, or an "explanation campaign," designed to educate parishioners as to the nature of the changes being made, and to solicit their input.[40]

The explanation campaign's first sermon described the new mural as part of a plan to permanently alter Pompei's sanctuary to suit Vatican II's revised liturgy. Re-doing the altar was first on a list of proposed interior refurbishments. The interior reconditioning was an extension of already-completed repairs of the church's exterior. The entire project was to be completed by 1976, the fiftieth anniversary of Pompei's plant.

Subsequent sermons clarified the role of change in Vatican II theology. Change was presented as a natural part of growth. In addition to natural changes, human hearts required supernatural changes for individuals to get closer to God. Willingness to change was a sign of obedience to the will of the Church expressed in Vatican II. The campaign's final section returned to Pompei's renovations, and summarized Vatican II's criteria for deciding which changes to incorporate into Catholic life.

After the campaign, Father Abbarno conducted a poll to use as a basis for decisions about proceeding with the renovations. On Sunday, November 24, 1974, parishioners attending Mass received packets containing flyers recapitulating the explanation campaign, and a ballot. The ballot gave the parishioners three options:

1) No further changes should be made at all.
2) Changes should be made, but in a very limited way.
3) Changes should be made completely in conformity with the Constitution on the Liturgy (Vatican Council II) and the style of our church.

There was also a space for opinions.

There were two areas of confusion in the ballots. Some parishioners considered repairs to be changes, and provided lists of changes that included refinishing the pews and replacing the front doors. Also, since the exterior had already been spruced up and the new mural already put on the ceiling, some parishioners voted for change, and explained that things should be changed back to the way they were. Even with the areas of confusion, the ballots preserved among Pompei's records are valuable historical documents of how the parishioners thought about the events taking place around them.[41]

Parishioners' comments divide into five groups. First there were people who wanted changes in conformity with Vatican II. Some, such as the respondent who wrote that "Innovation is a sign of progress socially and spiritually" indicated parishioners kept up with the trends of thought in Catholicism. Other respondents, such as the one who wrote "I pray that your efforts will succeed in whatever you desire in this matter" indicated they trusted the pastor's judgment in implementing changes. One touching example of the parishioners' cooperation was the respondent who outlined his reasoning on the matter of renovations and signed his name with "Your optimistic parishioner."

Second were those who voted for limited or no change for economic reasons. One of the few comments in Italian was *"Non tutti passano fare grandi donazioni Padre. I tempi non sono buoni cause dei prezzi che si alzuno tutti giorni."* ("Not everyone can give grand donations, Father. The times are not good because of the prices which go up every day.") Another respondent put the economic issue in theological perspective: "Can we in conscience make extensive and unnecessary changes in an already beautiful church when all over the world our brothers and sisters are starving[?] Haven't we misplaced our priorities? And isn't this completely contrary to Vatican II?"

A third group voted for limited or no change on the grounds that change wouldn't accomplish desired purposes. In these cases, a few parishioners responded to arguments that don't appear in the explanation campaign material but which they may have heard elsewhere. For example, none of the material in the packet accompanying the ballot advocated change as a tactic for attracting young people to Catholicism. However, several respondents wrote that if enticing youth to church was a reason for change, it was a misguided reason. As one parishioner explained, young people especially needed to see the statues and pictures in order to feel close to the saints to whom they prayed.

Except for a brief statement that Catholics should consider the caliber of works of art in decorating a church, the explanation campaign had not dealt with Pompei's interior's aesthetic qualities. The fourth and largest group, though, voted for limited or no change on the grounds that Pompei looked fine the way it was. Few parishioners believed Pompei was purely and simply a work of art. It was attractive for a reason. For several people, Pompei's interior was lovely because it performed its assigned function: it was conducive to prayer. "To me Our Lady of Pompei is a very warm and beautiful church. When I am at Mass or just making a visit, I feel the presence of God all around me."

For other parishioners, Pompei was well-suited to those who worshipped there. "We are Italians, warm and sensitive in nature. We do not want an antiseptic modern church . . . ." For those who remembered the lack of respect even their co-religionists had for the Italians' pious practices, this seemed like another attempt to pull the Italians away from their roots.

Most parishioners found Pompei beautiful because they knew it well: "True we come to Church to pray to God, but I feel I want to see the *familiar surroundings.*" Pompei reminded parishioners of their connection not only with God, but with their families: "My father and grandfather were around when Our Lady of Pompei stood on Sixth Avenue. They gave their all towards building it . . . ." The church was also a link to community history. Even though Father Demo died before the mural was even started, one respondent was confident that "I am sure that the members of *Our Lady of Pompei* want to keep the church the way *Father Demo* had it *built.*"

A fifth group voted for limited or no change, and gave one of two reasons that should be considered as the same reason in different wording. Some parishioners seemed inspired by Vatican II: "The decision as to what changes should be made should be left up to the congregation. After all the people ARE the Church!!!" Other seemed inspired by the American Revolution's slogan "no taxation without representation": "we're the one who have to pay from a small pay check income" for any improvements made.

Different as they sound, the two phrases point to the same facts. In 1973, the building was less than fifty years old, the mural less than forty. There were parishioners alive in 1973 who had watched funds go from their hands to the bricks, mortar and stained glass windows. Even those who had no financial connection to the building saw themselves in it. This architecture could have been chosen only for an Italian church; the ceiling pictures chosen only for a church dedicated to the Madonna of the Rosary; the mural chosen only for

Pompei. They knew, even before Vatican II told them, that "the people are the church."

The final count showed that 906 ballots had been distributed, and 220 returned. Of those 220, 40 chose the option to change in conformity with Vatican II, 66 preferred limited changes, and 114 chose to make no changes at all. Father Abbarno notified the Archdiocesan Building Commission that Pompei would discontinue its renovations.[42] Cancelling the renovations eliminated a source of tension, but it had negative consequences. Abandoning any project causes loss of morale, and this was only a year after Pompei abandoned its parish council. It was hard to look beyond the disappointments and to see the progress Pompei was making in other important areas.

Father Abbarno resigned his position as pastor in January 1975.[43] His successor, Father Giulivo Tessarolo holds Pompei's record for brevity of tenure. He was pastor for seven months, from January to July 1975. When Father Tessarolo was called to the Vatican to direct its Office of Migration and Tourism, Father Edward Marino was appointed administrator, and in 1976, appointed pastor.[44] Altogether, Pompei had six pastors in the twelve years from 1964 to 1975: Fathers Albanesi, Dal Balcon, Caverzan, Abbarno, Tessarolo, and Marino.

The rapid turnover in leadership would have posed problems even had everything else about Pompei remained the same. But everything else had changed. Catholicism changed, and so did Greenwich Village. In such an environment, Pompei had to experiment to see what would stabilize the parish. Inevitably, a few experiments wouldn't stand the test of time.

At the time, it was hard to overcome the demoralization accompanying the end of parish council and the incomplete renovations of Pompei's interior. From a longer perspective, it is easier to see that Pompei found new sources of stability in its Parish Advisory Board, its ministries to youth and to senior citizens, and its annual Festa Italiana. Even though the social and economic problems of the late 1960s and early 1970s continued into the late 1970s and early 1980s, Pompei had survived, and would continue to be a presence in Greenwich Village.

NOTES

[1] *Intercom* II:3 (June 1972), 1–11. This is the newsletter of the North American Province of the Scalabrinians.

[2] Abbarno to Elinor Ford, O.P., 19 November 1974, OLP Papers 1975–1980, loose papers.

[3] Abbarno to Captain Salmieri, 1 April and 3 May 1971, ibid., 1971 Folder.

[4] Weekly bulletin, 14 November 1971, OLP Bulletins I.

[5] Weekly bulletins, 12 December 1971 and 23 January 1972, ibid.

[6] Abbarno to William Herbert, 3 December 1973, OLP Papers before 1975, 1973 Folder; and Abbarno to Charles Roa, 30 January 1974, ibid., 1974 Folder.

[7] Invitation, before 18 July 1974, OLP Memorabilia before 1975, Abbarno Folder.

[8] Abbarno to Edward D. Head, undated, OLP Papers before 1975, 1971 Folder.

[9] *Village Bells* (Winter 1987), 2.

[10] *Village Bells* (Summer 1988), 3.

[11] *Village Bells* (Spring 1983), 3, and (Spring 1989), 2.

[12] Abbarno to Edward D. Corless, 26 November 1973, OLP Papers before 1975, 1973 Folder.

[13] Abbarno to Leland W. Lakritz, 8 May 1973, *ibid.*

[14] Weekly bulletin, 24 November 1973, OLP Bulletins I.

[15] "To Whom It May Concern," 2 July 1955, OLP Papers before 1975, 1950-1959 Folder; and *OLP Parish Bulletin* XXI:8 (October 1960), 14, and XXII:9 (November 1961), 7.

[16] Weekly bulletin 11 June 1972, OLP Bulletins I.

[17] *New York Times*, 29 June 1971, 1:1, 20:6. *See also* the related story at 20:5, which calls attention to a rumor that shopkeepers of Italian extraction were forced to close their stores in support of Colombo's Unity Day.

[18] OLP Papers before 1975, 1973 Folder.

[19] OLP Festa Italiana, Box 1, 1973 Folder.

[20] *Village Bells* (Summer 1981), 2–3.

[21] Dolores Musante, "The First 731 Days," undated typescript [1973?], OLP Memorabilia before 1975, Abbarno Folder.

[22] Abbarno to Thomas Checchia, 16 April 1971 and undated [1973?], OLP Papers before 1975, 1971 Folder; and weekly bulletin 3 December 1972, OLP Bulletins I.

[23] Weekly bulletin, 19 March 1972, OLP Bulletins I.

[24] Weekly bulletin, 1 April 1973, *ibid.*

[25] *OLP Parish Council Newsletter*, undated, OLP Memorabilia before 1975, Abbarno Folder.

[26] Weekly bulletin, 14 February 1971, OLP Bulletins I.

[27] Mock up of obituary in OLP Papers before 1975, 1972 Folder.

[28] Abbarno to 239 Bleecker, 9 November 1973, OLP Papers before 1975, 1973 Folder.

[29] Meeting of Advisory Board 11 March 1976, OLP Papers 1975–1980, Advisory Board Fr. Marino Folder.

[30] Caverzan to Joseph P. O'Brien, 29 January 1969, OLP Papers before 1975, 1960–1969 Folder; Caverzan to O'Brien, 15 January 1970, *ibid.*, 1970 Folder; O'Brien to Caverzan, 21 January 1970, *ibid.*; Abbarno to James P. Mahoney, 21 February 1973, *ibid.*, 1973 Folder; and Mahoney to Abbarno, 18 April 1974, Papers before 1975, 1974 Folder.

[31] "Annual Report of the Financial Committee," undated; Finance Committee Meeting Minutes, May 1970, 12 August 1970, and 25 September 1970, OLP Papers before 1975, 1970 Folder; and Finance Committee Meeting Minutes 16 February 1971, Papers before 1975, 1971 Folder.

[32] Scott Appleby, "Catholic Implementation of Vatican II at the Parish Level, 1965–1975," paper delivered at "American Catholicism in the Twentieth Century" conference, Notre Dame, Indiana, 1 November 1990. Professor Appleby compared the "Tridentine" model of the church which influenced church structure until Vatican II, with the "Vatican II" model of the church which, ironically, was based on a pre-Tridentine, biblical model. See also interview 0007.

[33] Weekly bulletin, 11 February 1973, OLP Bulletins I.

[34] Salvatore Gargiuolo to Abbarno, 2 May 1974, OLP Memorabilia before 1975, Abbarno Folder.

[35] Interview 0009.

[36] Fabian Zuccone to Abbarno, 2 August 1974, OLP Memorabilia before 1975, Abbarno Folder.

[37] Interview 0001.

[38] Abbarno to William J. McCormack, 5 September 1974, OLP Papers before 1975, 1974 Folder.

[39] Abbarno, circular, 15 September 1974, *ibid.*

[40] Abbarno to Parish Board Members, 6 December 1974, OLP Parish Memorabilia before 1975, Abbarno Folder. The explanation campaign material is also in this folder.

[41] Weekly bulletin, 8 December 1973, OLP Bulletins I. The next few paragraphs rely on the results of the parish opinion poll, in OLP Memorabilia before 1975, Abbarno Folder.

[42] Frank Woodruff to Abbarno, 21 November 1974, OLP Papers before 1975, 1974 Folder.

[43] Weekly bulletin, 5 January 1975, OLP Bulletins I.

[44] Weekly bulletin, 13 July 1975, *ibid.*

12

"The Unity We Reached by Rubbing Shoulders at the Wheel," 1975–1981

In 1975, after five pastors in ten years, Our Lady of Pompei began a stretch of almost fifteen years with just two pastors. The first, Father Edward Marino, was born in Chicago May 28, 1931, and ordained June 1, 1957. Father Marino was appointed administrator in August 12, 1975 and pastor February 22, 1976.[1] When he was reassigned in September 1980, he had been Pompei's pastor longer than any one since Father Albanesi.

Two months after becoming administrator, Father Marino issued his first report on "The Spiritual and Financial State of our Parish."[2] He counted only five hundred families. The next spring, when he posted the first issue of the parish newsletter, he had only two thousand names on the mailing list, one-sixth the parish population of the World War II era, and one-tenth the population before Sixth Avenue was widened. School expenditures exceeded income by $14,000, despite the fact that school population had decreased to the point that Father Marino had to squelch rumors of the school's closing.[3]

In his report on Pompei's spiritual state, Father Marino lamented the decline in regular attendance at Mass, and the fact that the more frequent communion encouraged as part of Vatican II had not caught on in the parish. He instituted two changes to stimulate parish spiritual life. In 1976, Pompei began scheduling its perpetual novena services in conjunction with the noon day Mass, thus making attendance more convenient for the elderly and office workers.[4] In 1979, Pompei experimented with training laymen in the parish as Scalabrinian Associates, to assist the pastor in several ways; this program's chief benefit was its creation of a group of extraordinary ministers of the Eucharist.[5]

There were other aspects of parish life which already worked fairly well. Every year, Father Marino sent the chancery a letter nominating for trustees men whom he described as "prudent, concerned businessmen . . . regular communicants and exemplary Catholics."[6] The trustees were two of the six members of the Parish Finance Committee. All Finance Committee members were men, most of whom had been parishioners a long time. New members were selected by the pastor, who took suggestions from those already on the committee.[7] Finance Committee members also appeared on the Parish Advisory Board, which was composed of men and women, religious and lay people who each took responsibility for some aspect of parish life.[8] About annually, the pastor called the heads of parish organizations together to report on activities and on plans for the coming year.[9] This may not have been the most representative system, but it was suitable for a parish with a core of experienced, dedicated parishioners.

Pompei needed those experienced, dedicated parishioners, because the city's faltering economy affected both individual parishioners and the parish as an institution. Like pastors before him, Father Marino tried to reduce expenditures, collect monies due more efficiently, and, above all, find new ways to raise funds. In October, 1975, he contacted archdiocesan officials regarding opening Pompei's school to non-Catholic pupils.[10] This entailed some expense as Pompei had to provide religious education for those students, but it also promised some income, as non-parishioners were charged a higher tuition. Besides, full schools discouraged any talk of saving money by closing schools.

Also in 1975, the Caring Community, the senior citizens' service begun under Father Abbarno, incorporated itself, and rented Father Demo Hall as one of four "sites" for its programs.[11] Demo Hall was the largest site, and so the Caring Community used it for annual events. There was already a Christmas party and, in 1976, the Caring Community began holding a Seder with a specially-written Haggadah, or Passover story, to emphasize the affinity of Judaism and Christianity.[12]

At this point, the Caring Community was the only organization renting space at Pompei. Greenwich Village Youth Council incorporated itself in 1977, but Pompei's pastor was its executive director.[13] However, a pattern was being established for the future. It was The Caring Community which served senior citizens; Pompei provided space at not-for-profit rental rates, participated on the Board of Trustees, and made other contributions.

Incorporating the Caring Community clarified the distinction between the social services this organization performed, and the pastoral care proper to the Church. Under Father Marino, Pompei added a new program to enhance senior citizens' devotional practice. In 1977, the bulletin announced that Pompei had held a successful Saint Joseph's Day celebration.[14] This may be the first mention of Pompei's Saint Joseph's Table, a Sicilian tradition involving setting a table with all of sorts of delicacies (except meat, since Saint Joseph's Day, March, 19, usually falls in Lent) in expectation of a visit from the Holy Family. Brother Michael La Mantia whose family's roots were partly in Sicily, organized the event for Pompei.

When Father Marino became pastor, Pompei had already booked parish events until October 1976, so much of Father Marino's first eighteen months was spent executing plans already made. The parish held its Festa '75 in October. The highlight of the activities was a procession with Saint Frances Cabrini's statue and a blessing of her new shrine.[15] The affair netted $61,000, $15,000 of which was immediately sent to the bank to repay a loan.[16]

The Festa Italiana's popularity provided a clue to Pompei's future: people who left the parish physically did not leave it spiritually. Even though she looked forward to her new home, the woman who wrote the letter quoted below knew what she was leaving behind at Pompei:

> *Prima di lasciare gli Stati Uniti per spendere il resto dei miei giorni con la mia famiglia in Italia, vorrei fare una donazione alla Madonna di Pompei alla quale sono particolarmente devota. Ho trascorso tutta la mia vita da adulta nel Villaggio, ho batezzato mio figlio nella nostra Parrocchia, ho sempre considerato Our Lady of Pompei come una "missione," ne ho sempre tratto conforto nelle mie preghiere e nelle mie visite e, ne sono sicura, sarà sempre nel meo cuore.*

> Before leaving the United States to spend the rest of my days with my family in Italy, I want to make a donation to Our Lady of Pompei, to whom I am particularly devoted. I have spent all my adult life in the Village, had my son baptized in our parish, have always considered Our Lady of Pompei as "mission," have always taken comfort in my prayers and my visits, and have always, will always, hold it in my heart.[17]

These were people whom Father Marino called "those far and near who wish to keep in touch with all the activities of the shrine-church."[18] Pompei was a "shrine" not only to the Madonna of the rosary, but to their own younger and more active years, to an immigrant generation that was passing away, and to the community in which they had grown up and grown old. Pompei developed new activities to foster this new shrine community. One new activity was a radio broadcast delivering a religious message to Italian listeners. Father Peter Polo was the first host of *La Voce di Pompei*, which began airing February 6, 1976, over station WEVD (97.8 FM).[19]

A second new activity came just before Easter 1976, when Pompei's senior citizens collated and mailed the first 2,000 copies of *The Village Bells*. The first edition included a schedule of upcoming events and invited readers to attend. When the publicity worked and people visited, their names were added to the mailing list, until the mailing list reached 12,000, and the collating and mailing had to be done by a firm hired for this purpose.[20]

Father Marino's most ambitious plan was to make it unnecessary for so many parishioners to move away. The plan first appears in the minutes of an April 8, 1976, Parish Advisory Board meeting, at which "Father Marino . . . spoke of the possibility of doing more for the Senior Citizens, such as building them a residence, etc."[21] This is the first mention of Demo Estates.

That October, Father Marino introduced a change into the Festa Italiana. Until 1976, the Festa coincided with a novena, but, as Father Marino explained,

"It is one of the contradictions of parish life. The Feast is necessary for survival because of the money it brings in, and at the same time we have to work around it for spiritual values."[22] In 1976, the novena was moved so that it ended the day Festa '76 began. Perhaps Pompei should not have moved the novena. Nine out of eleven days of Festa '76 were beset by freezing rain.[23]

Fortunately, the parish had another event scheduled for that year, the fiftieth anniversary of the church building. Under chairman Vincent Cifuni, the parish celebrated with a dinner dance on October 30, 1976, a Mass on October 31, a souvenir journal, and the release of a record featuring the anniversary Mass music.[24] It was for this anniversary that Pompei engraved an inscription on the central light pole in Father Demo Square: "This monument is dedicated to Reverend Antonio Demo, C.S., pastor of Our Lady of Pompei church from 1900 to 1933 and builder of the present Pompei church in 1926. He was a legend in his time, and is today honored by the Italian-American community he served with loyalty and love."[25]

In connection with the church's fiftieth anniversary, Pompei conducted a Special Donation Campaign and established a Special Altar Fund. The latter allowed for the completion of a renovation planned under Father Abbarno. When Vatican II directed that Catholics stress the importance of Mass as a community gathering, Pompei, like many parishes, installed a temporary free-standing altar which allowed the priest and congregation to face each other across a table. The "temporary" altar came in December 1964. Twelve years later, in June 1976, Pompei installed a permanent free-standing altar. The new altar was crafted in Italy of marble and of a size proportionate to Pompei's sanctuary space.[26]

The renovations made possible by the Special Donation Campaign allowed Father Marino to eliminate one outdated community service. Probably around 1961, when Soviet-American tensions ran high, federal authorities designated Pompei's basement a fall-out shelter in case of nuclear attack, and stored supplies there. Father Marino wrote the federal authorities to remove the supplies so Pompei could refurbish its basement.[27] By then the authorities concluded that few buildings adequately protected against atomic radiation, and once the fall-out shelter was cleaned, it was never restored.

All the while, progress continued on Father Marino's dream of affordable housing for senior citizens. By December, 1976, Father Marino had chosen a name for the project, "Demo Estates." Demo Estates would house the self-sufficient elderly in a rooming house or hotel atmosphere. The Scalabrinians, who already ran other homes for the aged, would manage the facility. Funds could come from the Federal Commission for the Aging, Italian-oriented philanthropies, and city and tri-state fund raising campaigns. Later, the parish could expand the facility to include senior citizens requiring nursing home care.[28]

In March 1977, Father Marino applied for an appointment to Community Board #2, which made decisions about new building, recreation space, and community services in the Village.[29] His application was turned down, but it is an important indication of how Father Marino thought about his work at Pompei. It was good for the parish to have an advocate on the community board, which made decisions that impacted aspects of Pompei's life, such as the Festa Italiana. It was also good for the community board to have someone from Pompei, which was one of the Village's more active and diversified community services.

Festa '77 was the first held in July. The July date made it easier to maintain a religious atmosphere at the October rosary feast, and it was hoped that visitors would be more numerous and the weather would be better. However, Festa 77's opening night, July 14, was also the night of a city-wide electrical blackout. During the festa, New York City set two records: the single hottest day of the year, and the most consecutive hot days.[30]

That August, the Federal Department of Housing and Urban Development approved the idea of Demo Estates, and Father Marino began looking for a place to put a foundation under his dream castle.[31] Meanwhile, he created a corporation to handle Demo Estates' business. After experimenting with the name Our Lady of Pompei Redevelopment Corporation , the organization was incorporated as the Our Lady of Pompei Demo Foundation. The date on the incorporation certificate was February 1, 1978.

Late in 1978 or early in 1979, the Demo Foundation discovered that former Public School 95, Food Trades Annex High School, was up for sale. The building was southwest of Pompei, in the block formed by West Houston, Hudson, Clarkson, and the point where Seventh Avenue met Varick Street. The foundation hired an architectural firm to write a request for a Housing and Urban Development Department grant to convert the school to a residence. The book-length application went to the Housing and Urban Development Department May 1, 1979.[32]

While waiting for Housing and Urban Development to decide, Father Marino continued working on strengthening the parish community and thinking up ways to convince those who had moved away to return for a visit. Following John Nicholls's death early in 1976, Pompei hired Charles Thomas as organist.[33] Under Mr. Thomas, Pompei added to its traditional Good Friday service a performance of Gioacchino Rossini's *Stabat Mater*. As Father Marino explained in a March 1979 press release, "The entire program is in Italian and Latin but the movements are evident in any language."[34]

Besides special programs, Father Marino took a unique opportunity to make Pompei a more attractive place for impromptu visits and private prayer. When in 1979 the Church of Saint Benedict the Moor was remodeling, its clergy realized that they had statues which had been taken along when that parish turned over its Bleecker Street church to Pompei. Saint Benedict's called Pompei, Brother Michael La Mantia visited the parish, and returned with the statues of the Blessed Mother and Saint John the Evangelist which used to stand at the foot of the Crucifix in the Bleecker Street church. The statues were placed at the foot of the same cross, now part of Pompei's Memorial Shrine.[35] (In 1991, the statues were moved to the side altar, near the purgatory scene.)

Shrinking population and continued inflation forced Father Marino to pay attention to every opportunity to save money or generate income. He leased candle stands rather than buying them.[36] He reminded parents to put their envelopes in the collection basket and to pay their tuition promptly.[37] He adjusted for inflation fees Pompei charged for services such as having an organist at funeral Masses.[38] He imposed a surcharge on tuition in lieu of having parochial school parents organize fund raisers.[39] In January 1980, he introduced a new system of Mass reservations, enabling people to request a Mass be said for their intention as much as three years in advance, and allowing the parish to book reservations and collect payments more methodically.[40]

And he found a second not-for-profit service agency to lease space at Pompei. The Scuola d'Italia was founded in 1977 as a school for youngsters whose parents were either Italians working temporarily in the United States, or who wanted their children to have a bilingual education. Father Marino leased two floors of the parochial school to the Scuola, which took up occupancy in September 1979, and remained until 1991.[41]

In October, the New York Area Office of the Department of Housing and Urban Development rejected the proposal for putting Demo Estates in P.S. 95. The site was considered unsuitable for senior citizens: too much noise from the traffic and from the loading bays in the area.[42] This was ironic, because there were plenty of elderly residents already living near the proposed site. Father Marino was reassigned soon after this, the Demo Foundation never found a site acceptable to the authorities, and it never did any official business.[43]

There was a second disappointment in 1979. The P.T.A. disbanded, leaving behind $2000 in scholarships for Pompei graduates going on to Catholic high schools.[44] Since Father Albanesi's day, the P.T.A. had been the vehicle for interesting mothers in the school, and, without interested parents, the school's education would not be as effective. Father Marino created a School Advisory Board to replace the P.T.A. as a way to keep the parents involved in the institution that educated their youngsters.[45]

In August 1980, after six years at Pompei, Father Marino was reassigned to a position as head of the Scalabrinians' Eastern United States Province development office, and superior of the community house on Staten Island.[46] As with Father Abbarno, his leaving had its demoralizing aspect: Pompei was still in debt, had not turned Demo Estates into a reality, and the renovations begun in 1974 were still incomplete. And, as with Father Abbarno, it was hard to look beyond the disappointments to see the permanent legacy. *La Voce di Pompei* and *The Village Bells* were the first steps in building a community that was larger than the Catholics living nearby in the Village. Renting space to the Caring Community and the Scuola d'Italia established a new source of funds and a new way to facilitate neighborhood services.

Finally, as Father Marino himself observed doing something difficult together could be useful in itself. In a circular letter written in 1978, Father Marino explained "that the unity we reached by rubbing shoulders at the wheel could become the center of unity in our spiritual life as well."[47] Through the 1980s, Pompei maintained its unity by having many people work together toward the common goal of maintaining Pompei as a presence in Greenwich Village.

NOTES

[1] Weekly bulletin 24 August 1975, OLP Bulletins I; and *Village Bells* (Easter 1976).

[2] Marino, circular, September 1975, OLP Papers 1975–1980, near Correspondence 1975 Folder.

[3] Weekly bulletin 23 January 1977, OLP Bulletins I.

[4] Weekly bulletin 4 January 1976, *ibid.*

[5] Weekly bulletin, 26 August 1979, *ibid.*

[6] Marino to Joseph P. Mahoney, 22 March 1976, OLP Papers 1975–1980, loose papers.

[7] Zanoni to 290 Sixth Avenue, 3 October 1983, OLP Papers 1980–1987, January 1983 Folder.

[8] "Meeting of Parish Advisory Board," 30 October 1975, OLP Papers 1975-1980, Advisory Board Father Marino Folder.

[9] Marino, circular, 7 January 1980, OLP Papers 1975–1980, Correspondence 1975 Folder; and "Meeting of Heads of Our Lady of Pompei Organizations," 12 November 1980, OLP Papers 1980–1987, 1980 Folder.

[10] Marino to James A. Feeney, 31 October 1975, and to Sister Anita Marie, A.S.C.J., undated, *ibid.,* Correspondence 1975 Folder.

[11] Weekly bulletin 27 July 1976, OLP Bulletins I.

[12] Undated news release advertising tenth annual seder for 28 April 1986, OLP Papers 1980–1987. January 1986 Folder.

[13] Greenwich Village Youth Council brochure, ca. 1987, OLP Memorabilia, 1989.

[14] Weekly bulletin, 27 March 1977, OLP Bulletins I.

[15] Marino to Joseph Pernicone, 19 May 1975, OLP Papers, 1975–1980, near Correspondence 1975 Folder.

[16] "Meeting of the Parish Advisory Board," minutes, 30 October 1975, *ibid.*, Advisory Board Father Marino.

[17] To Zanoni, 14 May 1985, OLP Papers, 1980–1987, January 1985 Folder.

[18] *Village Bells* (Easter 1976), 1.

[19] "Meeting of Advisory Board," minutes, 29 January 1976, OLP Papers 1975–1980, Advisory Board Father Marino Folder.

[20] *Village Bells* (Summer 1986), 3-4.

[21] "Meeting of Advisory Board," 8 April 1976, OLP Papers 1975–1980, Advisory Board Father Marino Folder.

[22] Marino to Dominic Grande, C.P., 17 February 1976, *ibid.*, loose papers.

[23] Marino, circular, January 1977, OLP Papers 1975–1980, near correspondence 1975.

[24] Fiftieth Anniversary Committee, circular, undated, OLP Papers 1975–1980, loose papers.

[25] Marino to Martin Lang, 14 July 1976, ibid.

[26] "Advisory Board Meeting," minutes, 14 June 1976, *ibid.*, Advisory Board Fr. Marino Folder.

[27] Marino to Mr. Guthrie, undated, ibid., loose papers.

[28] Edward J. Marino, "A Proposal for 'Demo Estates'," 6 December 1976, *ibid.*, in a report-type folder.

[29] Marino to Percy Sutton, 25 March 1977, OLP Papers 1975–1980, loose papers.

[30] Weekly bulletin for 31 July 1977. OLP Bulletins I.

[31] Marino, circular, 2 August 1977, OLP Papers 1975–1980, loose papers.

[32] Marino to Conklin and Rossant, 9 March 1979, *ibid.*, in an envelope labelled "Demo Foundation."

[33] Weekly bulletin for 11 April 1976, OLP Bulletins I.

[34] Marino to New York *Catholic News*, 30 March 1979, OLP Papers 1975–1980, yellow folder.

[35] *Village Bells* (Summer 1981), 3.

[36] Zanoni to Joseph Murphy, 18 March 1982, OLP Papers 1980–1987, January 1982 Folder.

[37] Marino to 224 Lafayette, undated; and to 32 Leroy Street, 17 October 1975, OLP Papers 1975–1980, Correspondence 1975 Folder.

[38] Marino, circular, 26 January 1976 and 21 December 1979, *ibid.*, loose papers.

[39] Zanoni to 6 MacDougal Alley, OLP Papers 1980–1987, 1981 Folder.

[40] Marino, circular, 10 January 1980, OLP Papers 1975–1980, Correspondence 1975 Folder.

[41] *Village Bells* (Winter 1983), 1–2.

[42] Alan H. Wiener to Marino, 4 October 1979, OLP Papers 1975–1980, loose business envelope.

[43] Edward J. Fontana to State of New York Department of Law, 25 July 1984, *ibid.*, loose papers.

[44] OLP Scrapbook.

[45] *Village Bells* (Autumn 1979).

[46] *Village Bells* (Winter, 1981), 1–2.

[47] Marino, circular, 29 October 1978, OLP Scrapbook.

13

A Shrine Church and a House of Service, 1981–1989

Father Marino's successor, who was officially appointed August 26, 1980, was Father Charles Zanoni. Father Zanoni was born December 27, 1935, in Melrose Park, Illinois. Bishop Joseph Pernicone ordained him a priest at a ceremony at Pompei April 7, 1962.[1] By the time he left in 1989, he had been at Pompei as long as the Scalabrinians' policies permitted.

Father Zanoni characterized the community he found at Pompei in a letter of recommendation for a parish family. In the letter he explained that the family had been parishioners for three generations. "This is something important to note since our Greenwich Village is an area where neighbors know neighbors for generations back."[2] Pompei was still Italian, but no longer composed of immigrants. The kind of spiritual life its parishioners led, and the kinds of services they required, were very different from Father Bandini's day. Pompei was a shrine community, a shrine to Our Lady of the Rosary of Pompei, and to the memory of Italian immigrant families. Pompei was also not only a house of worship, but a house of service.

Running a parish with such a long history and such a large mission was a complex project that required far more than just a pastor. Father Zanoni described Pompei's parish leadership as follows:

> I found in this parish several very good single entities: an advisory board of six people to counsel the pastor on finances, a school board of twelve people to help the principal and me in school matters, a committee of about twenty who care for the senior citizens of the area and two men who are totally dedicated to serving the parish as Saint Vincent de Paul members.[3]

Pompei was a sort of confederation composed of individuals and groups that in the course of the parish's history had maintained an interest in a particular part of parish life. Part of the pastor's job was to coordinate the efforts of the individual groups, and, when a new project was identified, to form a new group around it.

Pompei's parishioners provided the neighborhood leadership that non-Italian, non-Catholics at Greenwich House or the Children's Aid Society used to provide. The list of guests attending the William Church Osborn Club's annual dinner dance to benefit the Children's Aid Society, reads like a list of donors for a parish project at Pompei.[4] When Villagers organized to protect their neighborhood from "crack," a new and dangerous illegal drug, John Pettinato and Patricia Gardella Dawson of Pompei were the ones quoted and photographed for the newspapers.[5]

Funding an enterprise as huge as Pompei was equally complex. As of January 1, 1988, Pompei played its last game of bingo.[6] Without the funds twice-weekly bingo games once generated, Pompei's finances continued to require economy and efficiency. Father Zanoni replaced with electric stands the beeswax votive candle stands which were becoming too expensive to maintain.[7] He conducted an Increased Giving Program to shore up collections that eroded along with parish population.[8] He introduced a prize calendar, with multiple opportunities to win, as a fund raiser.[9] He paid off accumulated debts by selling the last of the real estate Father Cavicchi had acquired for the never-built high school. (As an example of how prices had changed, Father Cavicchi bought the house for about $10,000, probably during World War II. When giving permission to sell in 1973, archdiocesan authorities stipulated the selling price not be less than $225,000.[10])

But that was the last time Pompei could raise money by selling real estate. Father Zanoni built on Father Marino's precedent of leasing surplus space. The first mention of modern day care in the parish records came in 1976, when a "Pompei Playgroup" met on the premises.[11] Apparently the playgroup consisted of pre-schoolers whose mothers took turns supervising. However, there was an increasing need to revive the mission of the Asilo Scalabrini to care for working mothers' children. In 1983, Pompei Nursery Center became a separate organization with its own board of directors, leasing space at Pompei.[12]

Similarly, in 1984, Father Zanoni removed himself as Executive Director of the Greenwich Village Youth Council, which established itself as a separate organization renting space at Pompei.[13] The Youth Council's evolution shows why charities which used to be part of parish life became independent. A 1989 brochure listed the Youth Council's activities: aerobics, basketball, bowling, crisis counseling, debating, drama, drug abuse referrals, employment counseling, family counseling, field trips, group counseling, homelessness referrals, hot line, ice skating, job referral, photography, ping pong, softball, the Village Halloween parade, volleyball, weight lifting, and the *Youth Voice* newspaper.[14] Even if all the programs didn't run all the time, youth work cost money. The best source of money was the local government. However, in order to accept city funds, on had to accept city policies.[15] As an independent agency, the Youth Council could accept city money in good conscience, and was eligible for space in public buildings that were forbidden by law to rent to religious groups.

In the summer of 1985, *The Village Bells* listed for its readers the groups that met regularly at Pompei: Alcoholics Anonymous, The Caring Community, Greenwich Village Youth Council, Pompei Nursery Center, La Scuola d'Italia, Village Visiting Neighbors (for the home bound), and Victims for Victims (people touched by violent crime). Other organizations rented space only occasionally.[16] Pompei even rented space for a day's shooting for the comedy film *Legal Eagles*, which was produced by a profit-making agency but which was constrained in the places it could rent, since it needed to shoot a scene in the Village.[17]

The Caring Community, Pompei Nursery Center, and the Greenwich Village Youth Council were all charitable enterprises, but Pompei could not be just a "house of service," a not-for-profit landlord. Pompei's real mission was to be a house of prayer. And, amidst all the different organizations, how to create the community Catholicism valued?

One way to create a community was to lead people to realize they were on the giving as well as the receiving side of Pompei's services. The Caring Community always had people who came for help and became volunteers, or volunteers who became paid labor. In other organizations, the commitment to giving as well as receiving had to be fostered. Father Zanoni followed Father Marino's lead in working with the parents to develop their sense of responsibility for the institution educating their youngsters.[18] The Fathers' Club recruited younger members among the new fathers.[19] In 1987, Father Zanoni could tell archdiocesan officials that "Parents here take the school very seriously. They are directly involved in everything from the training of their children to the upkeep of the building."[20]

Another way to create a community was to bring together parishioners for opportunities for spiritual growth. Beginning about 1969 or 1970, Brother Michael La Mantia began taking senior citizens on summer trips to shrines as far away as Canada. Brother Michael's summer trips ended in 1977, when the Festa moved to July, but Father Zanoni noticed that senior citizens frequently took day-long bus trips to Atlantic City. He rented busses and held day-long retreats at nearby shrines. Archdiocesan authorities thought so highly of the idea that they contributed toward the cost and promoted day retreats as something other parishes might do for their seniors.[21] Father Zanoni also helped organize area parishes to provide funds to pay for a Catholic chaplain one day a week at the Village Nursing Home.[22]

In September 1988, the Reverend Bernebe Sison, or Father Bob, himself an immigrant from Samar in the Philippines, moved from the Diocese of Rockville Center to Our Lady of Pompei parish, and Pompei became a nucleus for the Filipino immigrant ministry. Like the Italians and like all immigrants, the Filipinos had their favored devotions and pious customs. At Pompei, they gathered on Wednesday night for a novena to Our Lady of Perpetual Help. Pompei was also the church to which they came for baptisms, and marriages.[23] In 1989, when the last two Italian shipping lines stopped sailing to New York, space at the Scalabrinians' Italian Seaman's Club was rented to the Filipino program.[24]

Pastoral care went beyond helping the people in the community service programs housed at Pompei. Acquired Immune Deficiency Syndrome, or AIDS, was first diagnosed in the United States in 1980. Pompei had no community service especially for people touched by AIDS, but, by 1987, Father Zanoni found that "Care for people with AIDS and their families and loved ones has become a significant part of my ministry," and Pompei's parochial school was studying ways to include AIDS education in the curriculum.[25]

Important as the pastoral care of community service program clients was, Pompei was a parish, with a distinct spiritual life revolving around its existence as a shrine church. Membership in the far-flung shrine community grew throughout the 1980s, and Pompei maintained and expanded parish activities designed to keep those at a distance in touch with the parish. In 1980, Father Joseph Cogo took over responsibility for *La Voce di Pompei*, which was then broadcast Thursdays at 2:50. That same year, the radio show became self-supporting, receiving contributions, as well as requests for prayers and advice.[26]

Father Zanoni himself took over editing *The Village Bells*. By 1981, The *Village Bells* carried four pages of photographs, historical sketches, parish personality profiles, reports on contemporary activities, and publicity for upcoming events. Putting together *The Village Bells* required a certain amount of research, and sometimes the research required a certain amount of stealth. In 1983, Father Zanoni wrote Father Cavicchi, then a missionary in Argentina:

> As you know I am the present pastor of Our Lady of Pompei Church. I am also fascinated by the history of the church, especially the way this parish was able to go through the depression years with such a large debt . . . . Would you also happen to have a picture of how you looked then? I would like to keep it on file, for such things as the parish's centennial here years from now.[27]

Actually, the photograph and Father Cavicchi's reminiscences appeared in the Spring 1984 *Village Bells*. This particular story underscored the importance of *The Village Bells* in preserving parish history. Father Cavicchi died shortly after the story appeared, and his memories of his years at Pompei were inaccessible forever.

In addition to *The Village Bells,* Father Zanoni issued two other publications about Pompei. The first, published in 1983, was a combination guide and prayer book. It took the reader around Pompei's interior, stopping at each statue and painting and providing a short prayer.[28] The second was published after the 1985 restoration of Pompei's interior.

Pompei encouraged its far-flung parishioners not just to read, but to visit. Pompei had its unique Good Friday service, and the parish occasionally hosted displays of unusual Christmas creches. In 1983, artist Franco Artese set up, in Pompei's basement, his "Natale a Grassano," which transplanted the Nativity from Bethlehem to a southern Italian village typical of those from which many immigrants came.[29] In 1986, Father Zanoni invited people to "a traditional nativity scene . . . with figures covered in actual garments."[30]

The Festa Italiana was *the* event which brought distant members of the shrine community to Pompei, and every time they came and brought their friends, the shrine community increased. Therefore, Father Zanoni used every available public relations outlet to entice visitors to the Festa. He contacted New York's Convention and Visitors Bureau to include the festa in its publicity.[31] Every summer *The Village Bells* ran a Festa edition, with pictures and copy extolling the good time to be had, and street maps showing how to plan a day in Greenwich Village.

The original idea had been that Pompei sponsored the Festa Italiana as a parish event. By the 1980s, it had grown so large, and the costs associated with it so high that no parish alone could sponsor it. In 1986, Father Zanoni received an inquiry from a brewery about "sponsoring" the Festa, meaning the brewery contributed to the costs and received the right to publicize its products and perhaps do some promotional activity. Father Zanoni checked with the Parish Advisory Board and the professionals who managed the Festa for the parish.[32] By the early 1990s, Pompei had picked up a valuable sponsor indeed, a radio station, which brought free publicity and more visitors.

The Festa called for tremendous commitment on the part of parishioners, especially when it was moved to the summer vacation period. Since vendors from outside the parish rented space for booths, and since sponsors sought to use the affair to further their sales, Pompei had to watch out for inappropriate commercialization. There was also the problem of making a nice place to visit a nice place to live. The Festa made the Village a nicer place to visit. It also made it, for a week or so, a noisier and more congested place to live, with flashing lights from the decorative arches and amusement park rides, the odors of an international food bazaar, and Italian brass bands striking up the music until ten o'clock at night. Every Festa was accompanied by a neighborhood debate as to whether it was worth it.[33]

There were four possible answers to the annual complaints. The first was that Pompei's parishioners sympathized, because they shared the noise and congestion, plus the Festa temporarily increased their commitment of time, effort, and money to their parish. Second, one week of being primarily a tourist attraction made the Village a nicer place to live in throughout the rest of the year, because Festa profits supported the church, school, and social services.[34] Third the complaints were older than the Festa. In the past the Protestant majority looked down upon Catholicism, and both Protestant and non-Italian Catholics looked down upon street festivals.[35]

Finally, the Festa was not the worst side effect of tourism. Traffic through the Village's already narrow streets increased with every tourist event, not just the Festa, disrupting residents' lives and endangering pedestrians.[36] The Village had long had a bohemian reputation, which was renewed when it became a center of gay life. Vendors happily exploited the Village's reputation for the off-beat by selling what one parishioner referred to as "exotic/erotic 'junque.'"[37]

Even a far-flung shrine congregation needed a church that was a visible symbol of its community. When Father Zanoni first arrived in the parish, parishioners let him know that there was a sentiment in favor of restoring the mural that had been above the altar. Father Zanoni agreed to pursue the matter with archdiocesan officials if he could be assured of parish support.[38] *The Village Bells* ran a headline on "An Attempt to Restore the Mural at Our Lady of Pompei Church."[39]

The parishioners, both those actually in the Village and those who had left, were delighted. "It was with great joy that I read in the latest edition of *The Village Bells* that there were plans to restore the beautiful mural of the church. I spent many years staring at those pictures of Our Lady and the angels and saints as I belonged to that parish from my baptism in 1944 to my marriage in 1966."[40] The finished results were such that the *New Yorker* ran a story about one of the artists who worked at Pompei.[41] People interested in New York City's history wrote asking to include Pompei on walking tours.[42]

A parishioner gave Father Zanoni the name and phone number of the D'Ambrosio Ecclesiastical Art Studios, which had done the original mural.[43] Professor Antonio D'Ambrosio, who directed the work, died in 1951, in a fall from a scaffold while working on a church. His son Anthony inherited the business, and the company worked on Pompei during Father Mario Albanesi's and Father Guido Caverzan's pastorates. By the 1980s, Anthony D'Ambrosio was training a third generation in the business, and his son George was one of the workers at Pompei. Pompei organized an ad hoc Art Committee, headed by Manuel Mergel and Sandra Di Pasqua to coordinate the parish's wishes and the art company's work.[44]

Pompei and D'Ambrosio Ecclesiastical Art Company signed a contract October 17, 1984. In January 1985, the art company trucks arrived with the scaffolding. Putting up the scaffolding alone was complicated job. Since practically all the ceiling was to be restored, the scaffolding had to allow the workers to reach everywhere safely—and Pompei's ceiling was some sixty feet above the floor. Also, although the workers had to be able to reach everywhere, there had to be space under the scaffolding for the congregation to attend services.

Once the scaffolding was up, workers primed the ceiling, stopped leaks and restored the elaborate mural. In the sanctuary below the mural, the workers touched up the altar so it blended with the scagliola on the rear wall. Out in the nave, they washed, sanded, and varnished the pews, cleaned and grouted the floor, and reconditioned the scagliola on the columns. Along the walls, they washed and polished the stained glass windows, repaired the window braces, and oiled the ventilators. They paid particular attention to the beauty, safety, and functioning of the lighting. They replaced the wiring between the main switch and ceiling lights, cleaned the glass in the lamps, inspected the chains suspending the lamps from the ceiling, and painted the chains. Finally, they took down the scaffolding and hauled it away.

The restored mural differed in some details from the original. The figure of Bishop Scalabrini was painted in next to that of Saint Charles Borromeo. The original mural had representative figures of priests, brothers, and sisters. In the restored version, the brother was recognizable as Saint Martin de Porres (1574–1634).

Pompei scheduled its rededication service for May 5, 1985, partly because that was when the scaffolding came down, but also because the first Sunday in May was the traditional date for reciting the "supplica" or special annual devotion to Our Lady of Pompei. Also, for a church that was increasingly interested in celebrating its history, early May was full of memories: the Mass celebrating the completion of the interior decoration in 1939, the move to the new church 1928, the move to Bleecker Street in 1898, and the first Mass in 1892. Scalabrinians came from all along the East Coast, and for the offertory there was a procession symbolic of the numerous groups that were part of parish life. At the end there were specially blessed roses—associated with the Blessed Mother—for everyone, and refreshments at Father Demo Hall. Those who could not attend read about the festivities in *The Village Bells* and in a commemorative booklet distributed in 1986.

Several other changes in the church's appearance (and sound) were made during Father Zanoni's pastorate. In 1981, the parish put in a new organ next to the one Father Demo had installed over fifty years earlier.[45] In 1983, Saint Vincent's Hospital gave Pompei the statue of Saint Gerard, patron saint of expectant mothers, that used to stand in the hospital's maternity ward.[46] At the time of the mural restoration Pompei built a new Saint Jude shrine. The stained glass windows above the main doors, depicting the Flight into Egypt, Columbus's arrival in America, and immigrants in New York Harbor, were mounted in 1986.[47] The new carillon was installed in 1988.[48]

In 1989, Father Zanoni filled out a questionnaire for the Scalabrinians that gave a snapshot of the parish. At that point, 12,000 people received *The Village Bells,* between 800 and 1000 attended weekend Masses, 400 students attended

Pompei's two schools, and about 150 people attended daily Mass. Pompei had 100 Vietnamese parishioners with their own community structures, plus 300 Filipinos, plus 300 parishioners who could be described as American-born, plus 500 who were American-born of Italian descent, plus 150 first-generation Italians.[49] This was the parish Father Zanoni left when he was reassigned to the position of director of the Scalabrinians' Villa Rosa Nursing Home.

At the time of Father Zanoni's departure, the most important upcoming event on the parish calendar was the 1992 centennial. One might think of a celebration of a hundred years of parish life as a time to reminiscence about the good times of the past. In Pompei's case, the celebration was also shaped by the social and economic situation of the present.

NOTES

[1] Brochure for Zanoni's silver jubilee, 5 April 1987, OLP Memorabilia 1985–1988, 1987 Folder.

[2] Zanoni letter dated 13 October 1986, OLP Papers 1980–1987, January 1986 Folder.

[3] Zanoni to Henry Mansell, 22 June 1981, ibid., June 1981 Folder.

[4] Helen Zarember and Bob Cardinale to Zanoni, 23 March 1982, *ibid.*, January 1982 Folder.

[5] New York *Post*, 28 February 1986; and *Catholic New York*, 3 April 1986.

[6] To Zanoni, 16 November 1987, OLP Papers 1980–1987, June 1987 Folder.

[7] Weekly Bulletin, 4 January 1981, OLP Bulletins I.

[8] Brochure for Increased Giving Program in OLP Memorabilia 1985–1988, 1987 and 1988 Folders.

[9] Zanoni, circular, 30 November 1987, OLP Papers 1980–1987 Folder.

[10] Zanoni to Timothy A. McDonnell, 8 October 1982, OLP Papers 1980–1987, June 1982 Folder; and McDonnell to Zanoni, 18 February 1983, *ibid.,* January 1983 Folder.

[11] Carol Walton to Marino, 14 June 1976, OLP Papers 1975–1980, loose papers.

[12] Zanoni to Robert A. Arpie, 16 November 1983, OLP Papers 1980–1987, January 1983 Folder.

[13] Zanoni to J[oseph] P. Murphy, 11 December 1984, *ibid.*, January 1984 Folder.

[14] Greenwich Village Youth Council brochure, OLP Memorabilia 1989.

[15] Kevin J. Colleran to Zanoni, 16 April 1985, OLP Papers 1980–1987, January 1985 Folder; and Zanoni to Susan Landgraf, 15 May 1986, *ibid.*, January 1986 Folder.

[16] Kim Huot Kret to Zanoni, 1 March 1989, OLP Papers 1988, January 1989 Folder.

[17] New York *Post*, 5 December 1985.

[18] Zanoni to Fred Nicomini, 5 January 1987, OLP Papers 1980–1987, January 1987 Folder.

[19] Interview 0007.

[20] Zanoni to Kevin O'Brien, 31 March 1988, OLP Papers 1988, January 1988 Folder.

[21] Interview 0001.

[22] Letters regarding Catholic chaplain service at the Village Nursing Home in OLP Papers 1988, January 1989 Folder.

[23] New York *Philippine News,* 17–13 September 1988 and 12–18 October 1988.

[24] Joseph A. Cogo, C.S., to "Dear Father," 24 March 1989, OLP Papers 1988, January 1989 Folder.

[25] Zanoni to Samuel T. Burneson, 11 June 1987, and to Sister Joyann, 4 November 1987, both in OLP Papers 1980–1987, June 1987 Folder.

[26] *Village Bells* (Fall–Winter [1981]), 1.

[27] Zanoni to Ugo Cavicchi, 20 February 1983, OLP Papers 1980–1987, January 1983 Folder.

[28] Copy in OLP Scrapbook.

[29] Post cards and clippings of Natale a Grassano in OLP Memorabilia 1980–1984, 1983 Folder.

[30] Zanoni, circular letter, 1 December 1986, OLP Papers 1980–1987, January 1987 Folder.

[31] Zanoni to New York Convention and Visitors Bureau, 20 June 1983, *ibid.*, January 1983 Folder.

[32] Stephen I. Siller to Zanoni, 24 September 1986, and Zanoni to Siller, 7 October 1986, *ibid.*, January 1986 Folder.

[33] Comments on Festa in each folder in OLP Papers 1980–1987 and 1988.

[34] Zanoni to 72 Carmine, 28 July 1984, OLP Papers 1980–1987, January 1984 Folder.

[35] Zanoni to 160 Prince Street, 11 July 1983, *ibid.*, January 1983 Folder.

[36]Zanoni to Carol Grietzer, 28 April 1987, *ibid.*, January 1987 Folder; and Zanoni to Benjamin Ward, 26 February 1988, OLP Papers 1988, January 1988 Folder.

[37] James Abbarno to John Bleecker, 14 November 1972, OLP Papers before 1975, 1972 Folder; Marino, circular, April 1977, OLP Bulletins I; and 65 Morton Street to Barbara Schwartz, 5 April 1984, OLP Papers 1980–1987, January 1984 Folder.

[38] Zanoni to Timothy A. McDonnell, 8 October 1982, OLP Papers 1980–1987, June 1982 Folder.

[39] *Village Bells* (Winter–Spring 1982/1983?), 1–2.

[40] To Zanoni, no address, 27 March 1982, OLP Papers 1980–1987, January 1982 Folder.

[41] *New Yorker* (6 February 1989), 24–26.

[42] Regina M. Kellerman to Zanoni, 4 June 1985, OLP Papers 1980–1987, January 1985 Folder.

[43] Much of the information that follows comes from Interviews 0001 and 0002, and from *Shrine Church of Our Lady of Pompei: Rededication* (New York: OLP, 1985).

[44] *Village Bells* (Summer 1985), 3.

[45] *Village Bells* (Fall 1984), 3.

[46] Sister Margaret Sweeney, S.C., to Zanoni, 21 October 1983, OLP Papers 1980–1987, January 1983 Folder.

[47] Zanoni to Gerard Hiemer, 19 December 1985, *ibid.*, January 1985 Folder.

[48] Ronald O. Beach to Zanoni, Sellersville, Pennsylvania, 12 February 1988, OLP Papers 1988, January 1988 Folder.

[49] Zanoni to Jose Arruda, 15 April 1989, *ibid.*, January 1989 Folder.

Altar mural in Our Lady of Pompei ceiling, originally installed in 1937, and restored in 1985.

Under Pastors James Abbarno (1970–1975), Edward Marino (1975–1981), and Charles Zanoni (1981–1989), Pompei developed its identity as a shrine church and a house of service. Brother Michael La Mantia mustered the members of Sacred Heart, Saint Rita, and Pompei societies for an October 1981 procession.

Pompei serves heterogeneous congregations of Italian and Italian American senior citizens and young Filipinos and Vietnamese immigrant families. Father Bernabe Sison preaches to Filipino listeners.

14

Ad Multos Annos: Pompei, 1989–1992

One can measure some of the changes in Pompei over the years by studying how Scalabrinian superiors chose pastors for the parish. When Father Bandini came to New York City in 1891, he knew some English and had lots of energy. When Father Tarcisio Bagatin came in 1989, he had more precise qualifications. Father Terry was born in Thiene, Vincenza, on April 5, 1928, and was ordained May 19, 1954. After a brief assignment in Genoa he acquired considerable experience in the United States and Canada before coming to Pompei. One assignment was at Saint Anthony's in Buffalo, New York, a parish whose experience with urban renewal introduced Father Terry to issues he encountered again at Pompei. Another was at Saint Anthony's in Ontario, Canada, where he had a weekly half-hour television program, preparation for speaking on *La Voce di Pompei*. Third, and perhaps most significant, he was assigned to Saint Michael's in New Haven, Connecticut, which celebrated its centennial during his time there.[1]

One can also measure the change over time by studying Pompei's big anniversaries over the years. The only evidence that there was any observance at all of Pompei's twenty-fifth anniversary are the anniversary prayer cards that some parishioners have saved since 1917. Probably World War I drained away much of the desire to celebrate, but one also has to remember that in 1917 Pompei's parishioners were still struggling immigrants. They didn't have the extra money for a nice commemoration, and there weren't many parishioners with the experience necessary to organize the events. When Pompei celebrated its fiftieth anniversary in 1942, World War II distracted the parishioners from fully enjoying their jubilee. Also, there still wasn't much input from the parishioners; the golden jubilee parish history was written by Father Constantino Sassi, and, even though the younger parishioners used English almost exclusively by then, the history was written in Italian.

By 1967, much had changed at Pompei. Instead of having pastors who stayed for long tenures, Pompei had pastors who stayed only a few years, and thus the parishioners provided the stability and continuity necessary to successful long-term planning. Also, the parishioners were not immigrants, but American-born, with the education and experience necessary for parish leadership. Pompei's diamond jubilee was much like similar celebrations carried at other parishes at the same time. The laity took an important role in the planning, and, since most parish organizations were either men's or women's groups, the planning was done by separate men's and women's committees. A layman wrote an English-language parish history. The celebration consisted of two main events, a Mass and a dinner-dance. In 1976, Pompei celebrated the fiftieth anniversary of its "new" church in a similar manner.

By 1989, much had changed again. The number of parishioners had dwindled, but they had also become more diverse: instead of one dinner dance for everyone, there was a year-long calendar of events for senior citizens, parochial school alumni, Italians, Filipinos, and Vietnamese. Instead of separate men's and women's committees, there was one main committee with a man and a woman—Mr. Michael Amorosa and Mrs. Lucy Cecere—as co-chairs.

Anniversaries tend to generate two ways of thinking. One emphasizes differences between past and present, and focuses on the anniversary as a way to remember "the good old days." Another way emphasizes differences between present and future, and focuses on the anniversary as a way of enjoying what will supposedly soon disappear forever. The truth of Pompei's situation lies somewhere between these two ways of celebrating an anniversary. "The good old days" had their difficult moments, and it is important to remember that. And, even though Pompei has changed over the years, the past still shapes the present, if one knows how to look for it, and the present will shape the future. One can see the interplay of past, present, and future when one looks at Pompei's history as an immigrant parish , as a specifically *Italian* immigrant parish, at the parish's economy, at its history as a house of service, and at its history as a house of worship.

How long can Pompei maintain its immigrant heritage? The answer depends not upon Pompei alone, but upon other factors. In the 1890s, American immigration law permitted hundreds of thousands of immigrants in every year. The immigrants formed parishes by settling in small communities close together. The Archdiocese of New York was still growing, and so there was room for new parishes. Anti-immigrant sentiments, present even within the Church, made separate parishes necessary.

In the 1990s, immigration law reduced the number of immigrants entering the United States. The use of subways, buses, and automobiles meant newcomers did not need to live together to get together. There is not enough land for new parishes, nor enough money to finance them. So, rather than separate parishes for each immigrant group, Pompei was shared by Italian, Vietnamese, and Filipino groups. Given the circumstances which encourage immigrants to find a place in existing parishes rather than create new ones, Pompei might continue to be an immigrant parish so long as there are immigrants.

What about Pompei's *Italian* immigrant heritage? That, too, depends not only on Pompei, but on other factors. In the 1890s, Greenwich Village was not an Italian neighborhood, but the Italians established themselves there. Housing wasn't of high quality, but it was affordable and close to work. Work in the warehouses or garment factories wasn't very good either, but those were the jobs the Italians could get. Once the Italians had houses and work, they developed the other institutions they needed followed. Shopkeepers sold Italian foodstuffs, clubs such as *Tiro a Segno* met social needs, and Pompei provided opportunities to meet spiritual obligations and to receive an education.

By the 1990s, appropriate housing was so difficult to find that Italian-Americans were moving out of the Village. The institutions they created though, remained behind. The bakeries, restaurants, and import shops originally intended to serve Italians became part of the Greenwich Village tourist scene. Pompei might continue to be an Italian church as long as tourists come to the Italian-American attractions in the Village. However, unless housing becomes easier to find and afford, Pompei will be an Italian outpost in a non-Italian Village.

What does Pompei's history contribute to its present economic situation? History has already determined how Pompei spends its money. Pompei has a parish plant capable of accommodating almost any type of activity. That plant's usefulness, and the parishioners' affection for their spiritual home, have prioritized expenditures. Pompei hasn't raised money for new construction for some time. Instead, it raises money to preserve the old. Father Terry's pastorate has been marked by a steady series of major repair jobs: pointing bricks, restoring electric wiring, replacing auditorium stage curtains, refurbishing class rooms, and replacing hot water equipment.[2] Similarly, Pompei's tradition of involvement in particular community services translates into an ongoing financial commitment.

Pompei's history does not suggest any one way of raising money to meets its obligations. In the 1890s, Pompei relied on wealthy non-parishioners such as Archbishop Corrigan and Miss Leary. By the 1910s, the Italians had their own community of businesses and families, and the few large donors gave way to many small ones. At that point, most donors lived in Greenwich Village. By the 1970s, people were moving out of Greenwich Village, and sending money back to Pompei; the parish still relied on numerous small donors, but not donors living in Greenwich Village. In the 1980s, Pompei began augmenting the many small donations with a few large sources of income. Rent earned from the Scuola d'Italia replaced the Archbishop Corrigans and Miss Learies of an earlier day.

The parish's economic health is tied to the people's economic health. In the 1890s, the Italians could not afford to build a church themselves, and other, more secure people stepped in. Even in the 1910s and 1920s, parishioners did not share the burden of supporting the parish evenly. One can see from the way Pompei financed building its present church that the parish expected prosperous local business to return some of their good fortune to the community in the form of donations to its church. For about twenty years after World War II, the middle class in Greenwich Village could generate enough donations to keep Pompei going. In the 1970s, when the middle class moved out of the Village, it could still donate enough to keep the parish going, if the parish made the effort to create a sense of community among its now scattered former parishioners. Since the 1970s, though, middle class income has eroded to the point that it may be unreasonable to expect these people to shoulder the main burden. On the other hand, people in a position to give large donations no longer think of a neighborhood parish as a suitable object for their generosity; they give to large projects such as Catholic Charities.

Pompei's history is most visible in its work as a "house of service". Its heritage of youth ministries is a good example. In the 1990s, AIDS, child abuse, drinking, drugs, educational crises, teen-age pregnancy, and unemployment made caring for youths one of the most difficult of social services. Yet, there has always been something for youth at Pompei: Sunday School, day care, elementary school, sodalities, sports, drama programs, and now the Greenwich Village Youth Council. Similarly, there has always been something for Italians, whether the Italians were recent immigrants or senior citizens.

There is room for innovation in Pompei's social service program, as its recent attention to senior citizens attests. Pompei will probably continue to be a place where new social needs first become known, because, as Father Terry noted, people call Pompei because they don't know how else to handle a problem, and so they want to talk to their pastor.[3] However, given the tendency toward greater specialization in American society, including social service, Pompei may increasingly emphasize its natural specialty: the pastoral care parishes traditionally provide.

How has the past shaped the present "shrine community" at Pompei? During Vatican II, one might have said Pompei's past didn't matter at all, because the Council changed the way Catholics had worshipped for centuries. Twenty years after the Council, one might have a better appreciation of its teachings. Vatican II emphasized the Church as "the people of God throughout the world." If the Church is a worldwide community, there has to be respect for the multiplicity of pious practices and spiritual customs in that large and varied population. Certainly, Pompei's experience is relevant here, for Pompei's history has been one of maintaining a particular identity within a universal Church.

If one spends time watching people come and go at Pompei, one might be able to draw up a list of all the different ways of expressing religious sentiments.

People come for Mass, for a particular novena, for the annual events such as the Good Friday service, or when Brother Michael is sweeping the floors. They find their favorite places: the Memorial Chapel, recently renovated to accommodate even more names, the Pieta, or somewhere that they can see the ceiling mural. They stand, they sit, they kneel. They favor certain prayers: the rosary, something from little booklets they carry with them, something from the books in the pew racks, something known only to themselves. They come over to the rectory to put a relative's name in the Memorial Shrine or to arrange a Mass for a special intention. Given the increasing respect paid to the variety of religious experience, Pompei might be in a good position to continue its pastoral mission in the Village *ad multos annos*.

NOTES

[1] *Village Bells* (Summer 1990), 1–2.

[2] Tarcisio Bagatin, C.S., "To Be Pastor," December 13, 1991.

[3] *Ibid.*

Brother Michael La Mantia coordinating the gift procession during the centennial celebration. The various gifts are presented by parishioners who wear the traditional dresses of the different ethnic groups who find in the church of Our Lady of Pompei a point of reference for their faith.

May 17, 1992. Centennial celebration: (Left to right) Fr. Tarcisio Bagatin, Bishop Lawrence Sabatini and Fr. Isaia Birollo.

Priests and parishioners after the celebration of the mass remembering the 100 years of ministering to migrants of the church of Our Lady of Pompei.

Bibliography

Apple, Rima D.
1987 *Mothers and Medicine: A Social History of Infant Feeding, 1890–1950*. Madison: The University of Wisconsin Press.

Bandini, P.M.A.
1892 *Relazione Della Società Italiana di San Raffaele in New York*. Piacenza: Marchesotti e L. Porta. This was reprinted in *Studi Emigrazione* V (1968), 303–323.

Bandini, Pietro
1983 *First Annual Report of Saint Raphael's Italian Benevolent Society*. N.p.

Barry, Colman, J., O.S.B.
1963 *The Catholic Church and German Americans*. Milwaukee: Bruce Publishing Company.

Berry, John M., and Frances Panchok
1987 "Church and Theatre," *U.S. Catholic Historian*, 6(2–3):151–179. Spring/Summer.

Blum, John Morton
1976 *V was for Victory: Politics and American Culture during World War II*. New York: Harcourt Brace Jovanovich.

Brace, Charles Loring
1880 *The Dangerous Classes of New York and Twenty Years' Work among Them*. New York: Wynkoop and Hallenbeck. Reprinted, Montclair, New Jersey: Patterson Smith, 1978.

Bremner, Robert H.
1956 *From the Depths: The Discovery of Poverty in the United States*. New York: New York University Press.

Brizzolara, Andrew, C.S.
1983 "One Hundred Days: The Visit of Bishop Scalabrini to the United States and its Effects on the Image of Italian Immigrants as Reflected in the American Press of 1901." Master's thesis, Fordham University.

Brumberg, Joan Jacobs
1980 *Mission for Life: The Story of the Family of Adoniram Judson, the Dramatic Events of the First American Foreign Mission, and the Course of Evangelical Religion in the Nineteenth Century*. New York: Free Press.

Caliaro, Marco, and Mario Francesconi
1977 *John Baptist Scalabrini: Apostle to Emigrants*. Translated by Alba I. Zizzamia. New York: CMS.

Candeloro, Dominic, *et al.*
1990   *Italian Ethnics: Their Languages, Literature and Lives.* New York: American Italian Historical Association.

Caroli, Betty Boyd
1973   *Italian Repatriation from the United States, 1900–1914.* New York: CMS.

———
1931   *Catholic Action: Encyclical Letter of His Holiness, Pope Pius XI.* Washington, D.C.: National Catholic Welfare Conference, 22.

Ciufoletti, Manlio, C.S.
1937   *John Baptist Scalabrini: Bishop of Piacenza, Apostle of Italian Immigrants.* N.p.

Cohen, Miriam
1977   "Italian-American Women in New York City, 1900–1950: Work and School." In Milton Cantor and Bruce Laurie, eds. *Class, Sex, and the Woman Worker.* Westport, Connecticut: Greenwood Press.

Coll, Jorge, T.O.R.
1989   *Una Iglesia Pionera.* New York: Privately published.

Cosenza, Michael A.
1967   *Our Lady of Pompei in Greenwich Village.* New York: OLP.

Cowell, Daniel David, M.D.
1985   "Funerals, Family, and Forefathers: A View of Italian-American Funeral Practices," *Omega* XVI:1.

Di Giovanni, Stephen Michael
1983   "Michael Augustine Corrigan and the Italian Immigrants: The Relationship between the Church and the Italians in the Archdiocese of New York, 1995–1902." Ph.D. Dissertation, Gregorian Pontifical University [Rome].

Dinnerstein, Leonard, and David M. Reimers
1988   *Ethnic Americans: A History of Immigration.* Third edition. New York: Harper and Row.

Dolan, Jay P.
1975   *The Immigrant Church: New York's Irish and German Catholics, 1815–1860.* Baltimore: Johns Hopkins University Press.

Foerster, Robert F.
1924   *The Italian Emigration of Our Times.* Harvard Economic Studies, Volume 20. Cambridge, Massachusetts: Harvard University Press.

Gannon, Robert I., S.J.
1962   *The Cardinal Spellman Story.* Garden City, New York: Doubleday.

Gold, Joyce
1988   *From Trout Stream to Bohemia: A Walking Guide to Greenwich Village History.*
       New York: Old Warren Road Press.

Greene, Victor R.
1987   *American Immigrant Leaders, 1800–1910: Marginality and Identity.* Baltimore:
       Johns Hopkins University Press.

Hayes, Patrick J.
1923   "The Unification of Catholic Charities," *Catholic World,* 117:145–153. May.

Higham, John
1984   *Send These to Me.* Second edition. Baltimore: Johns Hopkins University Press.

Higham, John
1969   *Strangers in the Land: Patterns of American Nativism, 1860–1925.* New York:
       Atheneum.

1906   *Gli Italiani negli Stati Uniti.* New York: Italian Chamber of Commerce.

Kauffman, Christopher J.
1982   *Faith and Fraternalism: The History of the Knights of Columbus, 1881–1982.* New
       York: Harper and Row.

Linkh, Richard M.
1975   *American Catholicism and European Immigrants, 1900–1924.* New York: CMS.

Mariano, John Horace
1921   *The Italian Contribution to American Democracy.* Boston: Christopher Publishing
       House.

Marraro, Howard R.
1949   "Italians in New York in the Eighteen–Fifties." *New York History,* 30:181–203,
       276–303.

McNab, John
1977   "Bethlehem Chapel: Presbyterians and Italian Americans in New York City,"
       Journal of Presbyterian History, 55:145–160.

McNaspy, C.J., S.J.
1965   "More Changes at Mass," *America,* (27 February), 281.

Meehan, Thomas F.
1903   "Evangelizing the Italians." *The Messenger,* 39:32.

1923   *La Messa D'Argento: Discorso Recitato Dal Rev.mo Francesco Canonico
       Castellano.* New York: Il Carroccio Publishing Company.

1906   "A Model Italian Colony in Arkansas." *Review of Reviews,* 34:361–362. September.

1963   "Modernizing the Mass," *Time* December 13.

More, Louise Boland
1907   *Wage Earner's Budgets: A Study of the Standard and Cost of Living in New York.* Greenwich House Series of Social Studies #1. New York: Henry Holt and Company.

Nelli, Humbert S.
1985   "The Economic Activities of Italian Americans." In Winston Van Horne and Thomas V. Tonnesen, eds. *Ethnicity and the Work Force.* Ethnicity and Public Policy Series. Madison: University of Wisconsin. Pp. 193–207.

New York Federal Writers' Project
1969   *The Italians of New York.* New York: Random House, 1938. Reprinted, New York: Arno.

Odencrantz, Louise C.
1919   *Italian Women in Industry.* New York: Russell Sage.

Orsi, Robert Anthony
1989   "What Did Women Really Think When They Prayed to St. Jude?" *U.S. Catholic Historian,* 8(1–2):67–79. Winter/Spring.

1959   "A Priest Campaigns against Delinquency," *Jubilee* (November), n.p.

Ravitch, Diane
1974   *The Great School Wars: New York City, 1805–1973: A History of the Public Schools as Battlefield of Social Change.* New York: Basic Books.

Rizzato, Remo, P.S.S.C.
1948   *Figure di Missionari Scalabriniani.* New York: D'Alatri's Press.

Rosenwaike, Ira
1972   *Population History of New York City.* Syracuse: Syracuse University Press.

1923   "Saint Benedict's Church," *Our Colored Missions,* 9(10):147–149. October.

Salvetti, Patrizia
1984   "Una parrocchia italiana di New York e i suoi fedeli: Nostra Signora di Pompei (1892–1933)." *Studi Emigrazione,* 21:43–64. March.

Schick, Robert
1947 "Father Bandini: Missionary in the Ozarks," *Ave Maria*, 65:782–786. December 20.

Simkhovitch, Mary Kingsbury
1935 *Neighborhood: My Story of Greenwich House*. New York: Norton.

———
1911 *Souvenir Journal, Grand Bazaar, Church of Our Lady of Pompei*. New York: L'Italiano in America.

Stein, Leon
1962 *The Triangle Fire*. Philadelphia: J.B. Lippincott.

Stibili, Edward Claude
1977 "The St. Raphael Society for the Protection of Italian Immigrants, 1887–1923." Ph.D. Dissertation, University of Notre Dame.

Sullivan, Mary Louise, M.S.C.
1987 "Mother Cabrini: Missionary to Italian Immigrants." *U.S. Catholic Historian*, 6(4):265–279. Fall.

Tessarolo, Giulivo, C.S.
1962 *The Church Magna Charta for Migrants*. New York: St. Charles Seminary.

Tomasi, Silvano M., C.S.
1975 *Piety and Power: The Role of the Italian Parishes in the New York Metropolitan Area, 1880–1930*. New York: CMS.

United States Department of Commerce, Bureau of the Census
1975 *Historical Statistics of the United States, Colonial Times to 1970*, Volume 1. Washington: Government Printing Office. Pp. 105–106.

Vecoli, Rudolph J.
1969 "Peasants and Prelates: Italian Immigrants and the Catholic Church," *Journal of Social History*, 2: 217–267.

Ware, Caroline
1965 *Greenwich Village, 1920–1930: A Comment on American Civilization in the Post-War Years*. New York: Houghton Mifflin, 1935. Reprinted, New York: Harper.

[Zanoni, Charles, C.S.]
1985 *Shrine Church of Our Lady of Pompei Rededication*. New York: OLP.

Index